'This book makes a unique contribution by focusing on gender-responsive budgeting (GRB) in Timor-Leste, a fragile state recently emerged from years of conflict. It shows how GRB can make a positive contribution to both gender equality and state resilience. It is highly original in its reflection on how knowledge is produced and communicated; and in identifying the contexts and actors that enable effective translation of gender analysis into improvements in opportunities for women and girls. Essential reading for scholars and students of feminist economics and gender and development; and for development practitioners in international NGOs, aid agencies and international financial institutions.'

Diane Elson, Emeritus Professor,
Department of Sociology, University of Essex, UK

'While women's gender equality claims can be slim in fragile states, Timor-Leste's engagement with gender responsive budgeting offers hope. This book demonstrates the critical role of women's participation in civil society and state institutions in establishing an agenda for integrating a gender perspective in the spending and revenue raising activities of government. Its untangling of complex relationships between researchers and policy actors increases our understanding of how policy and budgetary change is affected.'

Rhonda Sharp, Professor of Economics, University of
South Australia, Australia and former President of the
International Association for Feminist Economics

'Despite the progress made in women's political participation in Timor-Leste, gender inequality still persists, due to a lack of investment in the social and economic factors that impact on the status of women and girls. In 2016, Timor-Leste confirmed its commitment to leave no one behind by adopting the United Nations Sustainable Development Goals (SDGs) – with gender equality being recognized as key to the success of global development. Gender-responsive budgeting is an important mechanism to help the Timor-Leste government understand how to allocate and reallocate resources to more efficiently achieve their priorities including gender equality. This book shows that the participation of policy actors and civil society in engendering budgets is a concrete action for greater accountability to women's rights, which can improve access to resources and opportunities for women, girls, men and boys in a fragile state like Timor-Leste.'

Alita Verdial, former CEO of Alola Foundation, Timor-Leste

'The state of the economy and how the government spends its money in Timor-Leste remain deeply implicated in reproducing conditions of inequality for women, making them more vulnerable to violence. Costa outlines strategies and insights into how women in Timor are engaging in economic policy through budgetary decision making to reflect their concerns and priorities. She argues conclusively that gender-focused institutions are crucial in enabling women to become critical actors for change in budgetary policy and the economy in Timor-Leste. This is crucial for improving women's lives and makes this book an especially important one.'

Sara Niner, Lecturer & Researcher, Monash University, Australia

Gender-Responsive Budgeting in Fragile States

A growing number of governments have made commitments to achieving gender equality and women's rights, with many using gender-responsive budgeting (GRB) to allocate resources for the delivery of economic policy and governance that benefit men and women equally. At a time when GRB is growing in global traction, this book investigates what it can deliver for gender equality and state resilience in contexts where the state is weak or prone to violence, such as in Timor-Leste.

Gender-Responsive Budgeting in Fragile States: The Case of Timor-Leste uses the Timor-Leste case to investigate whether gender equality reform can be adopted at the same time as establishing economic and institutional fundamentals. While some may have thought that the adoption of a GRB strategy in 2008 was premature, Monica Costa argues that GRB initiatives have contributed to budget accountability and transparency, and ultimately improved policy and budget processes and decisions. This multi-disciplinary analysis of a decade of GRB demonstrates why GRB is important to inform the debate on state fragility-resilience and argues that fragile states cannot defer gender equality in the name of getting the economic and institutional basics right.

While a growing number of fragile states have taken steps to make their budget more gender-responsive, questions remain for economists and policy makers about what can be achieved, and how. *Gender-Responsive Budgeting in Fragile States* is the first international publication on GRB in fragile state contexts and will be of interest to researchers, upper level students, policy makers and NGOs with an interest in policy, economics, gender and development.

Monica Costa is a former international gender adviser to the government of Timor-Leste and holds a doctorate on gender equality and policy in Timor-Leste from the University of South Australia, Australia.

Routledge ISS Gender, Sexuality and Development Studies

The *Routledge ISS Gender, Sexuality and Development Studies* series explores the diverse ways in which topics of gender and sexuality relate to international development, both in theory and in practice. The book series aims to publish 'classical' gender, sexuality and development themes – such as the sexual and reproductive rights policy debates on population and sustainable development, adolescence and sex education, and policy on abortion – together with cutting edge work on embodiment, queer theory and innovative strategies of resistance to hegemonic discourses of sexuality and gender. The book series will pay special attention to the role of intergenerational power relations and how they interact with different gendered understandings of sexuality at diverse stages in the life cycle.

Wendy Harcourt leads the international editorial board with her colleagues from the renowned International Institute of Social Studies of Erasmus University, The Netherlands. The Board welcomes book proposals from researchers working in all geographic areas with special interest in research undertaken from feminist grounded theory and with marginalised groups in the global South and North.

To find out more about how to submit a book proposal, please contact the Development Studies Editor, Helena Hurd (Helena.Hurd@tandf.co.uk) or Wendy Harcourt (harcourt@iss.nl).

Global Trends in Land Tenure Reform
Gender Impacts
Edited by Caroline S. Archambault and Annelies Zoomers

Gender, Power and Knowledge for Development
Lata Narayanaswamy

Gender-Responsive Budgeting in Fragile States
The Case of Timor-Leste
Monica Costa

Gender-Responsive Budgeting in Fragile States

The Case of Timor-Leste

Monica Costa

First published 2018 by Routledge

2 Park Square, Milton Park, Abingdon, Oxfordshire OX14 4RN
52 Vanderbilt Avenue, New York, NY 10017

Routledge is an imprint of the Taylor & Francis Group, an informa business

First issued in paperback 2019

British Library Cataloguing-in-Publication Data
A catalogue record for this book is available from the British Library

Library of Congress Cataloging-in-Publication Data
A catalog record for this book has been requested

ISBN: 978-1-138-24065-0 (hbk)
ISBN: 978-0-367-88498-7 (pbk)

Typeset in Bembo
by Keystroke, Neville Lodge, Tettenhall, Wolverhampton

Contents

Contents

Figures

Abbreviations

AMP	Aliança com Maioria Parlamentar (Parliamentary Majority Alliance)
CAVR	Commission for Reception, Truth, and Reconciliation in Timor-Leste
CEDAW	Convention on the Elimination of All Forms of Discrimination against Women
CNRT	Conselho Nacional da Resistência Timorense (National Council of Timorese Resistance)
CPLP	Comunidade de Países de Lingua Portuguesa
EMIS	Education Management Information System
ETTA	East Timor Transitional Administration
FAR	Feminist action research
GAU	Gender Affairs Unit
GDP	Gross domestic product
GRB	Gender-responsive budgeting
IMF	International Monetary Fund
IPU	Inter-Parliamentary Union
MDG	Millennium Development Goals
MoE	Ministry of Education
MoF	Ministry of Finance
NWPA-CPLP	Network of Women at the Parliamentary Assembly of the Community of Portuguese-speaking Countries (Rede de Mulheres da Assembleia Parlamentar, Comunidade de Países de Lingua Portuguesa)
OECD	Organisation for Economic Co-operation and Development
OMT	Organização da Mulher Timorense (Organisation of Timorese Women)
OPE	Office for the Promotion of Equality
OPMT	Organização Popular da Mulher Timorense (Popular Organisation of East Timorese Women)
RDTL	República Democrática de Timor-Leste
SADC	Southern African Development Community
SDG	Sustainable Development Goals

SEPI	Secretary of State for the Promotion of Equality
TLLSS	Timor–Leste Living Standards Survey
UN	United Nations
UNDP	United Nations Development Programme
UNFPA	United Nations Population Fund
UNIFEM	United Nations Development Fund for Women
UNTAET	United Nations Transitional Administration in East Timor
UN Women	United Nations Entity for Gender Equality and the Empowerment of Women

Acknowledgements

I am very grateful to colleagues who have provided support and encouragement, research guidance, feedback and editorial advice, particularly Rhonda Sharp, Marian Sawer, Siobhan Austen and Sue Ingram. I could not have undertaken this study without the interest and generosity of many women and men in Timor-Leste: there are too many to name them all. Their experiences and reflections continue to inspire my curiosity. Specific thanks go to the Secretary of State for the Promotion of Equality, the Ministry of Education, the National Statistics Directorate and the Timor-Leste Parliament for being actively interested in my research. I would also like to acknowledge the support of the University of South Australia and the Australian National University. Finally, I owe many, many thanks to my family in Australia and in Portugal, who have in many different ways nourished me throughout this journey.

1 Introduction

Introducing the study

In 2011 the President of Liberia, Ellen Johnson Sirleaf, defended government investment in gender equality in poor contexts that are vulnerable to violence and conflict. Sirleaf gained recognition as the first female head of an African state and was awarded the Nobel Peace Prize in 2011. Speaking of women in poor African countries who are vulnerable to violence and conflict, she outlined links between financing for gender equality and a state's capacity to weather crisis and political instability:

> African women represent the real catalysing element in society. They have carried the burden of feeding the nation . . . They have been the ones that, when all things fail, they are there to promote peace, to advocate, to reduce tensions in society. And they have been so disadvantaged while they've carried these burdens. So today all the effort that is being made to enhance them, to empower them, to enable them to make an even greater contribution, but with much more abilities through education – and the statistics are very clear, where there are women's empowerment the country's economy expands, per capita income is increased, the level of tension in society is reduced, so any country that wants to prosper and to have sustained growth and development have got to come up with strategies that enable them to empower women.
>
> (Quoted in GREAT Initiative, 2011)

Her argument was straightforward: strategies that aim to produce better outcomes for girls and women can expand the economy and contribute to peace building. Gender-responsive budgeting (henceforth GRB) is one such strategy.[1] This defence by Sirleaf provides an important political contribution to an emerging discussion on the role of strategies for gender equality in post-conflict countries and contexts labelled as fragile. Fragile contexts are characterised by their vulnerability to state breakdown, including the failure to deliver services, a lack of budget control and a propensity to descend into violence.[2] Two opposing views feature in this discussion. One is the claim by mainstream economists that it is premature to embark on gender equality reforms before establishing economic and institutional fundamentals in a fragile context. A particular concern is that GRB is seen as adding to demands in a context of scarce resources and creating a diversion (see Joshi & Naidu, 2007). Feminist scholars however, contest this view and argue that adopting GRB strategies can contribute to equality and assist these countries to weather conflict and crisis. Their research however has primarily been conducted in well-established democracies, with a state that controls its budget, has the capacity to deliver services and possesses mechanisms to engage with actors outside government.

GRB initiatives are strategies for integrating a gender perspective into policies and budgets in order to promote gender equality and women's empowerment. This involves assessing policies and budget decisions and processes for differences and inequalities between women and men in terms of incomes, assets, decision-making power, service needs and responsibilities for care. Further to this, GRB involves political actors undertaking actions to bring about reprioritisation of budget decisions and changes to policies and budget processes. GRB was developed in the 1980s in Australia and is a strategy of 'following the money' to ensure that the rhetoric on gender equality translates into real and practical policies, legislation and budget allocations (UNIFEM, 2000: p. 111). Activists and scholars have explored the role of GRB in improving budget and policy processes and decisions, bringing about better services, and producing more efficient and equitable outcomes for men and women, boys and girls. In 2008 the United Nations Development Fund for Women (UNIFEM) reported that more than 90 countries have adopted elements of GRB (UNIFEM, 2008). These countries included many fragile states, such as Afghanistan, Rwanda, Uganda, Bangladesh, Ethiopia, Mali, Nepal, Pakistan, Sri Lanka and Zimbabwe (Stotsky, 2016). This study will focus on the experience of Timor-Leste as a case study of the contribution that GRB can make to gender equality and state building in a fragile context. Situated in the Asia-Pacific region, Timor-Leste is new, poor and vulnerable to conflict. It has a population of over 1 million. A 2016 International Monetary Fund (IMF) report identified Timor-Leste as a country with a prominent GRB effort, one of only four fragile states to be classified as having a significant GRB initiative (Stotsky, 2016: p. 38).

In Timor-Leste, a little-noticed gender statement included in the 2008 budget documents instigated GRB. At the time the government was led by former independence fighter Xanana Gusmão. This statement committed the government to a gender mainstreaming approach to promote gender equality and change views on gender issues within the government and across the Timorese society. This approach was to be articulated in the second national development plan and the 2009 budget. It outlined a link between gender equality, public policy and service delivery (Timor-Leste Ministry of Finance, 2008: p. 34). This gender statement saw the emergence of a political and institutional narrative for GRB in Timor-Leste and provided direction for embedding its practice.

These initial developments in GRB took place at a time of political and institutional transition. A new (coalition) government had been elected in the aftermath of the 2006 political and security crisis. The crisis displaced 150,000 people (United Nations, 2006), paralysed the bureaucracy and left the state apparatus vulnerable to collapse. Timor-Leste's fledgling democracy was (again) displaying the fragility of its governance institutions and rule of law.

The pursuit of improvements in budget decision making and processes to make it gender responsive raised a degree of concern in some government quarters. GRB appeared to be a sophisticated and highly technical concept and many pointed to the fact that Timor-Leste's new architecture for gender-focused machinery, in the Office of the Secretary of State, was not fully institutionalised. These concerns resonated with a 2000 New Year speech by Gusmão (2000) in which he criticised the 'obsessive acculturation to standards that hundreds of international experts try to convey to the East Timorese, who are hungry for values' (p. 2). He nominated gender equality as one such international value. He argued for a hierarchy of priorities as a path for state building and peace:

> What concerns me is the non-critical absorption of (universal) standards given the current stage of the historic process we are building. Old democracies are no longer like a smooth pavement or a linear social process where such standards slide along without the slightest friction. What concerns me is that the Timorese may become detached from their reality and, above all, try to copy something which is not yet clearly understood by them.
>
> (Gusmão, 2000: p. 2)

Gusmão's main point was that universal norms may not always align with the needs of the community. The implication is that some international norms are, to a degree, a distraction and would be better dealt with when the conditions are right. Extending his rationale to the adoption of GRB suggests that GRB was seen as detracting from the (more urgent) needs of the 'reality' of the Timorese community.

A priority has been to foster aspects of state resilience. A resilient state is one that has achieved and maintained peace and that has been able to strengthen national identity and institutions of citizenship, monopolise the use of legitimate force, reach across the territory and control the budget process so as to weather external crises and the challenges of economic development (Putzel & Di John, 2012: p. 8). This raises the 'chicken or the egg' dilemma: do the fundamentals need to be in place before GRB can contribute to state resilience or is GRB one of the contributors to state resilience?

At an Asia-Pacific regional forum economists Suhas Joshi and Sanjesh Naidu (2007) made a case that GRB should not be pursued in fragile states. In their view GRB would result in competition for a limited pool of resources and skills, ultimately detracting from the state-building and peace-building efforts.

They argued that higher priority should be assigned to getting public finance institutions and rules right:

> Once the basic systems are in place and have been embedded in the public service, the next step is to contemplate targeted spending, including gender budgeting. It takes considerable effort, resources and time to systematically implement a gender perspective in national policies and processes. It is therefore even more important to put in place a framework that allows measurement of results.
>
> (Joshi & Naidu, 2007: p. 4)

Their argument was that GRB is costly in terms of displacing resources and time from building the fundamentals of public finance. They advised that a country should first 'assess its readiness for embarking on a gender budgeting exercise' (Joshi & Naidu, 2007: p. 4). This position is reminiscent of past views that were made popular by Allen Schick in a 1998 presentation to the World Bank (see Allen, 2009). Schick's presentation was not published. In it he argued that certain preconditions should be met ahead of public finance reform (Allen, 2009: p. 16).

Economist Richard Allen (2009) has noted that fragile states are in a favourable position to fast-track institutional reforms. In a discussion paper on the challenges of budget reform in developing countries, Allen (2009: p. 10) argues that fragile states, such as Timor-Leste, are at ground zero for institution building:

> Post-conflict countries such as Afghanistan, East Timor, and Liberia are in a special category; conditions for institution building may be more favourable, at least in the initial stages, because of the vacuum created by the decline of previous institutions, strong political leadership and a powerful donor presence.

On the surface this view might support GRB. However, such conceptualising of states as devoid of institutional, political and economic history and an understanding of power fails to recognise the important interactions between the technical and political elements of economic reform and policy. These elements, including gender politics, are important for understanding the potential of GRB.

Feminist economics and gender-responsive budgeting: the story so far

Since it first emerged in the 1990s the study of GRB has grown into a rich theoretical and empirical field with contributions from several disciplines and areas of study including economics, sociology, and political and development studies. Feminist scholarship has made significant contributions to the GRB effort and has provided evidence of the structural nature of gender issues in the economy. It has expanded notions of the economy and the role of the state and understandings of the interactions between women and the state.

GRB has been bolstered by feminist research showing that the economy is dependent on the invisible work of women in the form of unpaid care, voluntary work in the community and informal work. The gender division of labour is not only the foundation of gender inequalities, but it is structural to the way the economy operates. However, in mainstream economics this invisible work is excluded from the formal market. Feminist economics has shown that if policy makers ignore the unpaid economy and fail to recognise the links between gender relations and macroeconomic policies the result will be unjust and inefficient outcomes. From this vantage point, feminists have positioned gender inequality as both a policy efficiency and an equity issue (see Elson, 2002; Sharp, 2003b; Himmelweit, 2002). This work has positioned gender equality as critical for better economics. Feminist critiques of mainstream economics have played an important role in expanding the debate on the interactions between growth and gender equality (see Kabeer & Natali, 2013; Berik et al., 2009) and have generated new theories of the economy that incorporate social reproduction and the care economy (Bakker, 2003, 2011; Bakker & Gill, 2003; Elson, 1995; Himmelweit, 2002, 2008).

The World Bank has provided support for this critique (World Bank, 2011a), but has been criticised for not going far enough.[3] The recent global financial and economic crisis has again brought to centre stage the links between gender order and inequality prevailing in the society and economy, and public policy responses. Women in Southern and Northern countries have found themselves under stress due to cuts in expenditure on social services (for more on the impact of the crisis on women see Karamessini & Rubery, 2013; Pearson & Sweetman, 2010). The feminist conceptualisation of the economy that incorporates social reproduction and the care economy is also relevant to fragile states where the state has had a limited footprint in the provision of social services, and its resources are under pressure. A study by the International Committee of the Red Cross (ICRC, 2011) into the links between violence and health care in sixteen countries found evidence of the duress health services are under, with 655 violent events against health-care staff and patients and the depletion of infrastructure. The consequence is that this care work is relegated to the sphere of the household and the community. Relevant research into the impact of the dismantling of social services during structural adjustment programmes in developing countries has shown its impact on poor women and their burden of social reproduction (see Elson, 1994, 1995).

More normative arguments for GRB have also gained some traction. GRB has been viewed as having a central role in improving accountability for implementation of international commitments, such as the United Nations Convention on the Elimination of All Forms of Discrimination against Women (CEDAW), the Millennium Development Goals (MDGs) and the more recent Sustainable Development Goals (SDGs) (see Elson, 2006; Jhamb & Sinha, 2010; Grown et al., 2008). An IMF report on GRB efforts found that two-thirds of the 23 countries with significant GRB initiatives had aligned their goals to the MDGs or a national development plan. In Afghanistan and Morocco this alignment was made explicit in the budget (Stotsky, 2016). Concerns over performance against the MDGs provided an important impetus for GRB work in Morocco with initial efforts focusing on sectoral budgets for education, health and agriculture and their role in achieving MDG goals (Kolovich & Shibuya, 2016). In Zimbabwe in 2011 ministries were instructed to consider MDGs in drafting their budgets (Stotsky et al., 2016). These connections have been enhanced by efforts to monitor performance against the MDGs and the spending that supports them. A report from Government Spending Watch, a non-government group that monitors government spending on the MDGs and SDGs (Martin & Walker, 2015), has shown that on average across countries less than 0.1 per cent has been targeted at realising women's rights or addressing gender equality. Of particular concern is the high level of debt service and defence spending, and its negative impact on allocation of resources to achieve the MDGs. Further, this report noted that government spending was at least US$1.5 trillion a year short of what was necessary to realise the SDGs (Martin & Walker, 2015). This research confirms the arguments of early proponents of GRB that attention should go beyond gender-specific budget allocations to consider the impact of the bulk of the budget, or general budget, on women's economic and social position (see Sharp & Broomhill, 2002; Grown et al., 2008).

Scholarship on GRB has contributed to debates on the role of the state in influencing women's economic position. Some feminist analysts see GRB as underpinning positive role for the state in improving women's economic position, observing that gender-sensitive policy holds limited reach if not paired with budget considerations (see Sawer, 1990). However, other feminist studies have observed that the role of the government in influencing women's economic position is ambivalent, complex and conflicting. The history of GRB provides evidence that women activists can press on with demands for institutional mechanisms to advance equality and policies to recognise women's distinct economic interests. This is true even when they are constrained by conservative forces, including gender-blind economic policy and bias against state intervention to eradicate gender inequality (see Sharp & Broomhill, 1990, 2002). These experiences offer significant insights to gender activists in fragile states as the path towards resilience is likely to involve significant reconstruction of the state and a broad political agreement about the role of the state and the nature of its engagement with citizens. Research into gender equality and aspects of fragile states suggests that women's engagement with the state is complex and often mediated by family and community institutions, religion and customs (Castillejo, 2011; Harcourt, 2009b). In such contexts women and girls may experience economic interruptions, insecurity, lack of government accountability, lack of access to services, and a state-building process that reinforces pre-existing disadvantage (see Baranyi & Powell, 2005a, 2005b; Koch, 2008; O'Connell, 2011; Paantjens, 2009).

The desire to make the state accountable to women has provided impetus for several GRB initiatives. By inserting women's voices into the economic agenda, these initiatives have expanded notions of transparency and accountability (Bakker, 2002). GRB research has shown the links between service delivery and the interests and needs of women, including assessing the adequacy of funding for achieving agreed policy aims and tracking the disbursement of funds to their planned use (see Sharp & Elson, 2008). The work of feminist scholars in South Africa, for example, has traced what monies have been effectively spent on pursuing and prosecuting perpetrators of violence against partners (Vetten, 2005) and in detailing and costing the implementation of domestic violence law (Vetten et al., 2005).

The remainder of this introductory chapter will expand on the context of Timor-Leste and the questions underlying my research. It will set out my approach to exploring the question of whether GRB can promote gender equality and women's empowerment in the context of a fragile state.

Gender inequality in contemporary Timor-Leste

Gender equality has been an integral part of the political discourse in Timor-Leste, where it has been associated with nation building and development. The way concepts such as gender, women and equality have been appropriated and redefined in this context suggests several different influences, and a degree of pragmatic and conceptual diversity (Cunha, 2011). Three particular influences have added to the debate: the history of women's activism, the gender-focused institutions and the support of the international aid community. Non-government actors have adopted a great diversity of approaches including a focus on the economic, political and social empowerment of women, and an emphasis on mainstreaming gender across the design and implementation of programmes (see Trembath & Grenfell, 2007). Some within civil society have described themselves as 'feminists', which they associate with the promotion of freedom from social controls and discrimination. Within the government, activists have drawn on the gender and development framework to mobilise a wide base of support for the women's agenda (see Cristalis & Scott, 2005). International institutions have made an important contribution to arguments on women's rights and their contribution to democratic governance (see Trembath & Grenfell, 2007). The participants in this study were comfortable with the use of the term 'gender' in reference to initiatives to change economic and political structures to increase gender equality, and to ensure both women and men benefited from the budget.

The literature on gender issues in Timor-Leste provides ample evidence of the gender economic structures at play and the unequal impact of key economic indicators on women and their dependent children. Timor-Leste has experienced a strong growth pattern with non-oil gross domestic product (GDP) in constant prices estimated to have grown by 7.8 per cent in 2012 (Timor-Leste Government, 2014). This growth pattern is explained primarily by natural resources, fiscal transfers and public investment and reflects the economy's low growth base (Nixon, 2011). Nevertheless, Timor-Leste remains a low-income country with non-oil GDP per capita of US$810 (Umapathi, Dale & Lepuschuetz, 2013). In 2007 about half of the population lived below the poverty line set at US$0.88 per person per day (Timor-Leste Government & UNDP, 2009). While there has been progress in the reduction of poverty in Timor-Leste, there remains a serious challenge in achieving the MDG target of 14 per cent of the population living below the poverty line by 2015 (Timor-Leste Government & UNDP, 2009; Timor-Leste Ministry of Finance, 2014). The percentage of underweight children under five years has fluctuated in the last decade. Between 2001 and 2007 the percentage of underweight children under five rose from 45 to 48.6 per cent (Timor-Leste Government & UNDP, 2009). However, by 2013 this had decreased to 37.7 per cent. This improvement remains short of the MDG target of 31 per cent by 2015 (Timor-Leste Ministry of Finance, 2014). A particular challenge is unemployment, with an estimated 15,000 new job seekers entering the labour market each year. This is especially an issue for young Timorese, with 90 per cent of the unemployed aged between 15 and 34 (Timor-Leste Government, 2010). The 2013 Human Development Index (United Nations Development Programme, 2013) ranked Timor-Leste's level of human development as medium at 134 out of 186 countries (estimated at 0.576).

While statistics are patchy (and some are dated), a picture of Timor-Leste's gender equality and women's empowerment can be developed using a range of national and international sources. The 2007 Timor-Leste Living Standards Survey (TLLSS) provides ample evidence of the gendered nature of the labour market in Timor-Leste. It suggests that women are less active in the labour force, with women's participation rates estimated at 48.5 per cent – well short of men's participation rate of 77.4 per cent (Timor-Leste Direcção Nacional de Estatística, 2008: p. 197). A further MDG indicator, the share of women in wage employment in the non-agricultural sector, was estimated at 36 per cent in 2007, suggesting that the labour market is male-dominated (Timor-Leste Government & UNDP, 2009).

Further compounding the gendered nature of the labour market, the 2007 TLLSS reported that women's unemployment was 9.2 per cent, nearly twice that of men at 5.1 per cent. Young women were particularly vulnerable, with unemployment for women aged between 15 and 24 years old recorded at 22.6 per cent (Timor-Leste Direcção Nacional de Estatística, 2008: p. 200). Such high levels of unemployment are further aggravated by high levels of underemployment (see Umapathi & Velamuri, 2013). Gender segmentation is also apparent in industries and occupations, notwithstanding limitations in available data; Civil Service Commission data showed that only 21 per cent of public servants are women (Secretary of State for the Promotion of Equality, 2014). In the labour market, women traditionally occupy lower salary levels and possess fewer benefits and opportunities to improve their professional opportunities. The United Nations Development Programme (2011) reported a significant gender gap when it found that, out of 70,000 paid employees earning a combined total of US$12 million dollars per month, women received a mere one-quarter of this total wages bill. There is limited data, however, on how women are faring in terms of working conditions and participation in the informal economy.

Women spend more time than men on care and household work; the 2007 TLLSS found that women spent more time than men caring for children, cooking, cleaning, washing clothes and fetching water (Timor-Leste Direcção Nacional de Estatística, 2008). Typically, women devote 50 per cent of their time to housework, compared to 36 per cent for men (United Nations Development Programme, 2011). With a greater proportion of the responsibility for care work, limited employment opportunities and lower earnings, women and their children experience higher rates of poverty.

Characteristics of Timor-Leste's fragile status, with limited service delivery across the territory, have undercut investments in women's 'human capital'. Women's illiteracy rate was estimated at 54.3 per cent for women above 18 years old. This is higher than the 36.8 per cent of men in the equivalent age bracket who reported being unable to read and write (Timor-Leste Direcção Nacional de Estatística, 2008). The ratio of literate women to men aged 15–24 decreased from 97 per cent in 2004 to 93 per cent in 2007. This indicator of gender parity suggests that the MDG target of 100 per cent of literate women to men by 2015 remains challenging (Timor-Leste Government & UNDP, 2009). Women in rural areas are particularly disadvantaged, with 61.1 per cent of women aged above 18 years reporting an inability to read and write (Timor-Leste Direcção Nacional de Estatística, 2008). This pattern is also apparent in school enrolment levels, with girls comprising 48 per cent of students enrolled in 2008–9 (Timor-Leste Ministry of Education and Culture, 2011).

Despite gains in some areas, data suggest that health services are failing Timorese women. While there have been significant improvements in the provision of antenatal and postnatal care in Timor-Leste (see Timor-Leste Government, 2010; United Nations Development Programme, 2011), the Timor-Leste Demographic and Health Survey 2009–10 estimated that in the previous seven years maternal mortality remained high at 557 deaths per 100,000 live births (Timor-Leste National Statistics Directorate & ICF Macro, 2010). These results fall far short of the MDG target for maternal health set at 252 per 100,000 by 2015 (Timor-Leste Government & UNDP, 2009). Improvements in access to health services have been critical for progress thus far; it has been estimated that the percentage of pregnant women receiving antenatal care from a health professional at least once increased from 42.5 per cent in 2001 to 86 per cent in 2009. The availability of health services remains uneven across the territory, with 93 per cent of women in urban areas receiving antenatal care at least once during the pregnancy, but only 84 per cent women in rural areas receiving equivalent care. Despite an increase of more than ten percentage points between 2003 and 2009 for deliveries assisted by skilled health staff, this figure lags behind the MDG targets (Timor-Leste Government, 2010).

The 2009–2010 demographic and health survey estimated that the number of births per woman was high at 5.7 for the three years that preceded the survey, representing one of the highest fertility rates in the South-East Asian and Asian regions (Timor-Leste National Statistics Directorate & ICF Macro, 2010). High fertility rates have been associated with increased risks to the health of the woman and child, their access to education opportunities and economic growth (see World Bank, 2010). Moreover, gender equality and women's empowerment – specifically higher levels of women's autonomy, education, wages and labour market participation – have been associated with progress in reproductive health (World Bank, 2011c). More research into the factors contributing to high fertility rates is important to inform future health policy.

One of the gendered impacts of a fragile state is widespread violence against women. This pattern is evident in Timor-Leste, where the Timor-Leste National Police reported that domestic violence represented 77 per cent of all crime reported in 2009 (United Nations Development Programme, 2011). Formal justice systems have failed women who have pursued justice for such crimes (Justice System Monitoring Programme, 2004). The 2009–2010 demographic and health survey found that, of 2,951 women aged 15–49, 38 per cent had experienced physical violence (Timor-Leste National Statistics Directorate & ICF Macro, 2010). Domestic violence has been linked to poorer outcomes for women's health – and that of children – including maternal death, low birth weights and greater risk of infant mortality (Taft & Watson, 2013). Women's vulnerability rose in the internally displaced persons camps that emerge in the aftermath of the 2006 political and security crisis (Ellsberg et al., 2008: p. 191).

Recent episodes of breakdown in the legitimate use of force by the Timorese state have highlighted the significant role that male political elites and the military leadership can play in the outbreak of violence on a national scale. Women were absent from both triggering and solving the political and security crisis (see Niner, 2011). The roots of women's political and economic marginalisation are long. A particular feature of the Portuguese colonial state in Timor-Leste was its military nature, with high military rank seen as a sign of status and authority in local society. During Indonesian occupation the continued and institutionalised violence targeting women significantly reframed women's engagement with the state and with public services (see Chapter 2). It was not only the Indonesian occupation that obscured women's public role, but also the nationalist movement within the territory. Old patriarchal norms prevented activist women from being recognised as having an equal standing to male Falintil guerrilla fighters (see Niner, 2009).

Militarised models of masculinity were also prominent during the United Nations administration (see Chapter 2). A particular feature of this militarisation was its influence on views within Timor-Leste on what sort of military force would suit the country. The Congress of the National Council of Timorese Resistance (Conselho Nacional da Resistência Timorense, CNRT) believed that a light infantry would be appropriate because it would release resources to be directed to the larger effort of building the state and its infrastructure. These views, however, were challenged by the experience of militarism under the United Nations Transitional Administration (henceforth UNTAET), when the military performed security and a range of civilian functions such as health and infrastructure (Joshi, 2005). By 2006–2007 budget allocations were directed towards security and defence representing 12.1 per cent of the total budget. This positioned security and defence as the second largest budget allocation behind public works, which represented 15.8 per cent of the budget (author's calculations using data in Timor-Leste Ministry of Planning and Finance, 2006).

Characteristics of Timor-Leste's fragile state have framed much of what is possible for the state in terms of achieving progress against development indicators, and specifically the MDGs (Timor-Leste Government & UNDP, 2009). Women and girls face additional disadvantage, with gender inequality featuring as a social, economic and political issue in Timor-Leste. The fact that state insecurity is a gender issue becomes clear in, for example, widespread records of violence against women. In such a political, economic and institutional context, it would not be surprising if women were to find it difficult to make gender equality claims.

The characterisation of Timor-Leste as a fragile state

The concept of fragile state has gained some conceptual and political relevance in Timor-Leste. First, since independence in 2002 the nation has experienced vulnerability to violence and political crises linked to issues of service delivery and budget control. Second, international bodies have designated Timor-Leste as a fragile state. Third, and most significantly, internal political debate has been heavily influenced by references to the idea of 'fragile' as a descriptor of the country's development status.

Over the past decade Timor-Leste has experienced multiple political and humanitarian crises. This was well captured by the Timor-Leste Government and OECD (2009: p. 10) in their description of the nation's context as 'one of constant change, with periods of progress interrupted by episodes of crisis and instability'. Since gaining independence in 2002, peace has been only fleeting. Two episodes illustrate Timor-Leste's fragile status. The 2006 political and security crisis pitted elements of political elites, defence forces, the police and disenfranchised youths against each other. Peace and security were restored following a significant expansion in the international presence including international peacekeeping forces and support to reinstate governance institutions and the rule of law. Two years later, political stability was again threatened with the attempted assassination of both President Ramos-Horta and Prime Minister Xanana Gusmão (see Chapter 2).

These features of fragile state status have also revealed themselves in recurrent episodes of poor coverage and quality of state service delivery. This is well illustrated by a speech in 2012 by the President of Timor-Leste, Taur Matan

Ruak, at the inauguration of the fifth government, led by Prime Minister Gusmão. At the time, the President gave a damaging assessment of the state's performance in improving the lives of the Timorese and 'serving' its citizens:

> State institutions contribute to the unbalanced development of the territory. Our centralized public administration has large, heavy structures in the capital, often providing poor quality services, and is almost absent from the districts where most of the population lives and social and economic deprivation is greatest. The state is not serving the vast majority of the Timorese people as yet.
>
> (Ruak, 2012)

The President echoed a broader concern that state institutions were failing the Timorese by providing poor quality services that did not cover the territory. Ultimately Ruak saw such service failures as undermining Timor-Leste's route towards peace and development, and referred to a range of strategies to promote change. Gender equality appeared within this menu of strategies to promote peace and stability. His was a call for unity 'to remove Timor-Leste from all lists of fragile states' (Ruak, 2012).

Timor-Leste has been classified as a fragile state by international bodies, such as the World Bank (2014). Such classifications are uncomfortable and stigmatising. Labels such as 'fragile state' and 'failed state' emphasise vulnerability and are perceived to have a severe impact on a state's international image, diplomatic standing, and economic and development opportunities (see Bertoli & Ticci, 2011; Stewart & Brown, 2009). In addition, the label 'fragile' is often used interchangeably with others such as 'failed', 'failing', 'crisis' or 'weak', without any clear rationale (see Cammack et al., 2006). The tension around these labels was visible in Timor-Leste when, in the heat of the 2006 political and security crisis, the acting President Fernando de Araujo 'Lasama' opposed such labels, declaring 'Timor-Leste is not a failed state' (East Timor Legal Information Site, 2008). Donors appear to have become mindful of this risk. In a report about how to work more effectively with fragile states, the British government's aid agency noted that 'no state likes to be labelled as fragile by the international community' (Department for International Development, 2005: p. 7).

The concept of fragile state has been prominent in domestic political debates in Timor-Leste. How the nation has come to understand its fragile status was well illustrated in a speech by Prime Minister Gusmão in 2013 at the Pacific Islands Development Forum meeting:

> Coming from a post-conflict situation with widespread poverty and very limited resources, we lacked governance experience and had no institutions of State. We had no human or financial resources and no infrastructure or capacity to build. We had no laws and yet we had to learn how to live in a democracy. All of this placed us at a terrible crossroad where there was

no quick and guaranteed way to respond to the many needs of our people who were suffering and who demanded – and deserved – to have their needs met.

Additionally, from the moment we were 'born' we – as the youngest member of the Community of Nations – had to absorb democratic values and their universal principles, which were conveyed to us by others without having being given the time to digest them. This resulted in a cycle of crisis, which led to the unrest of 2006 that came to its climax in 2008.

(Gusmão, 2013)

In this speech Gusmão drew a clear link between the difficulties of providing services to communities across Timor-Leste – 'terrible crossroads' with 'no quick and guaranteed way to respond to the many needs' – and Timor-Leste's fragile status, which he described as a 'cycle of crisis'. He also pointed to the contribution of the international community to Timor-Leste's status, with its emphasis on particular values – including small government and neo-liberal economic policies.

Recognition of the role of the international community in aggravating fragile status provided impetus for establishing an organisation of fragile states. In 2008, in the aftermath of the 2005 Paris Declaration on Aid Effectiveness, a small group of countries characterised as fragile mobilised to change the terms of their relationship with the international community. This group became known as the g7+. The g7+ emerged from the recognition that the international community had contributed to the failure of the development project in fragile contexts by pursuing international benchmarks prematurely, instead of the national development agenda and politically agreed priorities (Wyeth, 2012a). The g7+'s view of fragile status emphasises a process that enables a state to move from this status to resilience, describing a fragile status as 'a period of time during nationhood'. This definition emphasises activities such as inclusive political settlements, security, employment, good management of resources, and accountable and non-discriminatory service delivery (g7+, 2013: p. 4). These views establish a link between improving policy and budget processes and decisions, and the path to state resilience.

Timor-Leste was one of the founding members of the g7+ global platform of fragile states. Timor-Leste's leading role in the g7+ provides the strongest indication that it has endorsed the concept of fragile status as a political strategy. 'The "g7+"', Prime Minister Gusmão (2012) affirmed, 'provided an opportunity for fragile nations to meet, independently of our development partners, and to have a collective voice in the global development dialogue' (p. 1). While it is premature to assess the impact of the g7+, Vanessa Wyeth (2012b: p. 9) suggests that the g7+ 'made a splash' for they have framed the debate with an emphasis on their own context and priorities. Through this process, fragile states are claiming a more active role in the definition of national development policies and priorities, and are recentring the debate on the crucial features that make for a resilient state. Having commenced with a membership of seven countries, the g7+ has expanded, mobilising 20 countries in Africa, Caribbean and the Asia-Pacific region in 2016.

Fragile state contexts gained international attention in the mid-2000s as a reference to the poorest and most conflict-prone countries that were failing to meet minimum benchmarks set by the international community. The Organisation for Economic Co-operation and Development estimated that in 2015 fragile states were home to around 1.4 billion people or 20 per cent of the world's population. It was estimated that in 2013, 43 per cent of the world's people that are living on less than US$1.25/day were in fragile states (OECD, 2015). Research suggests that different social obligations and responsibilities, and exposure to violence, increases the effect of crises on women, marginalising them from access to the benefits of peace. Maternal mortality is an important indicator of gender inequality and discrimination in such contexts; it has been estimated that more than a third of maternal deaths worldwide occur in fragile states (World Health Organization, 2015).

Despite its currency, 'fragile state' remains a highly disputed concept. This concept was first circulated by international public institutions in the context of security concerns and became consolidated through an important body of primarily policy literature (see Bertoli & Ticci, 2011; Nay, 2012). This study draws on a working definition of fragile states that focuses on power and politics, following British researchers James Putzel and Jonathan Di John (2012). Their working definition highlights the following crucial features of fragile states: first, the failure of the state to operate basic bureaucratic machinery and control taxation and the budget process, and, second, its weak capacity to establish a presence throughout the territory including through service delivery. Their approach makes elements of economic policy a measure of fragile status, with the politics of taxation, macroeconomic policy and the degree of participation in the budget process linked to state legitimacy and resilience. Another important feature of this approach is the emphasis on fragile state status being on a spectrum that includes state resilience. Resilient states are those that hold the political tools to weather the tensions inherent in the development project. This construction of the fragile state as a stage on the path to resilience places the emphasis on the economic, social and political framing of local contexts and their impact on state building (Putzel & Di John, 2012). Another important feature of this approach is its focus on state capacity and capability and the recognition that several institutions, at times contradictory, can coexist, offering the possibility of actors switching between sets of rules (Di John, 2008). It is important to remember here that, despite its challenges to the concept of the fragile state, Timor-Leste has adopted a political version of the concept to express its vulnerability to crisis and its interactions with international organisations.

Feminists have joined those who critique current models, arguing they make gender power relations invisible (Castillejo, 2011). This invisibility comes from lack of recognition of gender as an analytical category of practical use for understanding fragile states (Jennings, 2010). The omission is significant as women's disadvantage, different social obligations and responsibilities, and exposure to violence implies that they are disproportionately affected by crisis and have less access to the benefits of the path to peace (UNDP, 2010). For example, one response to the state's vulnerability to violence and conflict has been the emergence of particular forms of the military state and with it the preservation of male privilege and female subordination (see Joan B. Kroc Institute, 2008; Turpin, 1998). Security is a particular priority in fragile and post-conflict state contexts, and feminist scholar Elisabeth Porter (2013) has found that security is also central to many women's views of empowerment. Also significant is the separation between the democratic governance agenda and the economic agenda, which will impact on opportunities for women to exercise their economic rights and to make the government accountable (UNDP, 2010). This research highlights that gender is central to a state that is legitimate, responsive and accountable (see OECD, 2013).

In summary, the concept of a fragile state in the Timor-Leste context has been politicised to draw attention to what the state can deliver, and has been reframed to underscore that the priorities of Timor-Leste need to reflect the particular context of the country. The Timor-Leste government has taken steps to engage with the principles of state resilience – including improving management and control of the budget and ensuring a presence throughout the territory – in its attempt to stamp fragile status away. The manner in which state fragility and resilience have been constructed and politicised in the Timor-Leste context is important for understanding the potential of GRB.

Learning from GRB experiences in fragile states

The expectations for GRB in fragile states are high. Proponents of GRB initiatives argue that they have a positive influence on policy processes and decision making, citizen–state relationships, state accountability and transparency, and gender equality (see Harcourt, 2009b; Khan, 2009). Their arguments have been derived primarily from contexts with an operating state, in command of its budget processes and decisions, capable of delivering services and with mechanisms to engage with actors outside government. Without a detailed study of GRB in a fragile state context it is impossible, with certainty, to make the case for GRB in such contexts. In this book I reflect on this question and investigate whether GRB can promote gender equality, women's empowerment and state resilience in a fragile state context. I examine the links between gender equality and fragile state status, with a focus on how the state controls the taxation and budget processes and reaches citizens though service delivery.

Despite the upsurge of GRB initiatives across the world, no country has addressed gender equality in the budget in its entirety. Instead, the degree of development or phases that GRB initiatives have reached is significantly mixed. Political, institutional, normative and relational factors, which Angela O'Hagan (2015: p. 234) termed a 'Framework of Favourable Conditions', offer some insights into the degree of adoption and implementation of GRB. O'Hagan

(2015) suggests that three sequential stages can be found: advocacy and agenda setting, formal adoption and implementation.

In the first phase of adoption of GRB the emphasis is on building a case for GRB as a strategy to address gender inequality. For example, in Pakistan budget and aid reforms created an opportunity for the gender equality institutions in government to pursue GRB. Since mid-2005 there have been significant efforts in awareness, training and gender analysis with targeted changes introduced to budget processes and key documents (see Chakraborty, 2016; Sharp et al., 2010). The evidence from Pakistan illustrates the shortcomings of a GRB project that was born out of aid reform processes, with ongoing problems of leadership and commitment and limited demand from civil society groups (Sharp et al., 2010). However, it supports other relevant research suggesting that important factors include a context of reform (see Budlender, 2009; Sharp, 2003a), a willingness to undertake reform that is meaningful to gender equality and a favourable macroeconomic context (see Sharp & Broomhill, 2002).

In some contexts, the approach to building a demand for GRB has involved a pilot initiative. This was the case in Fiji, a fragile democracy in the Pacific region, which in 1999 joined a Gender Budget Initiative of Commonwealth countries. Political instability, with the 2000 and the 2006 military coups, has severely undermined the potential for Fiji to adopt GRB initiatives (Costa & Sharp, 2011).

In other contexts, the formal adoption of GRB has been underpinned by a strong conceptual framework outlined in key policy and legislative documents, committed actors inside and outside government, and political will (O'Hagan, 2015: p. 238). Despite significant political and institutional change, Nepal's GRB initiative has produced important results including time-use statistics, and shed some light on the care economy (see Chakraborty, 2016; Sharp, Elson et al., 2009). The appointment in 2005 of a GRB expert and a permanent committee within the Ministry of Finance provided support to GRB, and the launch of a GRB framework for budget analysis a few years later provided further clarity to the GRB exercise in Nepal and showcased the political will that was behind it (Sharp, Elson et al., 2009). An important feature of this GRB effort was active local participation and research, which have played a role in sustaining the demand for GRB, and in the design of the approach to budget analysis (Chakraborty, 2016; Sharp, Elson, Costa & Vas Dev, 2009).

Some cases have reached the GRB implementation stage, with budget improvements including gender mainstreaming, and an application of gender analysis to support better decisions and processes (see O'Hagan, 2015: p. 238). There were some positive elements of the GRB initiative in Rwanda which dates back to 2002 when the key accountability instrument of gender budget statements was first developed. New momentum was gained in 2008 with an initiative supported by UN Women. It benefited from a context of budget reform with a move towards programme-based budgeting, and drew support from the commitment to GRB outlined in the national gender policy.

Important institutional steps were taken with the establishment of the Gender Monitoring Office, an accountability mechanism with authority to ensure that gender budget commitments were being met, and the inclusion of gender budget statements in the budget law (Stotsky et al., 2016; Stotsky, 2016). Despite some significant challenges there is some evidence of the intention to mainstream gender into policies, programmes and the budget (see Mirwobe, 2013; Mukunda, 2011).

Gender policy units, such as the Ministry of Gender and Family Promotion and the Gender Monitoring Office in Rwanda, have been identified as critical actors in the success and sustainability of GRB initiatives (see Sawer, 2002; Sharp & Broomhill, 2013). It is no coincidence that GRB strategies were first developed in Australia when feminists had a strong presence in the state through women's policy machinery (Sawer, 1990, 2002; Sharp & Broomhill, 2013; Sharp & Costa, 2011). This institutional model became popular, including in fragile states (Castillejo, 2011). There is, however, a relative silence on the contribution of gender-focused parliamentary bodies to challenging old norms and practices (see Sawer, 2014). This silence is all the more significant as there is a growing number of such bodies in parliaments across the world; the Inter-Parliamentary Union (IPU) has reported that almost half of 77 parliaments have a women's caucus (Ballington, 2008). There is also some evidence that such bodies are making economic policy more responsive to women (Byanyima, 2002; Wehner & Byanyima, 2004). The interest in theorising the role of parliamentary bodies in the promotion of gender equality is gaining traction (Sawer, 2014). However, the contribution of such bodies to GRB has rarely been examined in contexts where the state fails to deliver services and the parliament may struggle to make the government accountable. This is a significant problem as it would be expected that in such contexts, given weak processes and limited parliamentary oversight, gender-focused institutions in parliament would find it highly challenging to make a positive contribution to change.

In Uganda, the Forum for Women in Democracy, a non-government organisation (NGO) established by women parliamentarians, provided impetus for the first GRB initiative in the country (Stotsky et al., 2016). Research suggests that NGOs such as this can make a positive impression on the state (Budlender, 2002a; Costa et al., 2010). However, the case for women's organisations to engage with economic policy in fragile states is far from established. The challenge for women and their organisations in such contexts can be heightened by power arrangements that exclude non-government actors and the view that their actions may undermine the legitimacy and resilience of the state. In such contexts, women are faced with limited options to search for alternatives to government services, and demand for change might be their most feasible and effective strategy (UNIFEM, 2008). Other related literature highlights the political, cultural and material legacy of colonialism in the developing state context (Rai, 1996). Such legacies can undermine the perceived legitimacy of women engaging with economic policy. This literature reminds us that the path out of fragile status involves significant reconstruction of the state, and that part of this process is redefining the nature of the relationship between the state and women on economic policy.

International actors and covenants, and their underlying reporting processes, have been critical in fostering a pro-equality context, supporting the initiative of critical actors and bolstering gender knowledge (Bakker, 2007; Budlender, 2004; Elson, 2006). International organisations played an important role in bolstering a normative framework for GRB and providing technical and financial support for these initiatives in contexts such as Afghanistan (Kolovich & Shibuya, 2016). These interactions with international actors have taken a variety of forms. The GRB initiative in Mozambique has benefited from a collaboration with the Tanzanian Gender Network Program, a pioneer in GRB in Africa. This cooperation was under the auspices of the Southern African Development Community (SADC; see Stotsky et al., 2016). The SADC's work provides further evidence of the critical role that gender-focused institutions within such international institutions can play in the diffusion and adoption of GRB (see SADC, 2014). Despite these experiences, the contribution of international institutions in the diffusion and adoption of GRB has been a relatively neglected area of investigation.

Gender-relevant research and data are crucial to building the case for gender equality, improving policy and budgeting, and holding the state accountable for its political commitments (Moser, 2007). In Belgium, which has one of the most comprehensive and advanced GRB initiatives, there is a statutory requirement to collect and use sex-disaggregated data; this was included in its 2007 law on the integration of a gender dimension into all federal policies (Stotsky, 2016). GRB initiatives in Sub-Saharan Africa have been associated with more frequent time-use studies more and interest in unpaid care work (Stotsky et al., 2016: p. 39). Notwithstanding some success (see Sharp, Vas Dev et al., 2009), lack of data on the comparative situation of women and men, girls and boys (and their different sub-groups) continues to damage the potential of GRB to identify and respond to disadvantage (see Budlender & Hewitt, 2003). A particular area where feminist economists have been active is the call for unpaid care work to be counted in statistics, and made visible in representations of the economy and in policy-making processes (UNIFEM, 2000). The limited literature on data and indicators in fragile and post-conflict states suggests that those contexts face particular challenges including destroyed transport infrastructure, weak institutions, outdated systems and administrative structures, and the politicisation of data collection and use (see Fernández-Castilla, 2011). In the past two decades, indicators have become a fixture of development discourse, which places a premium on openness, transparency and participation. Indicators have become powerful tools to highlight state failure, and inspire nations to perform better and progress in the ranking. Indicators have also played a role in modern states in guiding decision making and reaching across the territory including supporting tax collection (see Merry, 2011; Porter, 1996). In this study I will focus on indicators that highlight how the state is failing women. I will investigate how gender analysis can shed some light on gender deficits in service delivery and support decisions on policy and resource allocations.

While the demand for research and data has gained momentum, it is less clear that this information has had an impact on policy decisions. The impact remains slight in developing countries, given low levels of capacity to engage with scientific evidence in policy debates and mistrust of scientific knowledge (Jones et al., 2008). Whether GRB can play a role in translating this technical and analytical work into policy change has been subject to academic debate. Some have suggested that the political and technical processes inherent in the gender mainstreaming enterprise can be complementary and that GRB provides a successful illustration of this (Sharp & Elson, 2008; Walby, 2005). Others propose that GRB is part of a portfolio of gender mainstreaming tools that have contributed to reducing gender equality to simple and short-term technical issues and processes. In doing so, GRB has diverted attention from the political and contested nature of gender, gender equality and gender mainstreaming (Kantola, 2010). Research into the factors that enable gender analysis to be an effective political tool in fragile contexts is only in its infancy (see Austen et al., 2013). In fragile states, bringing expertise and politics together may be a challenge given the weaknesses of political institutions and the bureaucracy. This study makes a contribution to research on the interface between research and policy change by investigating the factors that make gender analysis a part of the policy process and encourage accountability to women.

Change to the political economy of Egypt brought its initial GRB work to a halt (Kolovich & Shibuya, 2016) and is an important reminder of the way economic and political contexts determine the potential of GRB. In Australia, the election of a government in the 1970s with a reform agenda and an election commitment to make government more responsive to women provided an important anchor for the efforts of feminist bureaucrats and activists (Sawer, 2002; Sharp & Broomhill, 2013). It is likely that the path to state resilience may present opportunities to embed a gender equality agenda in economic and budget policy. 'Critical junctures' (Waylen, 2011: p. 149), such as transitions to democracy and peace, offer opportunities to advance gender equality in, for example, the negotiation of political settlements and constitutions. Flux in power relations in these moments of transition enables practices and institutions to be reshaped, and women's representation in formal politics and their economic contribution to increase (see Budlender et al., 2010; O'Connell, 2011; Porter, 2007; OECD, 2013). The literature, however, emphasises that progress in locking gender issues into new institutions can be undermined by old gender norms and the way political business has always been done (Mackay, 2009: p. 16). These tensions are particularly significant in fragile states where institutions are emerging from, and being framed by, masculinity, conflict and violence. In the post-Arab Spring of Egypt and Libya, governments took steps to curb the rights of women (see OECD, 2013).

The literature has built a strong economic, governance and equity case for GRB. It has highlighted its significant contribution to building more effective states and stronger democracies. This literature however has not engaged with fragile state contexts, leaving unanswered questions of whether such states should embark on such political and technical enterprises. These questions are all the more significant as recent literature on fragile states has failed to recognise gender as an analytical category of practical use. This omission is important as fragile states are setting the ground rules of their economic policy. Ignoring gender equality can produce unjust and inefficient outcomes. This study investigates two critical factors for successful GRB initiatives: the role of and interactions between policy actors, and the potential of gender analysis to bolster change. The remainder of this study answers the question whether the case for GRB can be extended to fragile state contexts by investigating its contribution to gender equality and state resilience. The literature relevant to the political and technical issues inherent to the success of GRB initiatives is discussed further in relevant chapters.

Research questions and approach

The growing literature on GRB suggests that it improves the lives of poor women, for example by improving economic indicators, allocating expenditure more effectively, counting the care economy and enhancing women's participation in economic policy (see Sharp & Elson, 2008). The literature suggests that such initiatives can contribute to strengthening governance, transparency and accountability (Bakker, 2002). These arguments have gained currency in Timor-Leste. The 2009 parliamentary resolution for the adoption of GRB in Timor-Leste (Parlamento de Timor-Leste, 2010) showcases the expectations around its potential contribution to economic growth and prosperity, accountability to women's interests and needs, budget transparency, and civil society participation in budget decisions. This resolution offers a unique insight into the economic and political rationale that moved women to pursue GRB. Women were looking for strategies that could support their political and technical efforts to bring about a more equitable, participatory, transparent and accountable development project. I will explore contextual, normative, institutional and social factors that enable (or constrain) the potential for GRB in a fragile state such as Timor-Leste.

Whether the GRB effort can realise aspirations depends on the political actors, their goals and view of the role of GRB, the strategies and tools they deploy and the broader economic, political and social context (O'Hagan, 2015). This research addresses the problem of whether GRB can promote gender equality and women's empowerment in a fragile state context. Using Timor-Leste as a case study, this study investigates:

• How do gender-focused institutions (in parliament, in the community and in government) engage with a fragile state to contribute to positive changes in budgets and policy processes and priorities?

• How can gender analysis, using administrative data, contribute to an understanding of the impact of the budget and foster policy and budget changes?

Feminist action research (FAR) provided a framework for this empirical investigation. FAR was useful for it emphasises understanding the views of women, the inclusion and participation of women in the research process, and, most importantly, a commitment to support action for positive change. Two particular reasons justify this choice: first, these FAR principles, specifically inclusion, participation, action and change (see Reid, 2004: p. 8), are central to the practice and scholarship of feminist economists on national budget policy. The theme of the inclusion of women in economic policy, for example, emerged strongly in the South African experience where organisations engaged in GRB produced simplified versions of their budget analysis to mobilise a wider community of women in the debate (Budlender, 2002b). Second, FAR offers a path to investigate the interface between research and action. Feminist scholarship – and specifically GRB – has recognised the significant role of research in informing positive policy and budget changes.

I used a combination of quantitative and qualitative methods in this study. My qualitative data collection involved interviews and focus groups in order to explore the practice and the meaning attributed to GRB and the potential for further action. The interviews were devised to develop an understanding of the meaning that men and women attach to GRB, its practice and, ultimately, its contribution to gender equality in a fragile state context such as that of Timor-Leste. I conducted and analysed 20 semi-structured interviews with key informants in Timor-Leste from a range of institutions engaged in budgeting and policy, and specifically GRB, including members of parliament (MPs), public officials engaged in policy-making, members of the women's movement and non-governmental, international policy advisers, and leading public opinion commentators. These interviews were conducted between 2011 and 2013. This study drew on additional interviews conducted as part of a two-year research project, called Gender-Responsive Budgeting in the Asia-Pacific Region. This project, funded by Australian aid, involved collaboration between economists Rhonda Sharp (University of South Australia), Diane Elson (University of Essex) and Siobhan Austen (Curtin University). In 2008–2010 this project examined the practices of, and potential for, integrating a gender perspective into budgetary processes in the Asia-Pacific region. These interviews provide a useful insight into the early days of the adoption of GRB.

Two focus group sessions were conducted with middle-level management in the Ministry of Education (MoE). A total of five participants were engaged in the focus groups. Participants were selected for their role in policy and data collection. Participants were drawn from the gender working group in the MoE and from the team responsible for managing the Education Management Information System (EMIS). The first focus group session took place in mid-2011 and involved three participants. At this session I presented the research project and provided preliminary results of performance of schools, showing how these compared across the country against gender-relevant indicators derived from EMIS. These indicators provided an impetus for a conversation on the usefulness of this approach for policy and budgeting. The second focus group session took place in mid-2013 and involved two participants. This focus group session considered the sort of socio-economic data that can be derived from TLLSS to shed light on the particular gender gaps that persist in education in Timor-Leste. The conversation dealt with issues related to the way that the gender analysis could be used to change the views of senior policy makers in relation to gender equality and to improve the gender responsiveness of budgets and policy.

The quantitative data included: (1) the use of an education administrative dataset, the EMIS, from the Timor-Leste MoE to produce a series of gender-relevant indicators, and (2) the use of a large household survey, the TLLSS from the Timor-Leste Ministry of Finance (MoF), to develop complementary socio-economic indicators. I aim to use this quantitative analysis to contribute to a debate on how to improve gender equality outcomes in education in Timor-Leste. This quantitative data analysis also provided the impetus for focus groups with public officials in the MoE in order to investigate the interface between gender analysis, positive policy and budget change. The combination of sources of data allowed the triangulation of evidence and the production of a comprehensive account of the research issues contributing to scholarship and theory on GRB and fragile states.

In short, quantitative (the EMIS and the TLLSS data) and qualitative methods (interviews, participant observation and focus groups) were used in a complementary manner to strengthen the robustness of the analysis, and capture a more complete, contextual and nuanced portrait of GRB in a context of fragility. Methods were applied with a degree of fluidity depending on the specific circumstances I encountered in Timor-Leste; to a lesser degree these methods influenced each other and informed the research questions.

The structure of the study

Chapter 2 traces the surfacing of GRB in Timor-Leste, initially as a government initiative. In this chapter I argue that the effort of institution building that supported a gender equality agenda made it possible for a narrative and a practice to emerge around GRB. This effort was framed as a strategy for gender mainstreaming and the promotion of Timor-Leste's economic sustainability. One particular strategy was mobilising high-level political support for changes to the way the budget is done. The focus of the initial stages of GRB adoption was on budget planning and its enactment including the annual action plans, budget statements, call circular and review processes. Timor-Leste's vulnerability to crisis undermined initial progress in women's engagement in economic policy, and this was worsened by the state's militarised and masculine nature, its failure to include a broad base of voices and its limited political presence.

Chapter 3 investigates the contribution of the parliament to Timor-Leste's GRB initiative. It examines the role of Timor-Leste's women's cross-party caucus in the passage of a parliamentary resolution on GRB. Much of the content of this chapter was previously published in 2013 in the *International Feminist Journal of Politics.*[4] Chapter 3 shows that the passage of the GRB resolution showcased the organisational skills of women parliamentarians and provided some evidence of their ability to influence policy, undertake scrutiny of the budget and encourage the participation of women's organisations and civil society.

Chapter 4 studies the conditions under which women activists can influence economic policy, making the government accountable for its policy commitments and encouraging active citizenship around the budget. I argue that women's strategic mobilisation around a cooperative and autonomous political platform, Rede Feto, has created opportunities for gender equality to become part of Timor-Leste's development project. Women's activism on economic policy is gaining shape, having benefited from a clear political agenda and some important political wins on representation and legislation to address violence against women. These positive steps have been constrained by a state that reflects masculine and militaristic privilege and the consolidation of power at the expense of spaces of participation.

Chapter 5 examines the contribution of international organisations to the pursuit of a gender equality agenda. Specifically, it studies the launch of a caucus of women parliamentarians in an international parliamentary institution, the Parliamentary Assembly of Portuguese-Speaking Countries. This chapter is based on an article that was published previously in 2016 in *Parliamentary Affairs.*[5] The experience of the Network of Women in this parliamentary assembly (NWPA-CPLP) provides an insight into the political, technical and financial challenges faced by women's collective action in the context of international parliamentary bodies.

Chapter 6 investigates the potential for further development of GRB in Timor-Leste. It reports on how the EMIS data can be used to develop gender-relevant indicators that measure and compare school performance across districts and sub-districts to guide policy and budget decisions. Such indicators were developed to identify gender inequality and gaps in the delivery of education services in Timor-Leste. Linking the EMIS data to household survey data (the TLLSS) enhances its value as a guide for policy and budget decision making in the education sector. I developed social and economic indicators using the TLLSS, providing policy makers with an insight into the social and economic context of each school. This provides an illustration of how EMIS can be used as a tool to influence policy and funding for improved gender responsiveness. Chapter 6 engages with the very limited research that exists on the EMIS data, the focus of which has been on its systemic and technical shortcomings. Such research has paid little attention to gender inequality and gaps exposed by the data. This chapter provides policy directions for improving gender equality outcomes in education in Timor-Leste.

Chapter 7 draws on the analysis outlined in Chapter 6 to explore the interactions between gender analysis and policy and budget decision making. Chapter 7 documents the reactions of policy makers in the MoE to the indicators developed using EMIS and the TLLSS. The views of these policy makers were collected in two focus groups and complemented by interviews. This chapter explores how a gender analysis of the EMIS could influence policy and budgeting, frame policy debate, foster changes in political discourses and processes, change policy and budgeting, and influence the behaviour of actors both inside and outside government. I argue that internal political interactions around policy making (including gender-focused institutional arrangements), together with issues of power and gender in public debate, determine which aspects of gender-relevant research are considered useful for policy. Characteristics of the research process and the relationship between feminist researchers and policy makers can determine whether research generates the momentum and support needed for positive change.

Concluding remarks in Chapter 8 discuss the potential of GRB for state building, economic efficiency and gender equality. This chapter explores the implications of this case study of a fragile state for GRB practice and research, and for global debates on development in contexts of state fragility or resilience.

Conclusion

The idea that fragile states should tackle gender inequality and gaps through economic policy is not yet widely accepted. Feminist scholars have documented the contribution of GRB to strengthening governance, accountability and transparency. However, other commentators have argued that gender equality reform should be delayed until economic and institutional fundamentals are established. Nonetheless, several fragile states have adopted elements of GRB by making changes to budget policy, decisions or administrative processes. A 2016 IMF report (Stotsky, 2016) found that four fragile states have undertaken prominent GBR efforts. Timor-Leste was one of those countries. My detailed study of GBR in Timor-Leste aims to contribute to these debates and shed some light on what GRB can deliver in fragile state contexts in terms of gender equality, women's empowerment and state resilience. The next chapter explores the emergence of a narrative and a practice for GRB in Timor-Leste.

Notes

1 In this study the terms 'gender-responsive budgeting', 'gender-sensitive budgeting', 'gender-sensitive public finances' and 'gender budgeting' will be used interchangeably.
2 In the context of this study, 'fragile states' and 'fragile contexts' will be used interchangeably.
3 See special issue of the journal *Global Social Policy*, 12 (2) for a discussion of the shortcomings of this report.
4 See Costa et al. (2013).
5 See Costa (2016).

2 The emergence of gender-responsive budgeting: gender machinery and the state

Since Timor-Leste gained independence in 2002, a narrative on GRB as a strategy to pursue gender mainstreaming has emerged that associates gender equality and women's empowerment with Timor-Leste's economic productivity, efficiency and sustainability. A range of practical initiatives to translate GRB into Timor-Leste's policy and budgeting decision making followed the first reference to GRB in a statement included in the 2008 budget papers.

The experience of Timor-Leste is not unique among fragile states. Gender-responsive budgeting has gained traction globally and has materialised in some fragile state contexts. Government-led GRB experiences have emerged in contexts such as Uganda, Mali and Pakistan. In Uganda the government officially endorsed GRB in 2004/2005 when it was incorporated in the budget call circular. Since then the budget call circular has been developed to strengthen the adoption of GRB, with the 2016/2017 circular encouraging detailed actions to respond to gender inequality and providing instructions on how to report sector plans (Stotsky, 2016; Stotsky et al., 2016). In 2010 a GRB initiative was adopted in Mali, with budget call circulars providing instructions for gender-responsive planning and budgeting. From 2011 a budget annex was integrated into the finance law, requiring an assessment of performance on programmes, objectives and indicators related to the national gender policy action plan (Stotsky et al., 2016). The government of Pakistan in 2005 adopted GRB with significant support from aid agencies. Since then, there have been some advances in awareness, training and skills on tools and approaches (Sharp et al., 2010). This initial work bolstered the analysis of the 2015/2016 budget and saw improvements in the 2016/2017 budget to promote gender equality in education and workforce participation (Chakraborty, 2016). Combined, these experiences highlight how governments in fragile states are setting up positive conditions for GRB (see O'Hagan, 2015) including raising awareness and providing training, channelling support from the international community, granting political commitment to gender equality and demonstrating the will to adopt GRB with the leadership of key ministries, not least the MoF.

This chapter tracks the emergence of GRB in Timor-Leste, which, in its early stages, was primarily a government initiative. In this chapter I seek to examine the political and institutional background to GRB in Timor-Leste. Legacies of

Portuguese colonisation, Indonesian occupation and UNTAET's state-building project offer important insights into what is possible for strategies for gender equality in Timor-Leste. I explore the internal feminist strategies that enabled the materialisation of GRB and the political legacies that have influenced the state in Timor-Leste. I argue that the characteristics of institution building for gender equality made it possible for a narrative to emerge around GRB. In this narrative, GRB was considered to be a strategy for gender mainstreaming and the promotion of Timor-Leste's economic sustainability. However, political instability has undermined initial progress in women's engagement in economic policy in Timor-Leste. This has been aggravated by the state's militarised and masculine nature, failure to include a broad base of voices and limited political presence. First, this chapter provides a brief account of the emergence of a political narrative around GRB, highlighting the changes to processes, training and awareness-raising opportunities that have followed. Second, it outlines the political architecture for gender equality in the government and its role in setting up a positive milieu for a government GRB initiative in Timor-Leste. Third, it considers the historical legacies of Timor-Leste's machinery of government and explores the influence of its key political and economic features on the emerging GRB initiative.

The advent of a narrative on gender-responsive budgeting

Gender-responsive budgeting (GRB) was first outlined in the 2008 budget papers by way of a short gender statement charting the commitment of the government to integrate a gender perspective into its annual plans and performance indicators (Timor-Leste Ministry of Finance, 2008). This gender statement contributed to fashioning an enduring political and institutional narrative for GRB in Timor-Leste and provided a direction for embedding its practice. It emphasised a gender mainstreaming approach ahead of the launch of the second national development plan and the 2009 budget. In addition, it identified particular areas of focus for public policy and service delivery:

> [w]omen are a particular priority for social policies where gender should be considered as part of all policies aimed at job creation, education and sports, vocational training and the development of entrepreneurship. The Government shall also promote the creation of mechanisms that will encourage the participation of women in political activities and address issues of domestic violence.
>
> (Timor-Leste Ministry of Finance, 2008: p. 34)

This statement charted a process to integrate gender issues into the budget through budget statements, annual action plans and the performance indicators of ministries (Timor-Leste Ministry of Finance, 2008). It was paired with a reference to gender equality as a cross-cutting issue for budgetary preparation in the budget speech by Prime Minister Gusmão (Timor-Leste Ministry of Finance, 2008: p. 16).

In March 2008 gender activists seized on the occasion of International Women's Day to further political support for GRB. Gathered for the celebrations, the government, members of parliament, civil society and religious groups pledged to increase resources and develop programmes, politics and legislation for the promotion of gender equality, including developing a strategy for the implementation of GRB and expanding the financial and human resources dedicated to gender equality. This political commitment, which became known as the Deklarasaun Kompromisu Dili (Timor-Leste Government, 2008), further anchored a political and institutional narrative for GRB. This pledge linked gender equality and women's empowerment to Timor-Leste's economic productivity, efficiency and sustainability. By making these associations more explicit the pledge strengthened the case for women to engage with economic policy. In the event, Prime Minister Gusmão gave his personal support to the pledge (United Nations Integrated Mission in Timor-Leste, 2008). The discussions that culminated in the pledge revealed how the government envisaged translating gender issues into the budget process. They provided a first insight into the links between gender equality, economic policy and service delivery and positioning these as part of an effort to improve the government's transparency and accountability to women.

Attempts to link gender equality and economic policy were not without precedent in Timor-Leste; earlier attempts to embed gender issues in the budget and planning processes can be traced to training conducted in 2003–2004, which targeted gender focal points and senior staff in the then Ministry of Finance and Planning. These training initiatives aimed to improve capacity to analyse budgets and policies from a gender perspective and translate gender issues into Timor-Leste's development planning process (Timor-Leste Secretary of State for the Promotion of Equality, 2007: p. 77). Also influential was the role of the Adviser for the Promotion of Equality as a permanent representative in the government's planning processes. At the time a particular proposal that was explored was the allocation of 5 per cent by each sector for technical assistance to implement gender mainstreaming, including capacity strengthening and monitoring and evaluation (Timor-Leste Secretary of State for the Promotion of Equality, 2007). This approach was reminiscent of the Philippines' gender and development budget (Sharp et al., 2011). In its *Initial report on the Convention on the Elimination of All Forms of Discrimination against Women* (2007), the Timor-Leste government laid out its plan to give the budget process a 'stronger gender perspective into their [sectors'] programmes, including increased provisions for funding' (Timor-Leste Secretary of State for the Promotion of Equality, 2007: p. 78). However, the process was tarnished by the limited skills within the country to include gender analysis in the planning process and by significant budget constraints (Timor-Leste Secretary of State for the Promotion of Equality, 2007).

The 2006 crisis halted the plans. When security was restored in 2007 the national gender-focused machinery was in disarray and most of its institutional knowledge and structure had deteriorated. Further to this, the existing planning and budgeting processes had been discontinued. The resignation of the Adviser for the Promotion of Equality, Maria Domingas Fernandes Alves, further aggravated this disruption of processes. This illustrates the way progress in making the budget and planning processes more gender responsive can be profoundly undermined by vulnerability to violence, and political and humanitarian crises.

Since GRB work has restarted it has gained the backing of consecutive governments. The annual action plans were the foundation of GRB in Timor-Leste. Since 2010 the budget circular has required the inclusion of gender issues in ministerial annual action plans and budgets (Christie & Thakur, 2016). In 2015 the budget circular required government agencies to emphasise gender equality and nutrition of children in line with Timor's international and national commitments (Budlender, 2015; Christie & Thakur, 2016). Budlender (2015: p. 35) has raised concerns about the lack of instructions on how such concerns should be addressed in the call circular. Instead, supporting guidelines regarding planning were provided by the Prime Minister's office. Additional detailed sectoral checklists from the national women's machinery were devised to provide directions on how to integrate a gender perspective into the planning and budgeting processes. These guidelines included issues around adoption of international norms, supporting gender analysis and data collection, and translating key laws into actions (Budlender, 2015; Christie & Thakur, 2016).

According to an IMF report (Christie & Thakur, 2016: p. 16), the integration of gender issues through the annual action plans 'had some success' with improvements in the number of agencies preparing action plans between 2013 and 2014 and in the quality of measures and actions relevant to gender equality. Timor-Leste's GRB initiative has been positioned in a rights-based framework (Christie & Thakur, 2016). An important boost to the role of the national women's machinery and the institutionalisation of GRB was its formal engagement in the review of the annual action plans. This role was bolstered with the inclusion of the Secretary of State and her office in the influential budget review committees. Her inclusion in 2012 was significant in affirming the role of this machinery in the budget and planning processes under the oversight of the Prime Minister (ADB, 2014; Christie & Thakur, 2016).

There have also been changes of course, with the gender statement in the budget discontinued after 2010 (Christie & Thakur, 2016). New opportunities may be generated with the budget documents with the 2016 budget making a reference to gender issues under a discussion of key global initiatives highlighting progress, and confirming its commitment to positive change (Timor-Leste Government, 2016: p. 39).

Institution building for gender equality

The national gender machinery, embodied in the Office of the Secretary of State for the Support and Socio-Economical Promotion of Women (SEM), has been a catalyst for GRB narrative and practice.[1] Its role was described in the first gender statement in the 2008 budget document in which the national women's machinery, then the Office of SEPI, was placed at the helm of gender mainstreaming for the government, with responsibility for activities including training the public service.

Two previous manifestations of gender machinery in the administration provided a framework for today's national women's machinery. First, elements of the mainstreaming rationale and institutional apparatus under the Gender Affairs Unit (GAU) in the UNTAET remain visible in practices such as gender focal points, the collection of gender-relevant data, analysis of regulations and consultation with women's organisations (see Charlesworth & Wood, 2002; Whittington, 2003). Second, the successors to the GAU, the Office for the Promotion of Equality (OPE) and the Adviser for the Promotion of Equality, achieved a degree of success in raising the profile of women, promoting the inclusion of a gender perspective in policy making and legislation, and building demand for critical legislation for women – specifically legislation against domestic violence.

Gender Affairs Unit (2000–2001)

Features of Timor-Leste's gender-focused institutions in government can be traced to institutional arrangements that first materialised in UNTAET through its Gender Affairs Unit (GAU). Established in 2000, the GAU aimed to advocate for gender equality and equity as endorsed by the UN and the Timorese women through their 2000 congress. The contribution of the UN in translating gender mainstreaming in Timor-Leste was touted as path breaking in international circles. Notwithstanding the contribution of some in the UN, women in Timor-Leste were instrumental in this first incarnation of a gender-focused machinery in the administration. Throughout the 1990s women activists pursued the inclusion of women in dialogues over the future of Timor-Leste including in the peace negotiations. Two events provided impetus for women's aspirations: a 1998 East Timorese National Convention in the Diaspora meeting, which adopted a formal statement on the freedoms, rights and duties of the Timorese people (the Magna Carta) and endorsed the Convention on the Elimination of All Forms of Discrimination against Women (CEDAW). Second, in 1999, a feminist activist in the Timorese diaspora and member of the CNRT, Milena Pires, introduced gender mainstreaming in a strategic planning conference held in Melbourne. Subsequently women activists actively campaigned and advocated for institutional arrangements with a focus on gender equality and for a gender mainstreaming agenda. They met with resistance from the UNTAET senior management but found backing in international NGOs (such as Oxfam), senior women activists in the UN and some in the donor community (see Alldén, 2009; Charlesworth & Wood, 2002; Cristalis & Scott, 2005; Roynestad, 2003; Whittington, 2000). This resistance to the creation of a gender unit suggests a difficulty in embedding gender equality in a militarised and masculine UNTAET administration.

When it was eventually established in 2000 the GAU had a small budget allocation and reduced staff and was located under the UN Deputy Special Representative of the Secretary General in the Governance and Public Administration pillar. East Timorese women were critical of GAU and its failure to provide a clear explanation of gender mainstreaming. However, GAU made a contribution to embedding gender mainstreaming in the transitional state bureaucracy and pursuing a strong presence for women in the political sphere and in the public service. As a result, it influenced the process of institution building that followed, including launching gender focal points in the districts and setting up the process and the rationale for the collection and analysis of gender-relevant data (see Charlesworth & Wood, 2002; Cristalis & Scott, 2005; Ospina, 2006b; Roynestad, 2003; Whittington, 2000).

The Women's Congress, first held in June 2000, lent substantial political impetus to the pursuit of positive change (see Chapter 4). This congress brought women activists together in Dili and adopted a political platform, the Platform for Action for the Advancement of Timorese Women, which outlined a menu of demands to expand women's choices and the enjoyment of rights. It was based on the 1995 Beijing Platform for Action and the Magna Carta (Cristalis & Scott, 2005). This political platform subsequently became integral to the mandate of GAU (Charlesworth & Wood, 2002; Roynestad, 2003; Whittington, 2000).

In parallel an umbrella network of sixteen organisations for which gender equality or women's empowerment were significant foci was launched (see Chapter 4). Rede Feto led the voicing of views of East Timorese women to UNTAET and was an active advocate for gender mainstreaming in the UN administration (Cristalis & Scott, 2005; Trembath & Grenfell, 2007). A significant result of the Women's Congress was the endorsement in August 2000 of a Resolution on Women's Rights by Conselho Nacional da Resistência Timorense (CNRT, National Council of Timorese Resistance). This resolution tasked elected members of CNRT to lobby UNTAET for gender equality including the adoption of a government mechanism to guarantee gender equity and the allocation of adequate resources for women's empowerment (Alldén, 2009; Charlesworth & Wood, 2002; Hall & True, 2009; Pires, 2004). These moves suggest that national political elites were endorsing the women's rights rhetoric, and suggest a recognition of the need to focus on the budget as a barometer of the political commitment towards gender equality.

Office for the Promotion of Equality (2001–2007)

Following the 2001 elections for the Constitutional Assembly, the East Timor Public Administration, a second transitional government was sworn in in

September 2001. This government was a model for the future independent government, with only Timorese holding executive positions. As part of this second transitional government, an Office for the Promotion of Equality (OPE) was established and an Adviser for the Promotion of Equality, reporting directly to the Chief Minister, was appointed. The international staff deployed under GAU assumed a mentorship role of the five new national staff (Ospina, 2006b).

A combination of national and international forces was behind the emergence of this first gender machinery, with women activists playing an instrumental role. A particular success of women activists was the appointment of well-known activist Maria Domingas Fernandes Alves as Adviser for the Promotion of Equality (Roynestad, 2003). It has also been suggested that UNTAET played a significant role in arguing the case for placing an institution for gender mainstreaming at the highest level. GAU and the UN Special Representative of the Secretary General, Sérgio Vieira de Mello, circulated a paper on the role of a women's ministry or office for the status of women located in the Office of the Prime Minister ahead of the elections in 2001 (Cristalis & Scott, 2005: p. 79). This was further reinforced by deliberate efforts to increase women's representation in decision making (see Ospina, 2006a).

OPE inherited GAU's broad concept of gender mainstreaming as a strategy for improving outcomes for women and girls, and its core functions. OPE expanded the 'wheel of women's affairs' by appointing gender focal points in all ministries and districts and an Inter-ministerial Group to mainstream gender within the public administration (Ospina, 2006b). It achieved a degree of success in raising the profile of women, promoting the inclusion of a gender perspective in policy making and legislation, and building demand for critical legislation for women – specifically legislation against domestic violence. To avoid backlash and resistance, the national gender machinery strategically emphasised the need to include women in the development process as a narrative for change. The Adviser for the Promotion of Equality, Maria Domingas Fernandes Alves, outlined this approach:

> We have found it easier to approach gender from the perspective that women should be included in development and able to participate and contribute, instead of saying it's women's human rights, which is harder to discuss. Men react by saying: 'What about us?'
>
> (Maria Domingas Fernandes Alves, quoted in Cristalis & Scott, 2005: p. 85)

Without a gender mainstreaming policy, OPE used the commitment to gender mainstreaming outlined in the national development plan to justify an agenda for policy change that included institutional capacity, and gender mainstreaming institutional arrangements and processes (Timor-Leste Secretary of State for the Promotion of Equality, 2007: p. 75).

A particular explanation for the success of OPE was the leadership of Alves (2002–2006). She gained prominence in 1997 when she founded the non-governmental organisation Fokupers to protect women survivors of violence and promote their interests, and to foster women's rights and empowerment. Her high profile was confirmed when, at the advent of independence, she was appointed by the then independence leader Gusmão to organise the First National Women's Congress in 2000. Widely respected by women activists and the senior political leadership alike, Alves was the first to leave public office in the 2006 political and security crisis in protest at the government's handling of the situation and the marginalisation of women from the political debate (Hall & True, 2009; Ospina, 2006a). Maria Domingas Fernandes Alves was later recruited as Minister of Social Solidarity in the first Gusmão-led government in 2007.

Office of the Secretary of State (from 2007)

A third generation of the gender machinery in government emerged in 2007 in the Office of SEPI. The office was located under the Office of the Prime Minister and maintained a broad advisory and advocacy mandate to develop, implement, coordinate and assess policy for the promotion of equality. It became a hub of Timor-Leste's women's policy machinery, anchoring gender equality units at both the ministerial and subnational levels of government. Since its early beginnings under GAU the wheel model has seen a significant institutional boost and has gained political and public visibility. It gained further institutional recognition when, in mid-September 2011, the Council of Ministers passed a resolution to establish gender working groups at the national and district levels (República Democrática de Timor-Leste, 2011). These groups were to become central to the implementation of gender mainstreaming strategies including GRB.

A distinct characteristic of this machinery was that the Secretary of State for the Promotion of Equality held a permanent seat in the Council of Ministers. This meant that the Secretary of State had direct access to and could contribute to policy design, and to budget planning and implementation. It also meant that she could mobilise high-level policy support for gender equality and equity and build a positive environment for the adoption of gender mainstreaming including GRB. It was her presence in the Council of Ministers that made it possible for this council to hold a debate about GRB. The Secretary of State for the Support and Socio-Economical Promotion of Women (SEM) (formerly the Secretary of State for the Promotion of Equality, SEPI) retained a position on the Council of Ministers.

The emergence of a state in Timor-Leste

Legacies of the Portuguese colonisation, the Indonesian occupation and UNTAET's state-building project offer important insights into what is possible for strategies for gender equality in Timor-Leste and point to the strong militarised and masculine culture of the state.

Portuguese presence

Portuguese traders arrived in the region in the sixteenth century. By the nineteenth century, the Portuguese administrative presence was still politically isolated, with chronic financial deficits, an indirect and minimal presence throughout the territory, and a divided, corrupt and disloyal bureaucracy (Roque, 2010: p. 319). A new push to make the colony profitable at the end of the nineteenth century led to the introduction of a head tax. This new tax provided impetus for the Timorese rebellion of 1910–1912, led by the local king Dom Boaventura. While the rebellion was crushed by the Portuguese, passive resistance to the colonial power grew and Dom Boaventura gained a particular place in Timor-Leste's political identity and contemporary nationalist movement. The colonial repression that followed resulted in the deaths of an estimated 15–25,000 Timorese, which represented more than 5 per cent of the population (Cristalis & Scott, 2005; Dunn, 1996; Durand, 2006; Niner, 2009; Roque, 2011).

Timorese participation in elections was limited by property and literacy requirements, and there was limited representation of Timorese in the Legislative Council and in the military leadership (Dunn, 1996). This repressive colonial administration had a profound effect on Timor-Leste's prospects of unity, governance and democracy:

> First, the colonisers' tactics of playing social groups against each other kept indigenous political alliances weak. This restricted development of the unity that is required for nation building. Second, no self-governing tradition was developed. Most East Timorese existed in subjugation to a feudal system. Third, the Portuguese colonial regime did not develop or institutionalise democratic and human rights values, though traditional cultural values already existed and the Church inculcated religious values . . . These factors all contributed to the disorder and internal conflict that emerged during the decolonization process in 1975 . . . [and ultimately] to Indonesia being able to invade Timor-Leste in 1975 with minimal international protest.
>
> (CAVR, 2005: p. 7)

This view of the Timor-Leste Commission for Reception, Truth and Reconciliation (CAVR) offers a sharp assessment of the adverse impact of the limited exposure of the Timorese to administration and governance institutions under Portuguese rule. The lack of a 'self-governing tradition' contributed to undermine Timor-Leste's emerging nationalist and democratic aspirations.

Indonesian occupation and the self-determination movement

In April 1974 the authoritarian regime in Portugal was toppled. News about these events was received with optimism in Timor. Domingos Oliveira described the mood in Dili:

> Before 25 April in Timor, we used to talk about our girlfriends, football and things like that . . . After 25 April, we only talked about the consequences of 25 April. What should we Timorese do? What is the right thing to do now in this new situation?
>
> (CAVR, 2005: p. 15)

Two weeks after the fall of the Portuguese authoritarian regime, political parties began to form in Timor-Leste. By the end of May 1974 three parties had emerged: União Democrática Timorese (UDT, Timor Democratic Union), Associação Social Democrática Timor (which became Fretilin, Revolutionary Front for an Independent East Timor, by September) and Apodeti (Timorese Popular Democratic Association) (Dunn, 1996; Durand, 2006; Jolliffe, 1978). UDT was a politically conservative party that held strong links with the Portuguese administration and initially supported progressive autonomy under Portuguese rule as a path towards independence. Its leadership was mostly drawn from an older cohort from private businesses or higher positions in the administration (CAVR, 2005; Dunn, 1996; Durand, 2006; Hill, 1978; Jolliffe, 1978). Fretilin supported independence and drew its founders primarily from families of local rulers or from families of administration officials, students in Portugal, officials from within the Portuguese administration and others from the clandestine anti-colonial collective of the early 1970s (Hill, 1978). In June 1974 the widow of Dom Boaventura endorsed Fretilin by becoming a member of the party, suggesting that women had a role as symbols of nationalist networks through marriage (Durand, 2006). Apodeti attracted its leadership from areas that had a strong geographic or political relationship with Indonesia and was linked to the Indonesian government and their annexation aspirations (CAVR, 2005; Dunn, 1996; Hill, 1978).

The Indonesian military saw an opportunity to occupy and annex Timor and began to devise a politico-military strategy, which included the recruitment of militia among Apodeti followers. The tension between UDT and Fretilin grew; on 11 August 1975, with backing from Indonesia, UDT staged a coup. A brief and violent civil war broke out until in mid-September Fretilin reclaimed a significant part of the territory. This conflict left between 1,500 and 3,000 dead (CAVR, 2005; Durand, 2006).

Following the outbreak of the civil war, Fretilin established an interim administration to fill the vacuum left by the withdrawal of the Portuguese administration to the island of Atauro. The task of establishing an interim administration was significant, with the departure of 80 per cent of the professional national and expatriate staff of the Portuguese administration. Hampered by a severe lack of financial and administrative capacity, and in the context of the political instability flowing from the August conflict and intensifying cross-border military operations by the Indonesian armed forces, this fledgling administration was under insurmountable pressures (CAVR, 2005).

It was in this context that Timor-Leste's first indigenous women's organisation was launched, the Organização Popular da Mulher Timorense (Popular Organisation of East Timorese Women, henceforth OPMT). It was founded on 28 August 1975 as part of the Fretilin party (Cristalis & Scott, 2005; Franks, 1996; Hill, 1978). Confronted with the prospect of an Indonesian invasion, Fretilin unilaterally declared independence on 28 November 1975. A new government was formed and called on the international community to avert the looming Indonesian invasion. Two days later, under pressure, representatives from the other political forces signed a declaration seeking the annexation of the Timorese territory by Indonesia. The 7 December Indonesian military attack on Dili realised the politico-military plan devised by the Indonesian government to annex Timor-Leste (CAVR, 2005; Dunn, 1996; Jolliffe, 1978).

The administration under Indonesian rule was primarily military in nature, with a high degree of corruption and with a budget that was primarily directed towards the 'pacification' of the population (see CAVR, 2005; Dunn, 1996; Durand, 2006; Kingsbury & Leach, 2007; Moxham, 2008). Over 24 years from 1975 to 1999, Indonesian rule produced one of the most horrific human rights records of the twentieth century. The report by the CAVR estimates that under the Indonesian occupation more than 102,800 people died (plus or minus 12,000). This report documented the pervasive displacement with more than 55 per cent of surveyed households indicating at least one displacement event and 2,011 displacement incidents reported (CAVR, 2005).

Sexual violence was widely used as a weapon of war; the CAVR (2005) report documents the widespread and systematic use of rape, sexual torture, sexual slavery and other forms of sexual violence by Indonesian forces in military installations and other official buildings, and the active encouragement of such practices by commanders and officials. The sexual violence experienced by East Timorese women under Indonesian occupation has been explained 'in part from a deep psychological need experienced by an insecure occupation force to prove their "potency" in the face of widespread local resistance and the fighting capacity of the male population' (Carey, 2001: p. 258). This widespread violence had profound implications for women's organisations, with women who were outspoken being seen as aligned with the resistance and being at greater risk of sexual violence (Joshi, 2005).

Institutionalised violence posed significant constraints on how women engaged with the state and with political life, and ultimately how they accessed public services. This is well documented by Milena Pires and Catherine Scott (1998), who argue that women were targeted by the Indonesian military, with numerous allegations of forced sterilisation under the Indonesian national population control programme Program Keluarga Berencana. This, combined with poor communication and insensitive administration, contributed to a fear of accessing health services and has been linked to high infant mortality at 149 per 1,000 births (Franks, 1996).

The resistance to the Indonesian occupation and its armed wing, Falintil, battled the Indonesian forces and had suffered major losses by the late 1970s. Gusmão emerged as the leader in the National Reorganisation Conference of March 1981 and commenced the reorganisation and broadening of the platform of the resistance to the Indonesian occupation with the Conselho da Resistência Revolucionário Nacional (Revolutionary Council of National Resistance). By 1988 a more inclusive resistance movement was consolidated with the launch of the Conselho Nacional da Resistência Maubere (National Council of Maubere Resistance), an umbrella organisation that brought together Fretilin, student groups, church and other groups around their support for independence. In a further sign of the move towards a broad political platform for independence, Gusmão, the leader of Falintil, resigned from Fretilin (Durand, 2006; Niner, 2009). Australian researcher Sara Niner (2009: p. 115) observed that the move away from Fretilin's socialist principles meant a loss of a clear idea of what the future independent state of Timor-Leste would look like and what sorts of policies it would implement to assist the most vulnerable. Behind these changes were significant political and strategic fault lines, which were to play out in Timor-Leste's political arena with the departure of Indonesia.

During the 1980s, clandestine groups multiplied, particularly among students in Timor-Leste and Indonesia. A visit by Pope John Paul II in late 1989 launched a cycle of demonstrations and crackdowns in the 1990s. Three events in the 1990s drew international attention to Timor-Leste's aspirations: the Santa Cruz Massacre (1991), the imprisonment of Gusmão (1992), and the award of the Nobel Peace Prize to Catholic Bishop Carlos Belo and José Ramos-Horta (1996). In 1998 the resistance held a landmark conference of the East Timorese diaspora in Portugal and established the Conselho Nacional da Resistência Timorense (National Council of Timorese Resistance, CNRT) in an effort to further widen the platform of the movement for independence (CAVR, 2005; Cristalis & Scott, 2005; Durand, 2006; Moxham, 2008; Niner, 2009). A particular achievement of this conference was the Magna Carta, which associated Timor-Leste's future policies with international practices and norms that emerged from UN conferences throughout the 1990s including those referring to gender equality and women's empowerment (Hill, 2006).

While women were said to represent 60 per cent of the clandestine resistance movement and some were active fighters among the guerrilla force, a gender-blind ideology framed the resistance struggle, resulting in discrimination against women former independence fighters. This is likely to have contributed to the scarcity of new roles for women in post-conflict Timor-Leste (Niner, 2011; Siapno, 2008). Instead, in the public memory, women are frequently equated with victims and martyrs (Carey, 2001). The marginalisation of women in the way the armed struggle had been constructed had profound ramifications for their role in the political structures of the Timorese resistance and in the leadership of Timor-Leste's diplomatic work. There was only one woman representative in the UN-sponsored All-Inclusive Intra-East Timorese Dialogue and only two women in active leadership roles in the two major political parties, UDT and Fretilin (Pires & Scott, 1998).

In the aftermath of the 1999 Asian financial crisis and the collapse of the Suharto presidency, the Indonesian government under the leadership of President B. J. Habibie announced a popular consultation on the future autonomy of Timor-Leste to be conducted under UN supervision (see Greenlees & Garran, 2002). In May 1999 a UN mission was deployed to organise and conduct the consultation. The voice of Timorese men and women was overwhelming; in a vote held on 30 August 1999 more than 78 per cent of Timorese rejected autonomy within Indonesia, signalling a commitment to independence (CAVR, 2005). What followed was a final act of violence and intimidation by militia gangs backed by the Indonesian military. This aggression left 550,000 people displaced, including the forced transfer of 250,000 to West Timor, and between 1,200 and 1,500 East Timorese dead including 900 immediately after the ballot (CAVR, 2005). With 70 per cent of the government infrastructure damaged and governmental records and files destroyed, and with the exit of non-Timorese who had provided public administration expertise, the structure of government institutions collapsed. Education and health services ceased. The violence came to a halt in September 1999 when a multilateral peacekeeping intervention was deployed (CAVR, 2005; Durand, 2006; World Bank Group & Independent Evaluation Group, 2011).

United Nations Administration

With the departure of Indonesia, the UN Security Council mandated a multi-dimensional peacekeeping operation, the United Nations Transitional Administration in East Timor (UNTAET) to administer the territory through to independence in 2002. UNTAET was located under the auspices of the UN Department of Peacekeeping Operations. As a peacekeeping mission, a disproportionate volume of monetary and human resources was allocated to UNTAET's military component. This military component of the peacekeeping budget was estimated to be a towering seven times greater than its civilian component. UNTAET engaged about 10,000 international peacekeeping personnel – one peacekeeper for every 80 Timorese. Delays in the recruitment of civilian staff further aggravated the relative importance of the military component of the mission (Joshi, 2005).

The arrival of the UN posed new challenges to the equality agenda in Timor. A combination of institutional arrangements, formal policies, norms and interactions reinforced the advantage of militarised masculinity (see Niner, 2016). Timorese gender activist Manuela Leong illustrates the new challenges to the equality agenda:

> The vote for independence was very important for women in East Timor. Ridding ourselves of Indonesian oppression has made our country free, but

there is still much work to be done . . . When the UN came, everyone thought of it as a freedom, and it is, freedom from Indonesia, but we still have military everywhere. Sure, it is a friendly military but even then, some of them have raped Timorese women, some of them have relationships with Timorese women and then leave the country. We have more challenges now, different challenges to what we had with the Indonesians.

(Quoted in Joshi, 2005: 6)

Leong points to the militarisation of aid when referring to 'military everywhere'. She also points to a shift in women's activism with an emphasis on the negative impact of peacekeeping forces.

In mid-2000 the East Timor Transitional Administration (ETTA) emerged from the UNTAET's Governance and Public Administration pillar, marking the beginning of the 'Timorisation' of the administration ahead of the 2001 elections for the Constitutional Assembly (Ospina, 2006b: p. 36). While women were included in the transitional administration, they failed to reach positions of seniority. The Cabinet of ETTA was composed of four positions held by Timorese (including one woman) and four held by expatriates (including one woman) (Alldén, 2009; Ospina, 2006b). The simultaneous formation of the National Council was more encouraging, with women representing 27 per cent of the membership. A second transitional government followed the election for the Constitutional Assembly, which was composed of 24 members and led by Fretilin's Mari Alkatiri. Two women were nominated for ministerial positions (Niner, 2009; Ospina, 2006b).

The record of UNTAET, which administered the territory between October 1999 and May 2002, is highly ambiguous. Elements of the security and governance mandate were achieved, specifically setting up the foundations of the state machinery (including tax and customs service), adopting a constitution, organising elections and maintaining security. However, these achievements were not sufficient to create the conditions for sustainable peace and economic prosperity (see Ingram, 2012; Porter & Rab, 2010). By the early 2000s political convergence around independence was showing some initial signals of instability and in 2002 violent riots rocked the capital (BBC, 2002; CNN, 2002). The UNTAET had underestimated the political context, it failed to consult widely and it set the state-building agenda upon its own views and imperatives. Ultimately UNTAET failed to build an inclusive political settlement that could anchor a stable and resilient state (Ingram, 2012).

The World Bank and IMF backed economic policies that emphasised an open economy and commitment to the US dollar, combined with policies that favoured small government, neo-liberal economic principles and private sector growth strategies. Officials within the World Bank recognised that some of its propositions were far from politically consensual. Senior officer at the World Bank Sarah Cliffe (2003: p. 238) described the pursuit of a smaller and more professional public service, offering higher salaries than those paid by Indonesia, as one of the most 'sensitive' recommendations of the Joint Assessment Mission and Reconstruction in East Timor, which occurred in late 1999. They left a small administration with its human resources under pressure from development partners to produce a sophisticated medium-term development plan. This small administration and the complex requirements imposed by development partners (for example, highly centralised fiduciary controls) constrained what could be delivered (Porter & Rab, 2010).

The influence of this brand of macroeconomic and public finance management policies was pervasive. The East Timor National Development Plan backed a small public service with the government described as an enabler of an environment in which the private sector could progress. The government was construed as 'limited to ensuring that physical and social infrastructure and services are provided and to establishing a growth enabling policy and legal environment; including the provision of macroeconomic stability' (Timor-Leste Planning Commission, 2002: p. 60). This indicates that the views of the World Bank and the IMF were codified into Timor-Leste's most significant development plan (Moxham, 2008). Despite a focus on setting up the core functions of the state between 1999 and 2005, little emphasis was placed on the budget and specifically budget execution, and as a result service delivery was hampered.

There were, nonetheless, profound political disagreements between the Timorese elites and international agencies on how Timor-Leste should be governed. Australian scholar Tim Anderson (2003) documents several instances of disagreements over Timorese-led development proposals, including investment in recovering agriculture infrastructure. Similar tensions led Gusmão to accuse the World Bank of 'at times trying to impose its own views on how the ravaged territory should be rebuilt' (Daley, 1999: p. 1). The Timorese elites believed that the international agencies were pursuing their own agenda. However, numerous public statements by the World Bank Director for Timor-Leste emphasised its commitment 'to help them [Timorese] without imposing our design on them' (Klaus Rohland, World Bank Director for East Timor, quoted in Dobell, 1999). More significantly, when asked to explain these contradictions Rohland argued that economics is not political (Anderson, 2003). These contradictions were in part explained by views of Timor-Leste as a blank canvas where economic policy, public finance management and governance models from other countries could be rolled out (Anderson, 2003; Chopra, 2002). The World Bank Director for East Timor described this view in an interview: 'there's not much you can build on because the past has been a different past, and this country really needs to be invented from scratch' (Rohland, quoted in Dobell, 1999).

These contradictions were intensified by delays in recruitment of Timorese for senior or middle management positions central to the reconstruction programme. A few months ahead of the celebration of independence, in late 2001, the civil service structure was not in place to ensure an effective government with the recruitment for lower levels prioritised (see Disch et al., 2007). This parallels the views of mainstream economics on the need to 'first get the basics right' in public finance (see Chapter 1), with politics alienated from the technical elements of economic reform and policy.

Independent state

The first independent administration inherited a small administration under significant domestic pressure to deliver services while constrained by aid-focused planning and finance management systems and rules (Porter & Rab, 2010). This was aggravated by the departure of the UN Mission of Support in East Timor in 2005, which meant a reduction in the amount of expatriate technical assistance. Politically appointed administrative officials and less experienced lower-level officials were then placed in senior positions to administer a complex and contradictory legacy of rules, systems and procedures. The leadership style developed by senior officials, framed by the years of clandestine work, shaped the way the state engaged with its citizens and the culture of the new administration. There were limited channels for citizens to influence the government and air their views, transparency was perceived as irrelevant and discouraged, and most ministers were resistant to divulging information outside a small group of advisers (Kaltenborn-Stachau, 2008). The first government faced significant challenges with an inexperienced civil service and a tight budget. It also seemed excessively centralist and non-inclusive of diverse voices (Scambary, 2015: p. 292).

The World Bank continued to exert significant influence over economic and fiscal policy through its role in the management of key budget support sources with for example, the Transitional Support Program accounting for 40 to 50 per cent of total government expenditure between 2003–2005 (Disch et al., 2007). Complex and centralised budget processes resulted in under-spending: 'complex and over-centralized processes . . . and weak human resource and institutional capacity on the one hand, and a high level of commitment to fiduciary account-ability on the other [resulted] in very low levels of budget execution' (IMF, 2005: p. 18).

This ultimately constrained the government's ability to deliver better outcomes for Timorese men and women. Rural communities were particularly penalised. The formal procedures to access funding were a constant reminder of Timor-Leste's limited control of policy and the budget; in practice project proposals had to follow the World Bank's procedures and gain formal approval from its Country Director and Regional Vice President (Davis, 2010).

Despite Timor-Leste's share of oil and gas revenues in the Joint Petroleum Development Area and the Greater Sunrise fields, royalties only started to flow substantially by 2005–2006 (Kingsbury & Leach, 2007). In 2004 the Alkatiri government undertook to devise a mechanism to accrue and manage the oil revenues in the Timor Sea in the Petroleum Fund. This fund placed a particular emphasis on the sustainability of these resources, detached the budget from the fund, and set an upper threshold for outflows at 3 per cent – the estimated sustainable income (ESI). Timor-Leste's Petroleum Fund has been regarded as best practice for good governance, economic prudence and transparency; and is a strong example of a sovereign wealth fund in a fragile or post-conflict context (Drysdale, 2007; McKechnie, 2013). The Petroleum Fund has expanded from US$1.7 billion in 2007 to US$16.6 billion in 2013 (Timor-Leste Central Bank, 2014; Timor-Leste Ministry of Finance, 2013b). A 2016 IMF report announced that the fund was expected to have reached its maximum in nominal terms that year. The prospects for the future are gloomy with Timor's position expected to weaken as oil production falls and ends by 2023, unless new reserves are developed (IMF, 2016). Revenue from resources continues to be the most important source of the budget, representing 86 per cent of the 2016 supplementary budget (see Timor-Leste MoF, 2016).

By 2006 social and economic gains remained limited. The unemployment rate was estimated in 2004 at 8.9 per cent, and as high as 23 per cent among the youth. Access to services was a challenge with an estimated 10 to 30 per cent of primary school-aged children, between the ages of 6 and 11, not enrolled in school in 2004 (United Nations Development Programme, 2006).

In 2006 Timor-Leste descended into intense communal violence and conflict. The sacking of close to 600 soldiers, the 'petitioners', triggered this unrest. These petitioners represented almost a third of the total military force and were predominantly from the western districts. Intergenerational disputes between former guerrilla fighters-turned-soldiers from the eastern districts and newly recruited soldiers in the western districts led these 600 soldiers to leave their barracks in protest over perceived discriminatory treatment. These men came to represent the concerns of a broader range of disaffected groups protesting against high levels of unemployment, the lack of democracy in appointments for public office, concerns over moves to curb freedom of the press, evidence of violations of human rights by the police, and allegations of corruption and intimidation. These issues were further aggravated by the tension between the police and the military, well illustrated by one of the most disturbing episodes of this period of unrest when soldiers massacred ten unarmed police after the UN attempted to reach an agreement on their secure passage (see Kingsbury & Leach, 2007).

Prime Minister Mari Alkatiri of the Fretilin party resigned in June 2006 and was replaced by Foreign Affairs Minister José Ramos-Horta. Security was improved with the arrival of multinational military and international police forces. While security was restored, the impact of the violence remained visible in Dili. It has been estimated that 38 people were killed and approximately 150,000 people were displaced, including 73,000 people in camps in and around Dili (see Kingsbury & Leach, 2007; United Nations, 2006). In the June 2007 elections Gusmão was elected as Prime Minister, leading a coalition of four parties, the Aliança com Maioria Parlamentar (Parliamentary Majority Alliance, AMP) (see Leach, 2009). Peace was short lived and, in 2008, Timor-Leste descended into further political instability when Nobel Peace Prize winner President José Ramos-Horta survived an assassination attempt that resulted in the death of Major Alfredo Reinado, who led the petitioners (see ABC/Reuters, 2008; MacKinnon, 2008).

In early 2015 Prime Minister Gusmão stood down, proposing a member of the Fretilin Party from the parliamentary opposition, the well-respected Dr Rui Maria de Araujo, as his successor. This move marked the beginning of a government of national unity, an idea that had been instigated by Gusmão with the informal backing of President Taur Matan Ruak. Behind it was the rapprochement between Prime Minister Gusmão and the secretary general of the opposition party Fretilin, Mari Alkatiri. One of the ways this has materialised was through the unanimous approval of the 2014 budget in parliament (Feijo, 2016; Ingram & Maia, 2015). Since then, hostilities have broken out once again between the government and the president, who has come to represent those that were discontented with current political directions. The 2016 budget provided the background for the president's challenge to the government when in the preparation for it the president argued for more resources for, among others, health and education and raised reservations over expenditure for veterans' privileges and large investment projects (Feijo, 2016).

Conclusion

In 2008 a narrative for GRB surfaced in the new and fragile state of Timor-Leste; it was described as a strategy to pursue gender mainstreaming, which linked gender equality and women's empowerment, to Timor-Leste's economic productivity, efficiency and sustainability. There were earlier attempts to link the budget to gender equality, which were brought to a halt by the political instability and violence that immobilised the government, leaving many displaced and dead. Despite its limitations, annual action plans have been the centrepiece of Timor-Leste's GRB initiative and have found support in the budget circular, references in the budget documents, training and lobbying. This emphasis on budget planning and enactment included the participation of the Office of SEPI in the budget review process. The mobilisation of high-level political support was central to efforts to change budget processes (see Christie & Thakur, 2016).

Gender-focused institutions in government have played a crucial role in facilitating women's engagement in economic policy. In less than a decade this machinery, in its distinct incarnations, had built a significant legitimacy for women's engagement with planning processes and drafting of legislation, and established a framework for gender mainstreaming. Also important have been gender working groups and arrangements such as representation of the Secretary of State in the government's ministerial council.

Combined, these strategies suggest that Timor-Leste has achieved a degree of formal adoption of GRB (see O'Hagan, 2015) supported by political statements, internal guidelines and key budget documentation that outline this commitment and its implementation. This suggests that there is a broad commitment towards gender equality, political will to translate this commitment into economic policy, leadership in the gender-focused machinery and key planning agencies, and strategic and active institutional arrangements. It is important to remember that activists inside and outside the government had to fight for legitimacy from a background of marginalisation from peace processes (see Cristalis & Scott, 2005) and the gender-blind ideology that framed the resistance struggle (Niner, 2011; Siapno, 2008). If the state is understood as a political settlement representing an arrangement of power relations (Putzel & Di John, 2012), it is significant that Timorese women were made invisible from its inception.

The new roles for women, and opportunities for making claims, in post-conflict Timor-Leste were significantly undermined by the broader historical and institutional context. The masculinisation and militarisation that have characterised Timor-Leste's state administration and history have reaffirmed the gender inequality in society and politics and have framed gender relations (Niner, 2011, 2016). These characteristics have further undermined the recognition of the legitimacy of women's voices, and have constrained women's engagement with the state, political life and public services. Another immediate impact of this militarisation is that violence and war have remained an attractive option for most men (Siapno, 2006).

Throughout Timor-Leste's history women's access to services has been a major concern. Under Indonesian occupation institutionalised violence placed significant constraints on how women engaged with the state, with political life and, ultimately, how they accessed public services. The presence of the administration had been an important issue for the Portuguese colonial power and Indonesian occupation who used the state administration as a means of control and a mechanism for extracting resources. The state was not only ineffective but also an avenue to control women's actions and their bodies. Concerns about accessibility and the presence of services across the territory were undermined by the prevailing views about economic policy that survived the UNTAET administration. These views further weakened the disaffection that was derived from the internal political settlement that emerged out of UNTAET and has been characterised as not inclusive (Ingram, 2012).

Since independence Timor-Leste has experienced several episodes of civil unrest and political instability. The institutional and political impact of Timor-Leste's vulnerability to violence has been significant, with leadership on gender equality and progress on mainstreaming gender in budget planning reversed by the events of 2006. The infrastructure for gender mainstreaming was dismantled and the fractures between activists in the bureaucracy were revealed. These fissures were raised as early as 2001 as a generation gap, tensions between activists in Timor and those from the diaspora, and family and party political conflicts begun to erode the relative unity around the independence project (see Cristalis & Scott, 2005: p. 7).

In this context, Timor-Leste's gender mainstreaming project was severely weakened and opportunities for women to make claims were modest. A particular challenge is the difficulty of tracking spending given the structure of the budget, the ability to shift allocations and limited available sex-disaggregated data (Christie & Thakur, 2016). The remainder of this book explores how Timorese women have created opportunities in a complex and challenging context to influence economic policy decisions and processes and to implement GRB as a gender mainstreaming strategy.

Note

1 'Gender machinery' refers to formal structures within a government mandated to promote gender equality and to advance the status and the rights of women (McBride & Mazur, 2011: p. 4). In this study, the terms 'gender machinery' and 'gender-focused institutions' are used interchangeably.

3 The influence of gender-focused parliamentary institutions in gender-responsive budgeting

Gender-responsive budgeting (GRB) has renewed interest in the participation of parliaments in budget processes and decisions. In some countries parliaments have played an important role in embedding a requirement for GRB in key legislation. This was the case in Mexico and Rwanda, where gender equality was incorporated into budget legislation. In Austria effective gender equality in budgeting is entrenched in the constitution (Pérez Fragoso & Rodríguez Enríquez, 2016; Stotsky, 2016). Parliaments have also contributed to ensuring that the government is accountable for its commitments to women's empowerment and gender equality. In Mexico the parliament, and women parliamentarians specifically, have collaborated with women activists to ensure that more resources are allocated to policies and programmes that address women's needs (Pérez Fragoso & Rodríguez Enríquez, 2016).

Experiences such as these suggest that women's collective action in parliament can have a positive effect on policies and budgets. Over the past two decades gender-focused institutions in parliament – whether cross-party caucuses, single-party caucuses, parliamentary committees or parliamentary friendship groups – have flourished across regions. Data collected by the IPU suggest that by 2013 over one in three parliaments had an active women's cross-party caucus. These institutions have had a disproportionate take-up in fragile state contexts, with an estimated three in five parliaments in fragile states in 2009 reporting a women's cross-party caucus. The role of these new institutions in bringing about positive changes to policies and budgets has rarely been examined in the expanding bodies of research into GRB and on women's collective action in parliaments. This chapter investigates the role of these gender-focused parliamentary institutions in representing women, pursuing a gender equality agenda in the parliament and collaborating with women activists. Specifically, it examines the role of Timor-Leste's women's cross-party caucus in the passage of a parliamentary resolution on GRB, and the caucus' ability to scrutinise policies and budgets and foster the participation of community groups in the legislative process.

This chapter is based on a manuscript published in 2013 in the *International Feminist Journal of Politics* (Costa et al., 2013). It provides an illustration of the positive contribution of women's cross-party caucuses to policy processes and decisions. The passage of the GRB resolution showcased their organisational skills and provided some evidence of their role in pursuing changes to budget outcomes. It provided an opportunity to strengthen women parliamentarians' skills, confidence and political currency. Limited institutional capacity, uneven commitment to a gender equality agenda, and a degree of political vulnerability have made it more difficult for the caucus to scrutinise the budget and influence changes to policy. Further, women parliamentarians' influence has been framed by the limited scrutinising powers of the parliament as enshrined in the constitution (Ingram, 2012) and undermined by the broader cultural values that construe women's engagement in the public sphere as illegitimate.

Women acting for women: gender-responsive budgeting in Timor-Leste

In the 1990s, the issue of women's presence in the political sphere, or descriptive representation, gained significant international traction, often fuelled by the suggestion that women would change the substance and style of politics and act in the interests of and in a manner responsive to women. The concept of acting to benefit women has been termed 'substantive representation', and there has been increased interest in how and when such substantive representation occurs (Celis & Childs, 2008; Franceschet & Piscopo, 2008; Sawer, 2006).

The concepts of critical actors and critical acts have been central to analyses of substantive representation. Critical actors influence the policy process and mobilise others around women's concerns, while critical acts are actions that lead to changes in the positions of minority groups (Dahlerup, 1988). It is argued here that gender-focused institutions can play a vital role in supporting critical actors and in enabling critical acts in the policy process.

Such gender-focused institutions may include women's movement organisations, women's wings within political parties, women's policy machinery in the bureaucracy, parliamentary institutions with a gender mandate and, importantly in the case of developing democracies, international agencies and donors.[1] Some scholars such as Laurel Weldon (2002) have already suggested that to understand substantive representation women's movements, women's state agencies and the interaction between them need to be brought into the picture.

There has been, to date, less scholarly interest in the role of parliamentary institutions mandated to focus on gender equality – whether cross-party caucuses, single-party caucuses, parliamentary committees or parliamentary friendship groups. The IPU has found a growing number of such bodies, and has observed that women's caucuses offer a unique avenue for women legislators to work with each other and with other partners, including women's groups. Significantly, the IPU notes that in countries with a women's caucus there is a strong sense that they have 'been successful at influencing parliamentary or legislative activities and providing oversight' (Ballington, 2008: p. 68). Broadly speaking, women's cross-party caucuses have emerged as an initiative of women legislators rather than being a permanent fixture of the parliament covered by standing orders.

A variety of models have been adopted in terms of structure, decision-making mechanisms, level of integration into the structure of the legislature, operating rules and scope (Gonzalez & Sample, 2010). Despite the enthusiasm of the IPU, so far there has been little academic study of such bodies.

The very small number of case studies that have been undertaken do suggest a positive link with substantive representation, but one that can be achieved in various ways (see Tripp, 2001). In the Philippines, women politicians in both houses of parliament, together with women's policy agencies and the women's movement, secured the passage of the Women in Development and Nation Building Act, 1991 (Reyes, 2002). The subsequent gender and development budget policy required each government agency to allocate a minimum of 5 per cent of its budget to gender equality initiatives (Sharp et al., 2011). In South Korea, a standing committee, the National Assembly's Gender Equality and Family Committee, and particularly its chair, were instrumental in achieving a legislated requirement for GRB (Elson et al., 2009). In Canada, both a single-party women's caucus and a standing committee (the House of Commons Standing Committee on the Status of Women) played a significant role in holding ministers accountable and auditing the performance of gender-based analysis in the federal government (Grace, 2011; Steele, 2002). In Australia, a single-party women's caucus similarly held ministers to account and was responsible for temporarily salvaging that country's women's budget statement (Sawer, 2002). Also in Australia, a parliamentary friendship group helped build trust across party lines that enabled co-sponsored legislation and the lifting of a ministerial veto on chemical abortion (Sawer, 2012).

Despite such evidence of the positive contribution of feminist institution building to the substantive representation of women, there is also need for caution. An emerging feminist institutional literature helps illuminate the constraints within which new institutions operate. Fiona Mackay's (2009) work on institutional reform in the Scottish parliament suggests that 'new' institutions 'are neither blank slates nor free-floating'; rather, they are shaped by 'past institutional legacies and by initial and ongoing interactions with already existing institutions . . . within which they are "nested" and interconnected' (p. 3). Her concept of 'nested newness' alerts us to how progress in locking gender equity issues into new institutions can be curtailed by old gender norms and the way political business has always been done (Mackay, 2009: p. 16).

Here the genesis of a critical act is examined, a parliamentary resolution on GRB in Timor-Leste. This chapter investigates the factors that made this critical act possible and, in particular, whether propositions that there is a positive link between the existence of women's caucuses and the substantive representation of women can be confirmed. This case study provides the most detailed evidence to date on this question. It is based on interviews conducted in Timor-Leste in 2008 and 2009. These interviews involved women legislators and other critical actors from NGOs, international agencies and the public service. Data were also collected from published academic research, grey literature and email communication with various stakeholders. The interviews and other data cover the themes of why, how and in what circumstances women legislators went about 'acting for' women by improving the scrutiny of policy and budgets.

The terms 'women' and 'gender' are both widely used in Timor-Leste. At the policy level, Timor-Leste is saturated with UN discourse and the interviewees were comfortable with using the term 'gender' in relation to initiatives to make policy more women-friendly and to ensure both women and men benefited from budgetary outlays. However, at the political level women mobilised around a collective identity as women in order to achieve these initiatives. The term 'feminist' is applied in this study to those advocating policies promoting gender equality and women's empowerment.

Women in parliament in Timor-Leste

Timor-Leste's political institutions are new, having emerged in little over a decade. The transition to democracy is a period of great change and a 'critical juncture' in terms of setting institutional trajectories (Waylen, 2011: p. 149). Within this transition, women's rights have been a striking feature of public discourse. The Platform for Action for the Advancement of Timorese Women gave impetus and political legitimacy to the demand for a quota of at least 30 per cent women in party lists, with women in winnable positions.

The campaign for a 30 per cent quota was a critical act that set in motion training in political leadership, incentives for parties to field women candidates and ultimately the reform of the electoral law. Criticism of the members of the National Council who voted against the quotas led some parties to embrace informal internal quotas in the 2001 Constituent Assembly elections (Pires, 2004). In the aftermath of these elections, women constituted 27 per cent of the 87 assembly members.

To maintain this presence, leading gender equality non-governmental organisations, along with the women's machinery and senior women in government and the UN, worked in combination ahead of the 2007 elections for the national parliament. The drafting of the 2006 electoral law offered a new opportunity to lock in gender equality. The new law (no. 6/2006), required that one woman be included in every four positions on party lists and that a *deputada* leaving parliament be replaced by another female candidate on the list (Parlamento de Timor-Leste, 2006a). *Deputada* is the term used in Timor-Leste to refer to a woman member of the parliament and is the term that I will use in this book. The struggle around quotas culminated in 2011 with another change in the electoral law ahead of the 2012 parliamentary elections. This now required that one woman be included in every three positions in the party lists (see Parlamento de Timor-Leste, 2011). In 2015 women constituted 38.5 per cent of the parliament and Timor-Leste was ahead of every country in the South-East Asian region, ranking sixteenth by the IPU (2015).

The Timor-Leste cross-party women's caucus in parliament

Given that numbers alone are not sufficient to guarantee attention to issues of gender equality, institution building within parliament can play a vital role in facilitating the substantive representation of women (Sawer, 2010: p. 219). The establishment of a cross-party women's caucus in Timor-Leste has proved to be a significant step in raising issues of gender equality in the legislature. Timing was critical, however. While a 2004 proposal for an ad-hoc committee on gender affairs, equality and children was rejected, a core group of activists persisted in sensitising their parties to the need for institutional arrangements for women. This advocacy was reinforced at the international level by the establishment of a network of *deputadas* from across the Portuguese-speaking world in 2005 (see Chapter 5). By March 2006, a cross-party women's caucus was formally established through a parliamentary resolution (Parlamento de Timor-Leste, 2006b) proposed by all but one *deputada* and approved by a majority of the parliament (Ospina, 2006a). A formal institutional space for women in parliament had finally been achieved.

A second generation of the women's caucus emerged in 2007 with the new legislature (Resolution no. 16/2007) and with support from all *deputadas* (Parlamento de Timor-Leste, 2007). It was backed by a political platform signed by the women's wings of 12 of the 14 political parties competing in the election (PST et al., 2007). For legitimacy it drew on both the Timorese constitution and a range of international frameworks, including CEDAW and the MDGs.

Comprising 21 members, the women's caucus retained a broad cross-party base with representatives of all major political parties. The histories of these women are diverse, and they include national heroes of the resistance, judges and former senior government members. Their education varies not only in terms of level but also in where it was obtained, including Indonesia, Timor-Leste and Australia. The caucus is led by a president, vice president and secretary, elected for a two-and-a-half-year period. To institutionalise the women's caucus within the parliament, significant efforts have been directed to laying out a five-year gender strategy and action plan 'to make concrete actions for the improvement of women's equal political participation and gender equality' (Costa, 2009: p. 4). Its current activities are ambitious, including both the development of a gender equality law and the development of a more inclusive approach to policy consultation and policy making. The 2007 resolution (Parlamento de Timor-Leste, 2007) that brought the women's caucus into being includes a specific provision that the budget should 'ensure to the Timorese Parliamentary Women Caucus the necessary means for its adequate functioning'.[2] It came into effect in 2009.

Strategic partnerships

The broader political institutional arrangements are important for understanding the context in which *deputadas* go about acting for women. Timor-Leste has adopted the brand of semi-presidentialism common to Portuguese-speaking countries. With seven parties represented among the 65 members of parliament, a genuine 'competitive multi-party system' emerged (Leach, 2009: p. 231). But political parties remain far from being structured along a left–right political spectrum, and political support relies on leaders' personalities and regional elites (Leach, 2009; Saldanha, 2008). Over the past decade the parliament has established a working organisational structure, including a parliamentary committee system. Gender equality was given formal institutional recognition in 2007 with the establishment of a specialised committee on poverty reduction, rural and regional development, and gender equality (designated Committee E). Committee E has a membership of nine members of parliament (MPs), of whom four are women (Costa, 2009: p. 4). An IPU report (2012) described Timor-Leste as a good example of the complementarity possible when a parliamentary committee on gender equality and a women's caucus work well together (Palmieri, 2012: p. 45).

With the separation between legislative and executive powers, ministers cannot serve as MPs; any MP appointed to a role in the executive has to be replaced in the parliament from the party list. Ministers are recruited by the prime minister and hence being elected is only one of the avenues for women to access senior political positions. In 2007, of the three women who gained senior ministerial briefs (16 per cent of the total), two were unelected. These women have gained significant international recognition: Minister for Social Solidarity, Maria Domingas Fernandes Alves, was nominated for a Nobel Peace Prize in 2005 for her work in the independence movement and for women's rights, and Minister of Finance, Emilia Pires, was appointed to the high-level panel to advise on a post MDG agenda (see Ellis, 2009; Peace Women across the Globe, 2011). The individual careers of these women and the way in which they were recruited for ministerial positions may have a significant impact on whether they pursue policies and practices that advance women's substantive representation. The lack of research on ministerial recruitment remains a major gap in understanding how such representation occurs.

The interactions between the national women's machinery in government, SEPI and the *deputadas* are another critical element of substantive representation in Timor-Leste. SEPI has made significant headway in establishing a gender mainstreaming structure across ministries (Rodrigues, 2011). SEPI's mandate is coordination and oversight of gender equality and women's empowerment policy. From a small unit in 2007, SEPI has expanded to a team of 47, of whom 31 are women, and resources have been invested in strengthening the capacity of its staff. The national women's machinery, with assistance from UN Women, has started training budget officers in gender analysis in preparation for the 2012 state budget.

As described above, the women's movement has been a critical actor in feminising the political agenda in Timor-Leste. One of the characteristics of the women's movement is its unity and strong umbrella organisation. By 2003 Rede Feto involved 20 women's organisations, including high-profile non-governmental organisations such as Fokupers and the Alola Foundation, as well as the women's wings of political movements and religious and cultural organisations (Pires, 2004). Another important feature of the women's movement in Timor-Leste is its agreed policy agenda, outlined in its Platform for Action and updated every four years through a broad consultation process with women and a national women's congress. The role of the women's movement in linking legislators and political parties with women was illustrated in the lead-up to the 2007 parliamentary elections, when Rede Feto conducted a range of activities to promote women candidates and the women's agenda (Rede Feto Timor-Leste, 2008). The women's movement has continued to press on the issue of women's unequal representation in politics, using CEDAW and its reporting processes as a conduit for this debate. The continuing campaign by gender equality advocates has given those women who are elected a mandate to voice women's concerns and bring about policy changes.

Another critical actor in institution building and supporting gender equality in Timor-Leste is the international community. This support goes beyond dissemination of norms of gender equality (see Hall, 2009) and includes significant technical assistance.[3] For example, the parliamentary women's caucus has received support from bodies such as the IPU, UN Women and the UN Development Programme (UNDP) as well as from bilateral donors such as Australia, Norway and Sweden. This support has included the establishment of a gender resource centre in the parliament to provide research and training in gender analysis (UN Women Southeast Asia, 2008). Some have criticised the effectiveness of the UN Transitional Administration in Timor-Leste (see Charlesworth & Wood, 2002); however, on balance this international presence has helped to open political and institutional spaces for women and for gendered claims making (see Myrttinen, 2009). Leading activist and current CEDAW committee member Milena Pires (2004) has pointed to the contradictions within UN agencies over quotas for women to illustrate how international pressure can work against women. Well aware of this, the Timorese women's movement has had to exert pressure at times to ensure that international agencies, in particular UN missions, give adequate attention to gender issues (Trembath & Grenfell, 2007).

The women's caucus and the road to gender-responsive budgeting

The existence of both parliamentary and government machinery with a mandate to focus on gender equality proved a significant enabling factor in the eventual adoption of GRB in Timor-Leste.

Their contribution to GRB was showcased in the Resolution no. 12/2010, drafted by the women's parliamentary caucus (Parlamento de Timor-Leste, 2010).[4] This resolution provided a framework for the introduction of GRB, assigning roles to the MoF, line ministries, the women's machinery in government, non-governmental organisations and international institutions. Specific recommendations were also made concerning the role of parliament. The women's caucus and Committee E were assigned central roles in assessing the implications of budget decisions, using 'tools and methods' of GRB such as gender-sensitive indicators and statistics (Parlamento de Timor-Leste, 2010: p. 4089). On 14 July 2009, the parliament made a historic commitment to GRB by passing the women's caucus resolution with 33 votes in favour, eight against and two abstentions (Parlamento de Timor-Leste, 2009: p. 4).

As outlined above, international influence has been very important in Timor-Leste, and the adoption of GRB drew strongly on rationales circulating within the international community. Resolution no. 12/2010 noted that GRB was central to meeting international commitments such as CEDAW. Further, the preamble outlined how integrating a gender perspective would ensure 'consistency between economic and social objectives . . . contributing to economic growth and prosperity . . . and improving governability along with promoting accountability, transparency and participation in decision making over budget policy' (Parlamento de Timor-Leste, 2010: p. 4088).

Apart from rationales for its introduction, international agencies have made a significant creative, financial and technical contribution to GRB in the Timor-Leste parliament. UN Women, for example, has provided support for the training of parliamentarians, government officials and non-governmental organisations in the use of tools to integrate a gender perspective into planning and budgeting. The Australian government has funded research on the practices and potential of GRB, including training and briefing for senior government officials. Events such as International Women's Day have been used to further the commitment to GRB. On 10 March 2008, the parliament held a special session to debate the theme of the International Women's Day celebrations, 'Financing for Gender Equality – Investing in Women and Girls: Investing in Equality' (United Nations Integrated Mission in Timor-Leste, 2008). On this occasion the chairperson of the parliamentary Committee E, with responsibility over gender equality, read out the pledge – the Deklarasaun Kompromisu Dili; this injected broader political support into the (emerging) GRB narrative. This pledge provided the impetus for a broad discussion on women's engagement in economic policy in a televised debate with representatives of civil society and the government. On this occasion concerns were raised over perceived inadequate budget allocations for the national gender machinery and over the failure to reach rural areas. Idelta Rodrigues, the Secretary of State for Promotion of Equality (SEPI), further stated that the government was adopting a gender mainstreaming approach, which involved allocating resources for women and children across line ministries (Rede Feto, 2008).

The passage of the resolution on gender-responsive budgeting in the Timor-Leste parliament

The GRB resolution of 2009 was first and foremost the product of the cross-party women's caucus of the Timor-Leste parliament, notwithstanding other actors being involved. The women's caucus saw GRB as a way to fulfil its gender equality mandate. The resolution on GRB was perceived as an effective strategy to draw attention to budget allocations and hence improve the status of women and girls. Importantly, the resolution was seen by a senior caucus member as a means to ensure that complaints and concerns over service delivery, particularly from women and girls, were integrated into the policy process (*Deputada*, Interview, 2009).

Paving the way for the resolution was a range of initiatives supported by international agencies to strengthen the capacity of the women's caucus. A *deputada* highlighted the role of this advice in 'giving us ideas' (*Deputada*, Interview, 2010). The drafting of the resolution appears to have been confined mainly to the women's caucus, although with significant input from international agencies. One *deputada* suggested the process involved wide consultation, with caucus members having 'to listen to the ideas of many people to develop a resolution that could be approved by the other MPs' (*Deputada*, Interview, 2010). Another *deputada* described the consultation process as encompassing male legislators and selected international organisations. This approach is consistent with what a *deputada* described as a recalibration of the focus of the women's caucus towards raising the 'awareness of the men' in the parliament (*Deputada*, Interview, 2009). Given that the goal of the consultation was to ensure the passage of the resolution, this stage of the process did not broadly encompass the women's movement or the women's machinery of government.

Women's caucus members tended to downplay their ideological differences and political divisions. One *deputada* suggested that within its structure there are no party lines because 'when we talk about raising the status of women . . . there are no parties'; almost all parties are committed to raising the status of women and voicing women's concerns through their women's wings (*Deputada*, Interview, 2010). Outside observers such as Michael Leach (2009) have made a similar point about the broad ideological consensus among political parties in Timor-Leste.

The president of the women's caucus emerged as a critical actor due in large part to her concurrent position as vice president of the parliament. As vice president of the parliament she was able to exert pressure that, combined with the caucus' lobbying work, resulted in a budget allocation for the women's caucus (*Deputada*, Interview, 2010). Since 2009 funding has been allocated in the state budget for the activities of the women's caucus. In the 2016 budget this was comparable to the budget allocations for standing committees and 14.11 per cent of the parliament's budget allocations to these types of structures (Timor-Leste Government, 2016). Through internal political pressure in the parliament presidency, the women's caucus was able to bring gender equality issues to the forefront of the political agenda. The case of the resolution on GRB illustrates that it is easier for *deputadas* to cooperate on specific issues. The lack of automatic solidarity among women was illustrated by the reluctance of some *deputadas* to participate in the early days of the caucus. The interest of these women had to be gained over time: 'after lobbying, training and my efforts to reach them, they are now engaged' (*Deputada*, Interview, 2009). Gradually the Timor-Leste's women's caucus consolidated and formalised its structures, becoming a well-organised body and an important actor in shaping debates and promoting legislation addressing women's concerns. The caucus is supported by an executive secretary, meets on a monthly basis and produces regular reports and planning documents (see Soetjipto 2014).

In 2010 the head of the parliamentary commission covering legislation and constitutional issues, public administration and local power – and a member of the women's caucus – sent a letter to the Prime Minister pressing the government to provide adequate funding for the implementation of the domestic violence law ahead of the 2011 budget. While the women's caucus has played a role in both GRB and the implementation of domestic violence law, the leadership of the women's caucus did not endorse the letter. Some observers saw in this event an indication of the political pressures the women face in their different parties that may curtail the women's caucus' effectiveness.

While a horseshoe layout of the parliamentary chamber tends to encourage less aggressive political behaviour, some commentators have observed that in Timor-Leste only a small number of *deputadas* are vocal and that gender issues are only haphazardly addressed in parliament (Ospina, 2006a). The presentation of the resolution on GRB to the parliament by the president of the women's caucus and vice president of the parliament, Maria Paixão da Costa, was met by robust opposition from many male MPs. In the discussion that followed, male MPs argued that GRB could be construed as special treatment for women, which in their view was in stark contrast with the parliament's commitment to defend gender equality. Representatives of the women's caucus responded that the resolution did not intend to erode men's rights and position but rather to support women's initiatives and strengthen women's position (Parlamento de Timor-Leste, 2009: p. 4). Male MPs have been slow to take ownership of the gender equality agenda. This was summarised well by one *deputada*: 'the women members of parliament – the male members of parliament not as much – always mention gender in their speeches' (*Deputada*, Interview, 2009). Resistance is often veiled (*Deputada*, Interview, 2009).

Deputadas drew strength from a safe women-only space and became 'more disciplined and . . . more organised . . . than the blokes' (*Deputada*, Interview, 2009). Some of the *deputadas* talked about the importance of having norms and practices established, a plan of action, for example to gain the political currency that enabled the passage of the resolution on GRB. Importantly, these *deputadas* have learned to use a range of tactics and strategies to increase their influence in parliament. These include indicating to their male colleagues that it is in their interests, personally and politically, to lend their support, and collecting data and personal accounts from women to bring about changes to legislation (*Deputada*, Interview, 2010).

This range of strategies was clearly displayed in the success of the women's caucus in negotiating a specific section for their comments in the overall parliamentary analysis of the budget, one of the most significant roles of the Timor-Leste parliament. The commentary is normally provided by parliamentary committees, and bodies such as the women's caucus would not normally be part of the process. During the 2010 budget debate, however, *deputadas* provided commentary on what could be done to improve the budget's responsiveness to gender. This was a critical act, illustrating the relationship between the women's caucus and the substantive representation of women. The women's caucus met opposition when its comments were read in the plenary. Some male MPs asked: 'Is the women's caucus a parliamentary committee?' to which the *deputadas* responded that while 'we are not a committee we ask you to consider that we have a double role' as MPs and women. Arguments as to why the commentary of the women's caucus on the budget should be included in the parliamentary analysis were crafted around the need to bring women's voice into the political debate: 'You [male MPs] agreed to our existence so now you need to give space for us to speak!' (*Deputada*, Interview, 2010).

Through its recommendations on the 2010 budget the women's caucus further feminised the political agenda. Initially the caucus focused on identifying areas for immediate action, such as health, education, agriculture, commerce and industry, and justice (*Deputada*, Interview, 2010). These sectors were viewed as directly connected to the gender mainstreaming priorities of the executive, illustrating the network character of substantive representation. By the 2011 budget the women's caucus' recommendations had expanded to areas including the national women's machinery in government, security, justice and social solidarity. Consistent with the GRB approach (see Sharp & Broomhill, 1990, 1999), the recommendations covered three types of outlays: expenditure specifically targeted to women and girls; expenditure directed to equal employment opportunity; and general or mainstream expenditure (Committee on Economy, 2011).

Another source of institutional support for the parliamentary representation of women is the women's movement. However, the women's movement does not appear to have made a specific contribution to the drafting of the GRB resolution. Nonetheless, the women's movement has been significant in assisting elected women to find common ground beyond their party affiliations. In a strong sign that *deputadas* are engaging in the responsiveness associated with substantive representation, consultations with the women's movement have been established to improve policy and budget decisions, to collect gender-disaggregated data and to raise awareness among politicians (*Deputadas*, Interview, 2009). Through such consultations the women's caucus is seeking to contribute to 'fiscal democracy' (Elson, 2004: p. 639) by making the budget process transparent, accountable and open to a range of participants, men and women, both inside and outside government. Some of the *deputadas* argued for iterative engagement with non-governmental organisations on the grounds that non-governmental organisations were well positioned to provide analytical input and to voice women and men's concerns as part of the legislative process (*Deputada*, Interview, 2009). Another *deputada* suggested that non-governmental organisations also need to strengthen their skills (*Deputada*, Interview, 2010).

The women's caucus saw its role as providing policy oversight and the monitoring of progress towards gender equality. In developing its resolution on GRB the women's caucus outlined a broad framework that would require considerable work from the Ministry of Finance, the women's machinery and line ministries in relation to technical detail and implementation. However, Timor-Leste's broad coalition of feminist advocates has successfully used this one-off resolution to change the way the government goes about its business. For example, the women's machinery of government drew on the GRB resolution to urge line ministries to show their commitment to implementing the domestic violence law.

Constraints on action

There are practical limits to the power of the women's caucus to initiate action. The women's caucus is politically and legally powerless to oblige the executive to act and its pressure over GRB has the potential to aggravate relations between parliament and government. One *deputada* noted: 'first I thought that it would be negative because the government is [was] not prepared' but she went on to say that the resolution was a first step to instigating change within the executive (*Deputada*, Interview, 2010).

In practice, parliamentary monitoring remains problematic due to the nature of the budget and planning documents, with MPs having 'no way of knowing what the money actually did go towards' and what 'sorts of results' were achieved (*Deputada*, Interview, 2009). Coupled with an underdeveloped policy debate, any effort to make the government accountable may fall short of improving services for women. On the other hand, the network of gender focal points could play a significant role. Well aware of the limits of their own sphere of action, the *deputadas* have asked for capacity building for the gender focal points to help enable inclusion of gender issues 'from planning to approval of the budget and its implementation' (*Deputada*, Interview, 2009). Women in parliament have been vital supporters of the women's machinery in government (SEPI) and the head of SEPI has made political use of the GRB resolution. However, the implications of the GRB resolution for the work of the public sector, and SEPI's role, while significant, are yet to be identified and capitalised on.

In terms of party support, while there may have been broad ideological consensus favouring women's political initiatives, the two largest parties have challenged each other's record on women's rights (Fretilin, 2007; National Congress for the Reconstruction of East Timor, 2007). An IPU (2012) report observed that *deputadas* are using existing arrangements with the party whips to prevent changes that are contrary to the women's agenda (Palmieri, 2012). Nonetheless, one *deputada* believed that women were 'not using their influence within their parties as best as they probably could', because the internal party mechanisms were not fully functioning and operating in a democratic way (*Deputada*, Interview, 2009). This was further canvassed by a president of the women's caucus, who called for more accountability from political parties for their gender equality commitments and better 'internal communication' among women's caucus members (Costa, 2009: p. 6).

Significantly one *deputada* linked accountability to political legitimacy. Drawing attention to the recently approved legislation (2010) on domestic violence, this *deputada* suggested that the success of this law rests on appropriate funding of services such as police and the justice system: '[If] we just have a law that's not implementable people will lose faith in it' (*Deputada*, Interview, 2009). Thanks to political pressure from activists, both inside and outside government, a special budget allocation for the implementation of the domestic violence law (see Rodrigues, 2011) was increased during the parliamentary debate over the 2011 budget. This achievement provides a further indication of the success of networking in generating more gender-sensitive legislation.

Conclusion

It seems obvious to say that Timor-Leste is a very new nation with new political and administrative institutions. Women activists were able to seize the opportunity presented by 'newness' to institutionalise a focus on gender equality. Timing was important: these new institutions were being created at a time when international agencies and donors were conduits for norms of gender equality. Local actors were able to utilise these international norms and GRB strategies effectively to gain more resources and greater representation for women. Characteristics of the women's movement that enabled it to speak with a united voice were also important, as were networks between the women's movement, women's machinery in government, and critical actors in parliament and the executive.

Since 2002 high levels of descriptive representation were achieved and a degree of commitment to gender equality was woven into the constitution and electoral laws. The need for *deputadas* to interact to bring about positive changes was recognised very early on. Soon they were initiating debate on the role of a gender-focused parliamentary institution. Since then, the women's caucus has built a significant presence as well as a plan of attack to bring women's concerns and perspectives into mainstream budget debates.

But while the new institution of the women's caucus has enhanced the power of the *deputadas* within the new parliament, it remains 'nested' within the traditional way of doing politics (see Mackay, 2009). Broader cultural values continue to hamper women's political legitimacy in Timor-Leste. Tribal leaders forewarned that the 'wrath of ancestors' could be incurred if the 'right' leader were not chosen (Palmieri, 2012: p. 11). Traditional attitudes continue to affect the inner workings of the parliament and the political parties. While the women's movement has been successful in improving the numbers, this does not necessarily indicate that party leaders believe in women's abilities (Forum Komunikasi untuk Perempuan Timor Lorosae (Fokupers), 2009). *Deputadas* recognise that, while there has been progress in gaining support in both political parties and the parliament, there is still resistance to a gender equality agenda. Such resistance came to a head when the caucus pushed for a formal institutional role within the budget process. The broader institutional environment is also critical to understanding the contradictions displayed by these new institutions. In particular, Timor-Leste's fragile state status, marked by weak institutional capacity, poor service delivery, crisis and instability, significantly hampers their potential, as have the varied degrees of commitment to gender equality. In a context marked by both a complex historical past and a large international footprint, more research is required to flesh out the ways in which new institutional designs and old institutional paradigms coexist and interact.

The contribution of this case study to the literature on substantive representation, and to international feminist politics more broadly, is in identifying the potential significance of parliamentary institutions in supporting critical actors and enabling critical acts, as well as providing a channel for women in the community to participate in the legislative process. The passage of the GRB resolution was a victory for the Timorese *deputadas* and the women's caucus. But it was also a win for women activists both inside and outside the political sphere. The resolution put the focus on gender as an integral part of policy and budget making, and paved the way for fiscal democracy along gender equality lines. This did not occur seamlessly, and the women's caucus leadership had to invest significant political capital to build this new gender-focused institution. Political tensions and policy debate are integral to the women's caucus. The GRB resolution, however, shows that *deputadas* have been able to move beyond these tensions and act collectively for women. They themselves are proud of this collective strength (Palmieri, 2012).

The collective work by the caucus on the GRB resolution helped build their skills, confidence and political currency. As a group, these women influenced the course of the parliament beyond what would have been possible for them as individuals. It was this enabling characteristic of the parliamentary caucus, including the networks surrounding it, that made it a significant player in the substantive representation of women. Such potential of gender-focused parliamentary institutions means that this case study has implications well beyond Timor-Leste for those seeking to ensure that the parliamentary representation of women moves 'beyond numbers' towards substantive achievements in advancing gender equality.

Notes

1 The IPU reported that of 77 parliaments almost half had a women's caucus. In 80 countries there were 93 parliamentary committees covering gender equality issues (Ballington, 2008).

2 Translated into English by the author.
3 The likelihood of synergies between international and local actors was enhanced when a prominent Timor-Leste activist, Milena Pires, became the head of UNIFEM in Dili, which had a strong track record in GRB work.
4 While the parliamentary resolution on GRB was approved in July 2009, it was officially published in 2010. For the purposes of clarity the resolution on GRB is referred to as a 2009 event (Parlamento de Timor-Leste, 2010).

4 The contribution of the women's movement to making economic policy more gender responsive

Civil society activism has played an important role in the adoption and implementation of GRB initiatives. Examples abound of the success of these endeavours. In South Africa and Tanzania the GRB initiatives were led primarily by women's organisations (Stotsky, 2016). In the fragile state of Zimbabwe a civil society organisation, Women's Resource Centre and Network, campaigned with some success for the adoption of GRB (Adebanjo, 2009; Stotsky et al., 2016). Despite some positive experiences, the literature on fragile states has observed that the interactions between the state and civil society can operate in contradictory directions. Some research has uncovered a positive role for political activism in democratic efforts in a fragile state context (see Norris, 2006). Other relevant research has highlighted the opposition between activists and the state and its effect in unsettling power and political stability (see Putzel & Di John, 2012; Okumu, 2011).

The stakes can be high for women's activism. Peace often fails to deliver better outcomes for gender equality, fragmentation places collective action under strain and political instability undermines opportunities for policy engagement. In this chapter I investigate how these contradictory forces operate in Timor-Leste to constrain (or expand) opportunities for women activists to influence economic policy from the outside. I reflect on the conditions under which women activists can influence economic policy, making the government accountable for their policy commitments and encouraging active citizenship on economic policy.

I argue that women's strategic mobilisation around an autonomous, well-organised and cooperative political platform has created opportunities to place gender equality in the context of Timor-Leste's development project. Women's activism on economic policy was strongly backed by a political agenda and some important political wins on representation and legislation to address violence against women. The experience of women's organisations in Timor-Leste shows that the nature and strategies of the movement, the politico-economic setting, its alliances with gender machinery and the nature of the changes pursued all mattered.

Women mobilising for change in fragile states

Research has provided an abundance of illustrations of the positive role of the women's movement on budget processes and decisions in fragile states. In Zimbabwe, civil society played a role in setting a positive context for GRB including a demonstration of its potential and the provision of technical support. Advocacy work by the Zimbabwe Women's Resource Centre and Network (ZWRCN), a civil society organisation, has been traced to 1999. It led to a commitment by the government to adopt GRB in 2007 with ZWRCN providing technical support. An outcome of this work was its inclusion in the 2007 call circular that instructed ministries to consider GRB objectives in budget planning (Adebanjo, 2009; Stotsky et al., 2016). In Bangladesh several civil society organisations have played a role in keeping the government accountable for its commitments and encouraging it to adopt a GRB initiative. These organisations collaborated with key policy makers to boost their understanding of GRB including outlining its contribution to transparency and accountability (Siddique, 2013). This chapter investigates the conditions under which women activists can influence economic policy, making the government accountable for its policy commitments and encouraging active citizenship on economic policy.

Research on fragile states has shown that the effect of the women's movement on gender equality and state resilience can be complex and at times contradictory. The positive role of civil society has been confirmed in a quantitative study on mass political activism in fragile state contexts conducted by Pippa Norris (2006). This analysis has shown that demonstrations, petitions and boycotts can contribute to a positive and effective democratic state in fragile democratic states (Norris, 2006: p. 16). Other research has urged caution about assuming that collective action has a positive effect. Such research suggests that activism can contribute to inciting or worsening violence and undermining political stability. One of the ways these organisations undermine political stability is by providing an alternative platform for those intending to challenge the state (Putzel & Di John, 2012: p. v). Another way is by raising expectations about what the state should deliver and how it should engage with society. Concerns about the role of these NGOs in increasing political instability has generated some resistance to civil activism and collective action among governments in South Sudan, Liberia, the Democratic Republic of Congo and Sierra Leone (Okumu, 2011: p. 21).

The literature on GRB has highlighted the contribution of autonomous, capable and well-organised women's organisations to realising equitable, transparent and accountable budget processes (Elson, 2004). Being autonomous, in terms of being self-governing and independent from political bodies, is central to the success of the women's movements in representing women and influencing policy (Weldon, 2002). The work of Shireen Hassim (2005) on South Africa shows that achieving gender equality is contingent on the presence of a women's movement with both autonomy and a political agenda. She distinguishes between 'weak' and 'strong' social movements, with strong movements being capable of voicing group interests, mobilising and determining strategies for action to further their interests (Hassim, 2005: p. 176). In some contexts, however, autonomy is not a choice but rather it is framed by the state. In Tanzania steps were taken to capture women's activism by bringing all women's organising under state control (Beckwith, 2007).

The women's movement, feminist or otherwise, is very broad and resorts to a diversity of strategies and tactics in its interactions with the state (see Beckwith, 2007). In the context of democratic transition in Chile, the women's movement realised some of its goals through a mix of insider and outsider strategies. It paired the autonomy to develop an agenda with insider tactics to place its demands on the public agenda in a 'double militancy' strategy (Franceschet, 2004: p. 501). How these women mobilise and interact is important to understanding the strategies deployed by activists and their political effectiveness in such contexts. The existence, or not, of a peak body, for example, can have a bearing on the unity of the women's movement and its deliberative capacity (see Andrew, 2008). Collective action in the context of a fragile state can be a challenge. These are contexts that are profoundly fragmented along ethnic, religious and class lines. Finding a platform for collective action in such contexts may be a fraught exercise. Fear and suspicion are obstacles to the networking and collaboration that are cornerstones of women's effective activism (see Benequista, 2010; Earle, 2011; Mcloughlin, 2009; Oosterom, 2009; Paffenholz, 2009). This fragmentation also has a significant impact on whose voice is seen as important and gets heard (see Hassim, 2005; Oosterom, 2009). Strategic and tactical alternatives for collective action may be significantly reduced in contexts that are highly fragmented and in states with limited capacity (see Earle, 2011; Mcloughlin, 2009; Rocha Menocal & Sharma, 2008).

The influence of women's representation and independence on the Mexican GRB initiative has received some attention. The mobilisation of non-government and community-based organisations, covering advocacy and research, led to the development of a GRB initiative in Mexico in the 1990s. While the engagement of a broad-based and nationwide network was a feature of this initiative, limited technical skills prevented it fulfilling its potential (Hofbauer, 2002). Economists Jennifer Cooper and Rhonda Sharp (2007) observed that the Mexican initiative struggled to engage women and grassroots communities, and instead became reliant on international agencies and the government. The representation of a broad range of views and the autonomy of the GRB initiative were seen as being at risk in Mexico. These patterns can be in part explained by the nature of some of the analytical work on the budget, which requires technical, negotiation and consultation skills (Heimans, 2002). This has led to the prevalence of elites with access to education and resources in the debate over policy and legislative changes. In Sierra Leone, educated and English-speaking activists were instrumental to the adoption of legislation relevant to gender equality (Castillejo, 2008: p. 13, 2011). Aid agencies have been seen to exacerbate these patterns because of their preference for dealing with primarily moderate and middle-class civil society and women's groups (Paffenholz, 2015).

The political and ideological context can influence the effectiveness of women's collective action (see Annesley, 2012; Franceschet, 2004; Sawer, 2002; Waylen, 2000). Spaces for women's collective action are framed by their interaction with the gender machinery, governance structures and women's political representation (see Beckwith, 2007), as well as informal institutions (Oosterom, 2009: p. 10). The transition to democracy and peace offers a real opportunity to move forward the women's rights agenda because it involves a redefinition of power sharing, setting up new governance institutions and rewriting rules and norms in electoral reform and the constitution. However, the realisation of these opportunities has been slow. In Burundi, Sierra Leone, Kosovo and Sudan men dominated negotiations to set out power-sharing arrangements, determine institutions for political governance and shape state–society relations. Women have found themselves excluded from public life at the end of conflict (Castillejo, 2011). Another study found that out of 585 peace agreements in 102 peace processes signed between 1990 and 2010, as few as 16 per cent made reference to women. This suggests that, from the outset, justice and equity are being forfeited to the prospect of achieving conflict resolution (Bell & O'Rourke, 2010). These patterns highlight the inherently precarious position of women in the public arena, given that the public sphere is framed by a male-biased distinction between public and private. Women's collective action is, in this context, a transgressive exercise (Weldon, 2004).

One of the ways women activists have attempted to change the political context from the outside is by mobilising for changes to electoral laws. They have successfully campaigned for the adoption of electoral quotas in Kosovo, North and South Sudan and Burundi. Yet they have found political parties to be profoundly flawed because they have failed to represent citizens' interests and to harness a significant policy agenda that could anchor gender equality (Castillejo, 2011). Practical challenges can further undermine the effectiveness of activism, including the difficulty of reaching regions where violence remains, the absence or collapse of infrastructure and limited financial resources (see Benequista, 2010; Earle, 2011). The cost to women activists can be significant with other relevant research finding that the presence of chronic violence severely compromises the opportunity for participation by closing sites of engagement with the state, arresting social interactions and homogenising communities (Pearce, 2007: p. 52).

State institutions with a remit over the promotion of gender equality have become integral to the broader set of governance institutions in post-conflict settings (Castillejo, 2011). This is important for the prospects of a gender equality agenda influencing policy. The literature points to the interaction between the women's movement and effective gender machinery as crucial to the movement's success (see Weldon, 2002). Research in Kosovo, Sierra Leone and Guatemala has documented the flaws of such machinery in fragile states given their unclear political agenda, limited resources and strong focus on capacity building and services. The weak and non-threatening nature of the leadership of these institutions can in part explain these flaws (Castillejo, 2011).

Importantly, however, research in Sierra Leone and Kosovo has found that the existence of a gender machinery that had adopted some of the women's movement's agenda was associated with a fall in activism (Castillejo, 2011).

The economic context and economic policy sanctioned by the government have also been found to influence the strategies deployed in women's activism (Annesley, 2012). In Australia, for example, neoliberalism has aggravated patterns of control over advocacy bodies funded by the government, broadly viewed as having a particular interest in raised public expenditure, and is seen to be a negative force in policy making (Sawer, 2002). Changes to the funding of women's organisations, including defunding of some of them, have changed the landscape of the Australian women's movement. Within the women's movement such moves were seen to have been intended to undermine the movement's advocacy capacity and to silence critical voices (Maddison & Partridge, 2007). This is a powerful illustration of one of the strategies the state can use to shape the women's movement (see Beckwith, 2007). Good economic performance makes it easier to pursue gender equality policies that have a high price tag. Also significant to the success of these initiatives are women's political presence (Annesley et al., 2014).

The emergence of the women's movement in Timor-Leste

The landscape of the Timor-Leste's women's movement has changed dramatically since its first incarnation at the dawn of the independence movement. Women's NGOs gained momentum under the strong repression by the Indonesian regime and thrived with its withdrawal and the influx of international resources and organisations under the UN administration. A defining feature of the Timorese women's movement was its mobilisation around a network and a policy agenda.

A precursor to women's NGOs in Timor-Leste was the first mass women's organisation, the Organização Popular das Mulheres Timorenses (OPMT). OPMT was established in 1975 and was integral to the pro-independence political party Fretilin. It endorsed a strong feminist agenda for the emancipation of women and the revision of cultural norms such as polygamy and 'bride price' practices (Trembath & Grenfell, 2007). It played an instrumental role in Fretilin's 1975 interim administration, including a role in literacy programmes and crèches. OPMT offered the first opportunity for many women to network, mobilise and contribute to the public sphere. The fight against the discrimination experienced by women under colonial rule was however subordinated to the struggle for independence (Cristalis & Scott, 2005; Franks, 1996; Hill, 1978, Smith, 2014). With the occupation of Timor by Indonesia in 1975, the emerging feminist project became increasingly subordinated to the self-determination project (Joshi, 2005; Niner, 2011).

The reorganisation and broadening of the resistance movement brought about by the development of the Conselho da Resistência Revolucionário

Nacional, under the leadership of Xanana Gusmão, allowed the emergence in 1998 of a platform for women's mobilisation through the Organização da Mulher Timorense (OMT). The OMT offered an avenue for the engagement of women across political parties and organisations with a mandate to mobilise activists at the grassroots level and support the resistance movement. It was an important change that provided a platform for women from a diversity of backgrounds and interests to collaborate. It also allowed women that were disenfranchised by political tensions within the resistance movement to mobilise (Cristalis & Scott, 2005).

The mid-1990s saw the arrival of NGOs and advocacy groups in Dili. Campaigning for self-determination was no longer women's organisations' principal focus (Cristalis & Scott, 2005). An early example of women voicing their rights as a distinctive political group was a 1998 protest rally denouncing the violence women experienced under the Indonesian regime. One of Fokupers' founding members was behind this campaign (Charlesworth & Wood, 2002; Hall, 2009). Also important to the development of a women's movement was the mobilisation of women in the diaspora and their engagement with the global women's movement. International sites such as the 1995 UN World Conference on Women were an important opportunity for women to network and campaign for Timor's independence (Cristalis & Scott, 2005; Smith, 2014).

The departure of the oppressive Indonesian regime and the arrival of inter-national organisations and resources saw the launch of a number of new local and national NGOs with a strong emphasis on women and their rights, needs and interests (Smith, 2014; Trembath & Grenfell, 2007). One concern of the emerging women's movement was ensuring that gender was main-streamed in the design of new political and electoral institutions. The transition to independence by 2002 offered new opportunities for women's participation including an opportunity to contribute to setting out the rules for election to the Constituent Assembly and the drafting of the Constitution (see Charlesworth & Wood, 2002).

While most of the political activity on gender equality issues is driven from Dili, there is great diversity among the organisations that work on addressing women's social, economic and political status. High-profile women's NGOs include Caucus Feto iha Politika, with a focus on promoting women's political participation, and Alola Foundation, founded in 2001 by the former First Lady, Kirsty Sword Gusmão, to address women's inequality and their marginalisation in the development process (Trembath & Grenfell, 2006, 2007). Local women's organisations have highlighted the role of women's mobilisation in changing community life. A particular example is Oan Kiak, a community-based enter-prise founded in 2003 in the isolated rural community of Barikafa. Their work has been found to have led to economic and cultural changes to the lives of women in this community (Trembath & Grenfell, 2007). These examples illustrate the organisational diversity of the women's movement and the strategies it has adopted. Australian researchers Trembath and Grenfell (2006) highlight that this diversity is reinforced by a multitude of factors including ideologies, organisations' politics and history, interactions with foreign workers, and conflicts between modernity and tradition.

Under the UN administration women's organisations moved swiftly to create a common political agenda and establish a formal structure in Rede Feto to lobby the political parties and leaders and international organisations. In June 2000 more than 400 East Timorese women from across the country convened the First National Women's Congress. This congress resulted in a policy document, the 2000 Platform for Action for the Advancement of Timorese Women, and the establishment of an umbrella network body, Rede Feto. The Platform for Action identified a series of long-term priority issues and recommendations, including those on poverty, education, violence against women, and decision making and institution building (Cristalis & Scott, 2005; Hunt, 2008: p. 103; Pires, 2004).

Rede Feto, an umbrella network body of the women's movement, mobilised national and local organisations concerned with gender or women's issues. It included religious organisations, NGOs and women's wings of political parties such as OPMT, OMT, Alola Foundation, Fokupers and Caucus Feto iha Politika. Its mandate was to promote women's interests, improve gender equality and women's rights, and contribute to broader national and international development issues (Abrantes, 2011; Hunt, 2008; Trembath & Grenfell, 2007). Since then, Rede Feto has held regular national women's congresses to review progress and outline a series of new policy priorities. These developments were integral to growing demands for a greater diversity of voices in the development project, and for alternative policies and development approaches (Hunt & Wigglesworth, 2014).

Claiming a role for women's organisations in gender-responsive budgeting

The mobilisation of women's organisations for greater budget participation, transparency and the adoption of a gender perspective gained momentum in 2010 when a working group on GRB was set up. These women's organisations have contributed to economic policy making on a number of fronts. One example is the representation of women's organisations in the Consultative Council of the Petroleum Fund, Timor-Leste's main revenue-raising mechanism. Working Women's Centre Timor-Leste is a further illustration of women's contribution to employment and industrial relations policy. The budget policy, however, offers the most longstanding example of the contribution of these women's organisations to economic policy (Costa & Sharp, 2017).

The endorsement of the 2008 government-led Dili Declaration, with its commitment to the implementation of GRB, is an early example of the role these organisations have played in setting a positive environment for changes to budgetary policy (Costa et al., 2009). A more recent development was an informal working group on GRB involving national organisations with a focus on women's status and gender equality. This working group was anchored on alliances with other NGOs that had experience in monitoring the government's budget and policy. Through this association, women's organisations tapped into their allies' methodological expertise, broader analytical approach and political strategies. The influence of these NGOs was evident in the strategies deployed by the GRB working group, which included lobbying the parliament through their budget committee debates, monitoring budget spending and raising community awareness about the budget and its gender impacts.

In 2010 the working group focused on the demand for more open access to budget documents, more equal outcomes and adequate resourcing for key elements of an agenda for gender equality. Practical steps involved gender analysis of the 2011–2013 budget proposals. This analysis and proposals for changes were submitted to parliament and the Office of SEPI. The group initially focused on sectors with obvious gender impacts such as health, education, the Office of SEPI and justice. Their experience in campaigning led them to act to change budget decisions and to mobilise the support of parliamentarians for an increase in the 2011 budget allocations for transport of victims of violence against women. By 2012 the working group on GRB had expanded its engagement with the budget to the audit and evaluation stages of the budget process. Using scorecards and a baseline survey, the women's organisations attempted to assess the implementation of the law against domestic violence at the community level (Female activist, Interview, 2013).

Increasingly the focus was on demanding information on whether the budget was being spent as planned and in engaging communities in the process. This was in part stimulated by concerns that underspending and reallocation were undermining arguments for a more gender-responsive budget. A range of explanations of budget underspending has been suggested, including poor planning, lack of technical support for budget initiatives and rules on spending. Investigating whether the money was actually spent as planned complemented existing efforts to monitor how services were responding to women's needs and interests through reporting on CEDAW and the Platform for Action. Similar issues were uncovered in 2005 by Mexican NGO Fundar, which found that funding for HIV/AIDS was being given to hospitals that did not specialise in treating HIV/AIDS. When they probed this information further, they found that a significant proportion of the hospitals that received these funds were using them for financial services, cleaning, security and maintenance (Hofbauer, cited in UNFPA & UNIFEM, 2006).

Women's activism on economic policy in a context of change

Women's activism on economic policy was bolstered by some important political wins, leading to recognition of women's organisations as a legitimate and autonomous voice for women. Storm clouds were now gathering, with the budget under growing stress, evidence of the prevalence of masculinity and the military in the state, and a contraction of spaces for participation.

Rede Feto, the Women's Congress and its Platform for Action all had important roles in shaping the women's movement and the strategies it has deployed (see Abrantes, 2011). Every four years since 2000, women's organisations have gathered around the Women's Congress to develop a Platform for Action. The approach that was deployed to develop these Platforms for Action was important. Ahead of the 2008 congress facilitators were trained and workshops were conducted across the territory. Themes for consultation were set by Rede Feto and informed by CEDAW. These district discussions informed the Platform for Action endorsed by the 2008 National Women's Congress.

This consultative approach was important to distil diverse interests and needs into a united agenda, mobilise women across the territory around a women's plan and energise the women's movement. It can be argued that the Platform for Action and the national congress are critical in giving political legitimacy and autonomy to the women's movement with Rede Feto and activists in Dili playing a leading role. This is partly because of the methodology adopted, in particular consultations at the district and national levels. This is not to say that all women were engaged in this exercise; however, the approach suggests that the political agenda engaged a broad collective of Timorese women in both the districts and the capital. Despite its political meaning, the Platform for Action has an important shortcoming in that it fails to provide depth of analysis and as a result it did little to reactivate the connections between activists and policy makers. What it did was to highlight where policy outcomes are failing women and girls (see Austen et al., 2013). Ahead of the 2007 elections the women's movement took steps to lobby political parties to adopt the Platform for Action. This resulted in 12 political parties endorsing a women's political platform that included issues such as education and the economy (Chinaud, 2007; Rede Feto Timor-Leste, 2008a; PST et al., 2007). Combined, this work provides an example of how the women's movement has at times adopted a 'double militancy' strategy (Franceschet, 2004), using its autonomy to outline its political agenda and active engagement with political parties to influence policy.

Since independence, women's activism has grown more confident, sophisticated and resourceful, having contributed to the adoption of quotas in party lists in the electoral law and the passage of the law addressing domestic violence. Changes such as the introduction of quotas in the electoral law were significant to the broader gender equality agenda. The links between women's representation and policy were outlined by a representative of the women's movement when she argued that 'the [former] Prime Minister is a veteran – so most of his work pays attention to veterans' (Women activist, Interview, 2008). This activist suggests that the success of women's gender equality agenda needs the support of women in political and governance structures.

Demands for improvements in women's presence in politics were accompanied by a sense of impatience with women's silence in the public sphere (Victorino-Soriano, 2004: p. 21). The view that women are too 'shy' to participate needs to be understood in the context of Timor-Leste's traditional social hierarchy, which assigns women to the home and expects their silence. The implication of these patterns is that women activists in the districts are rare, and educated women tend to be concentrated in Dili where they can find a role as effective and free activists (see Wigglesworth, 2009: p. 245). These patterns have raised concerns over who is being represented by women's activism. Researcher Nina Hall (2009: p. 319) argued that new norms and discourses of gender equality and women's rights are not embraced by the women's movement as a whole. Instead Dili-based urban middle-class activists appear to have led the mediation of these norms, drawing on the alliances with international NGOs and the UN to make their actions more effective (Hall, 2009).

Women's organisations have emerged as experts, as a source of information and research on women and their needs and interests. This positive view was clearly expressed by a Timorese *deputada* who commented that the women's movement was 'very well equipped . . . and independent' (*Deputada*, Interview, 2009). Women's organisations have collected data on the nature of assaults, and the relationship of the perpetrator to the victim, for inclusion in the government's CEDAW report (Timor-Leste Secretary of State for the Promotion of Equality, 2007). Another example is the collaboration between the University of New South Wales, James Cook University and the Timorese Alola Foundation on the link between experiences of violence, abuse, injustice and explosive anger among women in post-conflict contexts (Rees et al., 2013). Research such as this was important to build the agenda for legislation against domestic violence and the allocation of resources to survivors. These organisations rose to the challenge and provided detailed information on gender inequality and gaps that was important for informing parliamentarians. This research has been particularly important to legitimise the voice of women's organisations in budget policy making by framing their contribution around knowledge and expertise.

Activists had grown concerned that key achievements such as legislation addressing violence against women would be ineffective without adequate funding. The broader context was important, with the budget escalating from US$348 million in 2008 to US$1,953 million in 2016 (see Chapter 2). This 'big money' approach adopted by Gusmão's AMP government was coherent with the economic liberalism agenda circulated by international financial organisations (Anderson, 2012: p. 229). Elements of the women's agenda such as funding of the women's parliamentary caucus and the women's machinery in government were early beneficiaries of this shift. However, the risk is that GRB is only seen as possible when funds are abundant, as noted by a male activist: 'No petroleum fund, no gender budgeting' (Male activist, Interview, 2013).

The positive association between economic growth and gender equality has been supported by relevant research (see Annesley, 2012). However even when the economy of the United Kingdom was performing well under New Labour, the United Kingdom Women's Budget Group was only able to challenge the efficiency elements of the budget and was prevented from intervening in policy decisions if the cost was considered to be high (see Annesley, 2012: p. 19). The actions of the women's movement were significant in positioning changes to the budget in line with the women's political agenda as a less risky political business.

A growing concern, however, has been the sustainability of the budget and the 'primacy of militarized masculine privilege' (Niner, 2016: p. 503) that underpins it. One of the ways this primacy has materialised is in a largesse of welfare allocations directed towards (male) veterans' pensions, social services, scholarships and irregular contracts related to the national electrification scheme (Scambary, 2015). In the 2015 budget US$130 million was allocated to veterans' pensions, representing 8 per cent of the total budget (Timor-Leste MoF, 2015) for a mere 1 per cent of the population (Scambary, 2015: p. 295). Many voices have been critical of these choices, one of the most vocal being President Taur Matan Ruak. The 2016 supplementary budget was received with consternation by the President with an argument that the credibility of the state was at stake given that the commitment to more conservative spending was not carried through (Ruak, 2016). Other research has found that these cash transfers, designed to increase stability and prevent conflict, are imperfect avenues for poverty reduction. Instead, a case has been made that small cash grants for children in vulnerable families are a stronger basis for an anti-poverty programme (Dale, Lepuschuetz & Umapathi, 2014).

Women's activism has had to operate within the confines of great political uncertainty. The first independent Timor-Leste government was unsure, and at times suspicious, of the role of civil society. By 2004, the interactions between NGOs and the state were a 'significant concern' (Hunt, 2008: p. 254). The 2006 crisis interrupted policy, legislation and programmes. Women's organisations collaborated and reallocated their resources to support women affected by violence and political instability, and in effect responded to gaps in state services (Trembath & Grenfell, 2007). More recently sites of participation are being redefined by the formation of a 'national unity' government. An implication of having all parties sitting in the government is the lack of effective opposition in the parliament (Feijo, 2016). In this setting the parliament might be reduced to 'rubber-stamping government decisions and discharge [of] its functions of controlling and monitoring the action of the government' (Feijo, 2016: p. 11). The impetus for engaging with NGOs and creating sites in which they can participate may also be significantly compromised. Women's organisations have found support for their demands in the women's cross-party caucus and opposition parties. The political changes may seriously undermine their levers for engaging with the parliament.

Without an effective opposition the value of activism may be significantly diminished. This has been evident in Timor-Leste, where the 2014–2017 budgets have been approved by a unanimous vote (see Feijo, 2016). The development of a closed-door ad-hoc committee ahead of the 2013 budget to consider amendments provided further indication of the vulnerability of fiscal transparency in Timor-Leste. These patterns have been worsened with for example a contraction in the number of hearings with advocacy organisations, ahead of the 2014 and 2015 budget discussions (see La'o Hamutuk, 2014, 2016a). This is a significant concern, with the 2015 Open Budget Survey finding that opportunities to participate were weak and primarily limited to the parliament (see IBP, 2016). The space to influence the budget might be in flux, and access to budget decisions and processes been significantly impaired. Further compounding the difficulty of participating, policies and legislation are often presented in Portuguese, and attracting and maintaining the qualified and skilled staff that are essential for high quality analysis and engagement with policy making and budgeting remains a challenge (see Hunt & Wigglesworth, 2014). These concerns have an important bearing on the prospects of making the budget more gender responsive.

Since the 2012 withdrawal of the UN and some development agencies the Timor-Leste government has established a fund for women's organisations, making grants available to local organisations. These allocations are set to change the landscape of NGOs and women's organisations. Concerns over autonomy have been raised, with similar grants to NGOs reported to benefit particular organisations and to soften their criticisms of the government (Hunt & Wigglesworth, 2014).

The cooperation between the women's movement and the gender machinery is also not without its challenges. Personal relations, family past history, roles in the resistance and the women's movement, and the legacy of old power structures all shape the tone of these interactions (Hunt, 2008). Bolstering the women's case are women activists who moved from women's organisations to senior political positions in government (see Piscopo, 2011). An example is the former Minister for Social Solidarity, Maria Domingas Fernandes Alves, who led the women's machinery in government before 2006 and was a founder of the NGO Fokupers. The women's movement has also played an important role in service delivery, often in an attempt to address state failure. A particular example is the work of Fokupers, an NGO that has played a role in mediation, counselling, and in the provision of safe houses for long-term stays for survivors of violence (Trembath & Grenfell, 2007).

Timor-Leste's dependency on revenue from natural resources makes tax collection and its link to state resilience a particular concern. In 2008 the government cut a range of taxes in a decision that aimed to draw foreign investment and had the support of international agencies. The result, however, was a significant worsening of Timor-Leste's dependency on the Petroleum Fund (Anderson, 2012). Arguments for a more diversified revenue base have been raised by NGOs: 'everyone [should pay direct tax, as] this can teach all our citizens that they share responsibility to contribute to development, and . . . [can remind] the government of its responsibility to our citizens' (La'o Hamutuk, 2008: p. 4).

These arguments rehearse the debate over the links between taxation and state performance (see Putzel & Di John, 2012). Feminist scholars have raised concern over the gender impact of tax regimes. This research has highlighted the inherent explicit and implicit gender biases that prevail in both indirect and direct tax (see Barnett & Grown, 2004; Casale, 2012; Grown, 2005; Grown & Valodia, 2010;

Stotsky, 1997). Explicit biases were on display in Argentina where the tax code assigns income earned on jointly owned assets by default to the husband. In this way the tax system is reinforcing gender inequalities in the allocation and control of income earned jointly. Research has also uncovered implicit biases. In many countries, contributions to pension funds generate tax benefits and men benefit the most from these, given that they are disproportionately in formal employment and earn higher incomes (Valodia, 2010).

NGOs have praised the political commitment and language of the government in support of GRB; however, they have judged its practical adoption as inadequate. In an interview a male activist suggested that GRB is 'just a jargon' term (Male activist, Interview, 2013), undermined by the intricacies of policy and budget planning and implementation. Framed this way, these organisations are highlighting the tension between new strategies such as GRB and traditional norms about gender and the way politics has always been played (see Mackay, 2009). While the women's movement has fostered a positive political environment for the emergence of a GRB initiative in the government, this political work needs to be supported by access to budget documents and processes, and strong technical skills that highlight the impact of the budget on different groups of men and women. In Timor-Leste, women's organisations have estimated the resources required to address violence against women, with support from UN Women, to successfully advocate for an increase in funding for shelters for survivors of violence (see Silva Alves, cited in Rugkhla & Alvarado, 2016).

Conclusion

Examples of women's activism on economic policy in contexts such as Bangladesh, South Africa, Tanzania and Zimbabwe suggest that women's organisations have a positive role in economic policy making. The reality is messier. This chapter provides an insight into women's collective action in Timor-Leste and how it has contributed to important forms of feminist engagement in economic policy. It indicates that women activists have achieved this despite a context of political fractures, changing institutional spaces, limited technical capacity and growing concerns over the sustainability of Timor-Leste's budget.

The experience of women activists in Timor-Leste shows that characteristics of the movement and the strategies it deployed were important. It highlights how women have framed the women's movement's autonomy from political and governance institutions around Rede Feto, its women's congresses and the Platform for Action. These were critical spaces for women to delineate and express their views, bringing together a very culturally, politically and socially diverse group of women. These provided legitimacy to Rede Feto and its membership, enabling them to pursue changes to the electoral law, a gender policy machinery and a law against domestic violence. These approaches have been important for the emergence of a capable and 'strong' women's movement (Hassim, 2005) in Timor-Leste.

In the late 2000s, some women's organisations established a working group for the adoption of GRB. This was underpinned by significant political achievements including the institutionalisation of gender-focused institutions in government, improvements in women's political representation and the passage of the law against domestic violence. Growing concerns that this positive legislative change was failing to attract the right resources provided the impetus for women activists to engage with economic policy more actively. This working group has campaigned for more open access to budget documents, more equal outcomes and adequate resourcing for its agenda. In a short period this group has supported budget changes and encouraged budget monitoring.

While activists have praised the government's commitment to adopting GRB, they have judged that the practice has fallen short of the political commitments. A growing concern has been the 'primacy of militarized masculine privilege in Timor-Leste's post-war society' (Niner, 2016: p. 503) and its impact on the security of women, overall budget sustainability and economic growth. Opportunities for women to engage with the budget are in flux with the formation of a 'national unity' government and the contraction of spaces for participation in budget discussions in the parliament. Without strong investment in analysing the impact of the budget on groups of men and women, the contribution of women's organisations to GRB might struggle to go beyond a timid contribution to sectors traditionally associated with women.

5 The role of international parliamentary bodies in supporting gender-responsive budgeting

This chapter examines the launch of a caucus of women parliamentarians in the Network of Women at the Parliamentary Assembly of the Community of Portuguese-speaking Countries (NWPA-CPLP). This institution was established in the 2000s and holds a mandate to coordinate and cooperate on matters related to gender equality and equity. Timor-Leste is a member and the NWPA-CPLP provided a framework and lent legitimacy to Timorese *deputadas'* collective action (see Chapter 3). This chapter is based on a manuscript published in 2016 in *Parliamentary Affairs* (Costa, 2016). There is reason to believe that gender machinery within international institutions can play a significant part in the diffusion of GRB. The Commonwealth played an important role in the diffusion of GRB with the introduction of an initiative on GRB in its 1996 annual meeting of Ministers for the Status of Women. GRB was positioned as a strategy for advancing gender equality and eradicating poverty through the national budgetary process. At that time pilot initiatives were implemented in several countries, including Barbados, Fiji, St Kitts and Nevis, Sri Lanka and South Africa (Hewitt & Mukhopadhyay, 2002; Sharp, 2000; Spence, 2002). Commonwealth Women Parliamentarians has also furthered the diffusion of GRB by supporting debate on GRB in national parliaments. For example, in the 2013 Commonwealth Workshop on Women's Political Party Caucusing, participants discussed the role of parliaments and parliamentarians in advocating for gender mainstreaming and acknowledged a role in encouraging debate in national parliaments on GRB (Commonwealth Women Parliamentarians, 2013).

Gender-focused bodies have multiplied in parliaments across the world, and also among international associations that link national parliaments. Bodies with an emphasis on gender equality have emerged in a range of international parliamentary institutions like the IPU, which has a Coordinating Committee of Women Parliamentarians. In the Commonwealth of Nations there is Commonwealth Women Parliamentarians, and in the Southern African Development Community (SADC) Parliamentary Forum there is a women's caucus. The women's caucus, typically an informal body established by women parliamentarians, has gained particular traction in these international institutions. Another format that has proliferated is the international extension of cross-party parliamentary groups with a gender mandate. An example of this is the Asian Forum of Parliamentarians on Population and Development, linking cross-party groups in almost 30 parliaments and itself having standing committees on the status of women, and on the involvement of men in the elimination of violence against women (see Sawer & Turner, 2016).

These gender-focused bodies have been shown to boost the capacity and influence of women parliamentarians, to validate norms distinct from those that dominate the parliament and to encourage the participation of the women's movement and civil society in parliamentary processes. Such bodies give important political legitimacy to critical acts that seek to promote gender equality. Women's cross-party caucuses have been found to contribute to building cross-party consensus around a particular issue, and create a network of support and mentoring for parliamentarians (Sawer, 2014). The literature on such parliamentary institution building, however, has generally neglected international parliamentary bodies. Other relevant literature highlights the role of transnational networks, specifically the transnational feminist movement, in the diffusion of gender equality norms and strategies to national policy contexts (see Keck & Sikkink, 1998; True & Mintrom, 2001). Recent research highlights feminist institution building in parliaments as part of the mobilisation of the women's movement (see Sawer & Turner, 2016).

This chapter examines the launch of a caucus of women parliamentarians in a new and relatively unknown international parliamentary institution, the Parliamentary Assembly of Portuguese-Speaking Countries. I draw on interview data conducted with women parliamentarians from five Portuguese-speaking countries: Timor-Leste, Mozambique, Guinea-Bissau, Angola and São Tomé e Príncipe. These women were involved in the NWPA-CPLP. It examines the Network of Women in this Parliamentary Assembly (NWPA-CPLP) and its role in mainstreaming and supporting its membership through capacity building and networking. This chapter reflects on the conflicting forces at play; with women pursuing in this new institution another avenue to transform politics and policy, and a political context where patriarchal norms are prevailing and contradictory views of strategies to address gender inequality and gaps have not been tested. The present chapter suggests that this women's caucus can play a role in furthering elements of an agenda for GRB in national contexts. It has pursued this in three different ways: first it recommended that national governments adopt GRB, providing a policy framework and leverage for action in the national context; second it created opportunities for transfer of knowledge and capacity building on how to 'do' GRB; and third it encouraged nationally driven gender equality agendas to improve women's economic and political status. An example of this was a 2016 UNDP initiative that brought a former leader from the women's cross-party caucus of the Cape Verde parliament to train Timor-Leste's women's cross-party caucus (UNDP, 2016).

The advent of the NWPA-CPLP

The women's caucus in the Parliamentary Assembly of the Community of Portuguese-Speaking Countries is a relatively new enterprise. Formally recognised in the Parliamentary Assembly's statute, this caucus mobilises women across a range of political parties and development contexts to mainstream gender equality and equity across the work of the assembly, as well as member national parliaments. *Deputadas* of Portuguese-speaking countries first mobilised in 2003 under the framework of the Forum of Parliaments of Portuguese Language (2002–2007) (CPLP, 2011). This forum was the first incarnation of an international association of parliaments from these countries. By late 2007 it had been replaced by the Parliamentary Assembly of the Community of Portuguese-speaking Countries, linking the national parliaments of Angola, Brazil, Cape Verde, Guinea-Bissau, Mozambique, São Tomé e Príncipe and Portugal (Conselho de Ministros da Comunidade dos Países de Lingua Portuguesa, 2007). Timor-Leste joined in 2002 upon its independence. This assembly was designed to promote the Portuguese language, and to foster stronger diplomatic and political ties and collaboration on a range of issues including public administration and education.

The mandate of the NWPA-CPLP is extensive. It aspires to play a role in strengthening the capacity of *deputadas*, as well as promoting policy changes that advance gender equality and equity including in maternal and child health, gender-based violence, care work, conflict prevention and politics. It also seeks to play a role in sharing and harmonising legislation, an example of which is the introduction of gender electoral quotas in São Tomé e Príncipe (Rede das Mulheres da Assembleia Parlamentar da CPLP, 2010). The NWPA-CPLP has provided a framework for *deputadas* to engage with economic policy, and in particular budgetary policy.

Gender equality and equity were recognised as objectives in the statute of the new Parliamentary Assembly. A review of the statute of the Parliamentary Assembly in 2009 provided an opportunity for the formal recognition of NWPA-CPLP as a cross-party body for coordination and cooperation on matters related to gender equality and equity and as a vehicle for human development and peace building (Assembleia Parlamentar da Comunidade dos Países de Lingua Portuguesa, 2009). Another important feature of the codification of gender equality is the commitment, inscribed in the Parliamentary Assembly statute, that each group representing a national parliament in the activities of the Parliamentary Assembly should consist of at least 30 per cent women (Assembleia Parlamentar da Comunidade dos Países de Lingua Portuguesa, 2009). The *deputada* from the small African island state of São Tomé e Príncipe described the sentiment that provided the impetus for the materialisation of the caucus: 'It was necessary that women had a space; that women can reflect on questions that concern them, questions that relate to gender equality and equity' (*Deputada* São Tomé e Príncipe, Interview, 2011). Primarily, this *deputada* suggests, the arguments for the advent of the women's caucus were born out of the need to build a supportive network, create a route for the development of a gender equality and equity agenda, and ultimately boost their representational capacity.

With representation across Europe, Africa, Asia-Pacific and the Americas, this Parliamentary Assembly brings together economically and culturally diverse territories that were in the past part of the Portuguese colonial empire. The UN has classified Angola, Mozambique, Guinea-Bissau, São Tomé e Príncipe and Timor-Leste as least developed countries (United Nations, 2014). Guinea-Bissau has been classified as a fragile state and has joined Timor-Leste on the g7+ platform of fragile states. Brazil, however, has joined the G20 as one of the 20 largest economies. Mozambique and Timor-Leste have made significant progress in women's representation in parliament, ranking thirteenth and sixteenth in the world with 39.6 per cent and 38.5 per cent of parliamentarians being women (IPU, 2015). This relatively high level of representation suggests a degree of success in engaging women in post-conflict political settlements and weaving special measures into electoral laws and party practices to boost women's descriptive representation (Waring, 2010). Brazil presented the poorest showing for women, ranking 116th, with 9 per cent of parliamentarians being women (IPU, 2015).

When the broader community of countries (CPLP) was established in 1996, many had reservations. The historical basis for this community made for challenging relationships, not least the violent opposition between the Portuguese colonial power and anti-colonial political movements in Mozambique, Angola and Guinea-Bissau. By the mid-1990s Portugal had undergone significant economic and political modernisation with its integration into the European Union, and former Portuguese colonies were more focused on their political and economic future. In this context it was possible to reframe the relationship between Portugal and these new countries (MacQueen, 2003).

Different views were emerging on the relevance of a community built around the Portuguese language, with Mozambique seeing its membership of the Commonwealth as central to its regional aspirations (MacQueen, 2003). The ambivalence of Brazil was significant to the future of the CPLP. While it had an important role in the creation of the CPLP, Brazil had emphasised bilateral economic relationships, particularly with African countries (Varela & Costa, 2009). Among Portuguese elites the enthusiasm for this political project vacillated, with concerns that the CPLP would be seen as a form of neo-colonialism and a recasting of Portugal's colonial past. Political and economic instability in contexts such as Guinea-Bissau further undermined the policy potential of the CPLP and its institutions (Redondo, 2008). These economic and political differences combined with uneven degrees of enthusiasm have added to the challenge of the political project of the CPLP and its Parliamentary Assembly.

Making the caucus work for women

Establishing a women's caucus was only a first step. To make this international network work for women, *deputadas* and the NWPA-CPLP have engaged in the internal politics of the Parliamentary Assembly to enhance the avenues available to pursue gender equality and women's rights. Particular concerns have been the expansion of the gender architecture and adoption of practices that enhance gender equality. The NWPA-CPLP has also provided opportunities for capacity strengthening, and has promoted women's political representation and legislation to protect the rights of women.

Deputadas inserted gender equality and women's rights into the debate over the role and shape of standing committees. These committees were established to operationalise the Parliamentary Assembly and strengthen the links between the assembly and other bodies within the community of Portuguese-speaking countries. A *deputada* from São Tomé e Príncipe argued that standing committees were central for women to pursue their agenda, as they expanded the space available to women to present their issues. This view suggests a complementarity between the role of the NWPA-CPLP and that of the standing committee (*Deputada* São Tomé e Príncipe, Interview, 2011). The work of Marian Sawer (2014) has shown the potential complementarity between such specialised bodies, with a women's caucus holding the more informal role of supporting its members, and standing committees operating in a more institutionalised role, applying a gender lens to the legislative process. In the Parliamentary Assembly of the CPLP, gender equality was allocated to a multi-portfolio committee with responsibility for issues of policy, strategy, legislation, citizenship and mobility. This may suggest an emphasis on gender mainstreaming and its application to a broader range of policy and legislative issues. Gender equality, however, has failed to reach the standing committee responsible for economic policy. While these standing committees are in an embryonic stage, policy collaboration between the NWPA-CPLP and the standing committee could magnify the effectiveness of the *deputadas* in the Parliamentary Assembly.

Another issue that *deputadas* sought to address was continuity of NWPA-CPLP activity. Typically, the women's caucus meets annually as part of the undertakings of the Parliamentary Assembly. Without additional support, further activity has been limited. *Deputadas* have sought to expand opportunities to interact and network through parliamentary workshops. Since the first workshop in São Tomé e Príncipe in 2010, the regularity of such workshops has been inconsistent. A more recent event occurred in 2013 when *deputadas* met in Angola ahead of the Parliamentary Assembly to consider discrimination against women. Issues covered included violence against women and maternal health, as well as strategies to integrate a gender perspective in budget policy (see Agencia Angola Press, 2013). These issues, particularly gender-based violence, had featured in previous meetings including the 2010 workshop and have been outlined in its mandate.

Economic policy, with a specific focus on budgetary policy, has been an area of interest for the NWPA-CPLP and provides an insight into the role of the caucus in supporting *deputadas*. The women's caucus has nominated budgetary policy as a key strategy for promoting gender equality and provided training on how to 'do' GRB. Three documents underline the interest in GRB. First, article 4 of the statutes of the NWPA-CPLP, agreed on 8 March 2010, includes the object of fostering the adoption of GRB to realise gender equality and equity (Rede das Mulheres da Assembleia Parlamentar da CPLP, 2010). Second, the 2010 Declaration of São Tomé recommends that governments adopt detailed and objective measures to allocate resources for the implementation of gender-responsive policies (*Jornal São Tomé*, 2010). Third, the 2009–2010 annual report of the NWPA-CPLP recommends that adequate resources be made available for the support of women, as a pathway to equality and equity (Rede das Mulheres da Assembleia Parlamentar da CPLP, 2011). These political statements reflect an attempt by the NWPA-CPLP to provide a policy framework and leverage for action at the national level. However, these statements do not in themselves bring about measures to make national budgets more responsive to women. Instead the CPLP has been shown to hold a limited influence on national policies partly because of the lack of CPLP-sponsored policies, including those concerning economic policy (Varela & Costa, 2009).

These statements provide a framework for support for national women's parliamentary caucuses and for strengthening the capacity of *deputadas*. An example of this are visits of a representative of the Cape Verdean parliament's women's caucus to women's caucuses in Angola and Guinea-Bissau, to share their experience of analysing the differential impact of the budget on men and women. With support from the UN, these initiatives provide an illustration of the potential of the NWPA-CPLP to strengthen the capacity of *deputadas* and their contribution to national policy (see Semana, 2015).

In Angola, women in parliament and government have found positive ways to engage with expenditure on social issues at both the planning and monitoring stages of the budget cycle (*Deputadas* Angola, Interview, 2011).[1] These *deputadas* saw themselves as 'insiders' of the women's movement who have performed in a range of political roles, and construe their engagement with civil society and communities as a source of their legitimacy. These views highlight the role of these gender-focused institutions in parliaments in consulting with communities and civil society and fostering inclusiveness (see Sawer, 2014). The role of women's caucuses as gateways to community organisations and women's groups (see Sawer & Turner, 2016) has also emerged at the CPLP level. In a 2013 workshop in Angola, the NWPA-CPLP brought civil society and government together to consider gender equality issues (see Agencia Angola Press, 2013).

The passage of the law against genital mutilation in Guinea-Bissau in 2011 provides a further illustration of the role of the NWPA-CPLP in strengthening the capacity and confidence of parliamentarians and raising gender equality issues relating to its member states. The practice of female genital mutilation in Guinea-Bissau was discussed in the 2010 parliamentary workshop of the NWPA-CPLP in São Tomé e Príncipe. On this occasion, the women's caucus recorded their opposition to this practice and recommended that resources be directed towards its eradication and to the provision of reproductive health services to women (Jornal São Tomé, 2010).

The political context within which the parliamentarians of Guinea-Bissau have had to navigate is very complex, with not one elected prime minister having finished their term of office since the mid-1990s (see IRIN News,

2012). The NWPA-CPLP contributed to building the capacity and confidence of *deputadas*. A *deputada* from Guinea-Bissau suggested that by being involved in the NWPA-CPLP she had 'more weapons' in terms of knowledge and skills, 'more initiative, more courage to fight for the law against genital mutilation' (*Deputada* Guinea-Bissau, Interview, 2011). Despite this important legislative success, firm budget allocations for implementing the new law are yet to be forth-coming. Beyond political resistance to addressing gender equality, the particular economic and political circumstances of Guinea-Bissau offer some insights into the challenges in implementing the new law. Guinea-Bissau has been in political turmoil for over two decades and the 2012 military coup d'état caused a con-traction of its economic opportunities and fiscal revenues, including the reduction of aid and a disruption in cashew exports. Opportunities for new budget expenditure were constrained by cuts to domestically funded capital spending and increases in defence expenditure (IMF, 2013). In this context, the potential for budget allocations to be redirected towards elements of the women's agenda is much reduced. The particular national economic context can trump international efforts to bring about positive changes for women.

As well as introducing new elements, the NWPA-CPLP has had a role to play in supporting critical acts in national parliamentary contexts. This is well illustrated by the endorsement lent to a 2009 parliamentary resolution in São Tomé e Príncipe recommending that political parties take the necessary steps to improve women's representation in eligible positions by at least 30 per cent. The resolution also recommended that government and civil society take steps to improve women's representation and to recognise a role for the women's movement in raising awareness of women's political rights (São Tomé e Príncipe Assembleia Nacional, 2009). There were no illusions over the shortcomings of the resolution, with its emphasis on self-regulation. The NWPA-CPLP publically voiced its concern about the adoption of voluntary quotas in a workshop in 2010 (Jornal São Tomé, 2010). This public position served to underscore the lobbying work of women activists in the country, and drew the attention of political parties and the government to their poor performance on indicators of women's representation. Another way the NWPA-CPLP supported national activists was by lobbying political leaders in São Tomé e Príncipe, placing them under political pressure. This episode provided *deputadas* with practical experience of working collectively, supporting the efforts of national parliamentarians and placing a national issue on an international platform. This contribution to the work of activists in São Tomé e Príncipe illustrates the role of networks such as NWPA-CPLP in lending personal and political support to critical acts and validating norms on gender equality and women's empowerment.

Despite failing to reach the target of 30 per cent representation of women in parliament, on balance this resolution has had a positive impact on women's representation. In one election, São Tomé e Príncipe moved from one to eleven *deputadas*, equivalent to 20 per cent of the parliament. In parallel, there were significant improvements in the representation of women in senior leadership positions in parliament with the election of women to the positions of vice president, secretary and vice secretary.

Resisting change

The positive steps represented by the launch of the NWPA-CPLP and the adoption of quotas for the representation of women in national groups in the Parliamentary Assembly have been nested in old ways of doing politics and the traditional gender order. Gender equality has had limited traction, remaining construed as a women's issue of limited policy significance. The nature of the CPLP posed particular institutional challenges. With limited financial support and a geographically, economically and politically diverse community, the NWPA-CPLP has seen its influence diminished. A particular challenge is that of geopolitical power, with *deputadas* in the South having different approaches to gender equality to the politically dominant members in the global North.

As it was conceived, the NWPA-CPLP involves all active *deputadas* in the member countries of the Parliamentary Assembly (Rede das Mulheres da Assembleia Parlamentar da CPLP, 2010). Occasionally, men have also taken part. The absence of women from national delegations, however, is not uncommon. This issue surfaced in 2011 when Portuguese male parliamentarians addressed the women's caucus and acknowledged the absence of women in their national delegation. They were met with condemnation from the leadership of the NWPA-CPLP. The resistance to implementing the 30 per cent quota for women in national delegations has been a source of frustration for the *deputadas* in the NWPA-CPLP. For some *deputadas* this continued resistance to the inclusion of women in national delegations is strong evidence of the lack of seriousness with which gender equality is treated within the Parliamentary Assembly of the CPLP. A *deputada* from Mozambique summarised her frustration with what she saw as symptomatic of the vulnerable position of gender issues within the Parliamentary Assembly: 'if in an organisation we are still talking about the statutes that establishes [the Parliamentary Assembly] then we have a long way to go!' (*Deputada* Mozambique, Interview, 2011). *Deputadas* have actively voiced their frustration with the way some countries have failed to implement the 30 per cent quota for women in national delegations. This resistance within the membership of the Parliamentary Assembly suggests that much of the work of *deputadas* remains in the realm of educating their peers on the need for gender equality in this institution.

Men's lack of engagement with gender equality issues has featured as a particular concern among *deputadas*. Efforts to mainstream gender equality within the architecture of the Parliamentary Assembly have been pursued to counteract views that gender equality is a women's issue. Such positive steps have been undermined by deep-rooted gender bias, gendered power inequities and the way political business has always been conducted in traditional political institutions (Mackay, 2014). A *deputada* from Mozambique highlighted this tension between new and old norms by observing that there is a lack of debate on gender issues and the work of the NWPA-CPLP within the broader assembly:

> [What] I find frustrating is that the women get together and that in plenary there is no opportunity to discuss our problems, the problems are of men and women, and if the men don't understand, don't take up our problems the leverage of the NWPA-CPLP will be constrained.
>
> (*Deputada* Mozambique, Interview, 2011)

The nature of the CPLP poses particular challenges, with a *deputada* remarking that its geographic dispersion and economic and political diversity hampers the depth of learning and exchange within the women's caucus. Opportunities for thoughtful relationships may be undermined by the diversity of contexts; priorities and interests of *deputadas* in a crisis context such as Guinea-Bissau are substantially distinct from those in one of the largest economies, Brazil. In addition, the emphasis on a shared cultural system among Portuguese-speaking countries, with its origins in Portuguese imperialism, has been contested (McMahon, 2014).

Gender equality is one of the battlegrounds where what is shared and what is different within this diverse community of countries is being played out. A particular fracture line has been divergent approaches to gender-focused bodies in national parliaments. In Mozambique and Angola *deputadas* opted for the development of caucuses and have drawn on regional platforms such as the SADC for inspiration. *Deputadas* from these countries believed that gender equality was taken seriously by SADC. The SADC was taken seriously not only because of its gender equality initiatives but because of its regional significance; for example, Mozambique's affiliation with CPLP was seen as subordinate to its regional membership with the SADC (McMahon, 2014). In contrast to the SADC model, in Portugal gender equality has been integrated into a standing parliamentary committee with remit over citizenship and constitutional issues. The absence of a women's caucus in the Portuguese parliament has raised concerns over whether Portuguese parliamentarians can represent the broader views of *deputadas* of their parliament. These distinct approaches have led to fractures within the NWPA-CPLP over the best way to pursue gender equality. Opposing views over strategies for reaching out to women, in particular the creation of a centre to support women within the CPLP, have brought these tensions to a head. The organised women's caucuses in the South are effectively positioned in opposition to the old order, which nonetheless continues to wield substantial influence over the Parliamentary Assembly. This suggests that postcolonial power relations influence the political agenda of women's caucuses within international bodies.

Issues around the budget of the Parliamentary Assembly and how it funds the NWPA-CPLP have featured as a particular concern. The lack of funding for the women's caucus within the Parliamentary Assembly budget was raised in the annual report for 2009–2010 (Rede das Mulheres da Assembleia Parlamentar da CPLP, 2010). The effectiveness of the NWPA-CPLP comes at a cost; it requires funds to hold regular meetings and to provide technical and political support to national initiatives, as well as to provide technical support between meetings to further its national and international agenda. The NWPA-CPLP faces significant financial challenges given that the costs it incurs are met directly by the annual contributions of national parliaments, and are vulnerable to appropriation for other priorities. This lack of a secure budget allocation has led some *deputadas* to talk about a mere symbolic commitment to gender equality within the Parliamentary Assembly. As the debate broadens to consider how the Parliamentary Assembly will allocate its budget, specifically the budget for its standing committees, a new frontline will emerge for *deputadas* to ensure that the NWPA-CPLP secures a regular flow of funds. The positive experiences of national and regional women's parliamentary caucuses (such as that of Timor-Leste) may play an important role in shaping this debate.

Central to the effectiveness of the NWPA-CPLP is its relationship with the CPLP forum, which brings together ministers who have portfolio responsibility for gender equality at the national level and those who have a closer link to the implementation of policy and budgeting. This forum is part of the CPLP's gender architecture. Set up in the mid-2000s, this forum provides a regular and permanent mechanism for the meeting of CPLP ministers to ensure the cooperation and adoption of gender mainstreaming, and monitoring of gender equality. The importance of the representation of women in the executive was highlighted by the experiences of several *deputadas* in national policy debates. In Angola *deputadas* felt that progress on funding of social areas was heavily influenced by the presence of activists in leadership positions, principally the Minister for Planning and the Secretary of State for the Budget, who created the conditions for a national debate on gender equality norms and strategies. The mobilisation that brought about the passage of the law against domestic violence was described at the time as evidence of the positive collaboration between the executive and the legislature (O Pais Online, 2011). This collaboration is significant as the separation between legislative and executive powers means that ministers recruited by the Prime Minister of Angola cannot serve as parliamentarians. The role of one of the world's most respected African women leaders, Luisa Dias Diogo, former Mozambique Prime Minister (2004–2010), provides a further illustration of the positive bearing of women in leadership. Dias Diogo became well known for her actions to increase the number of women in parliament and the executive, and her support for the provision of free reproductive and sexual health services (Waring, 2010).

The *deputada* from Guinea-Bissau remarked that the absence of women and gender activists in the executive would be likely to undermine efforts to pursue gender equality. She claimed that any attempt to gain funding for the implementation of the law against female genital mutilation faced political resistance because 'the President of the Republic is a man, the Prime Minister is a man, the President of the Parliament is a man' (*Deputada* Guinea-Bissau, Interview, 2011).

The degree of engagement of men with gender equality has been one concern of the NWPA-CPLP. Strategies to mobilise men have included reading the caucus' annual reports in the plenary of the Parliamentary Assembly. The honest assessment of a *deputada* from Mozambique was that these strategies have failed to produce a change in gender power relations, and instead a commitment to gender equality endorsed by the NWPA-CPLP coexists alongside deep-rooted gender bias, gendered power inequities and traditional views of politics.

Political and financial issues have undermined the interaction between the NWPA-CPLP and another gender-focused body within the CPLP – the forum of ministers for gender equality. The Portuguese Secretary of State for Parliamentary Affairs and Equality, Teresa Morais, explained the poor performance of this forum of ministers by the lack of an ongoing executive support infrastructure within the CPLP Secretariat (Lusa, 2014). Since then, an agreement has been reached on a permanent technical secretariat for gender equality and gender focal points to support cooperation between ministries and the implementation of the CPLP's 2014–16 work plan. Another area of concern has been the allocation of resources and its impact on men and women (Ministros Responsáveis pela Igualdade de Género da CPLP, 2014; Simão, 2011). An example of a positive step in this area is the commitment by the forum of ministers for gender equality to identify and mobilise resources to fund initiatives against domestic violence (Ministros Responsáveis pela Igualdade de Género da CPLP, 2014). Despite some positive actions taken by the forum of ministers, political and financial issues have hampered efforts to entrench gender equality within the CPLP's permanent structure. Without a coordinated, funded and effective forum of ministers the role of the NWPA-CPLP in the diffusion of gender equality norms and strategies may be significantly undermined.

Conclusion

It is too early to provide a definitive assessment of the contribution of the NWPA-CPLP to leveraging gender equality strategies and norms, and furthering women's substantive representation. The *deputadas'* assessment of the NWPA-CPLP has generally been positive, with the functioning of the caucus proving to be relevant to women parliamentarians. What is possible at this time is to reflect on the challenges to women's organising in an international parliamentary body and difficulties they face in gaining political traction for their agenda.

This gender-focused body has played a role in building the capacity of members and in information sharing and discussion. *Deputadas* have been able to contribute to the development of the assembly by inserting new gender norms such as a quota for women's representation in national groups. The caucus had an impact on gender machinery in some national parliaments, having supported the emergence of a women's caucus in the Timor-Leste parliament (see Chapter 3). This caucus has provided a platform for debate on gender equality including GRB, and supported critical acts to change national legislation. This case study confirms the findings in the literature on the generally positive role of these bodies (see Sawer, 2014). It highlights the contribution of those in international parliamentary bodies by inspiring and supporting national initiatives and applying a degree of peer pressure. When *deputadas* found themselves in small numbers in the parliament of São Tomé e Príncipe they drew on the NWPA-CPLP to bolster their efforts to improve women's representation.

Geographic dispersal and economic and political diversity have undermined the potential for learning, collaboration and exchange of the NWPA-CPLP. The continuity and effectiveness of the NWPA-CPLP has been further undermined by the lack of financial and ongoing technical support for its activities. To overcome these problems, *deputadas* have drawn on international bodies such as the UN. With their support, parliamentarians have been engaged in inter-country exchange and learning. Ultimately, however, the characteristics of domestic politics and the economic context can trump international gender-focused bodies.

Nonetheless, *deputadas* have attempted to gain traction for gender mainstreaming. Representation of women within the Parliamentary Assembly has been a particular battlefield for the NWPA-CPLP. The resistance to a quota for women in national delegations has emphasised the lack of political will to improve gender equality. Also central to effectiveness is the relationship of the NWPA-CPLP to the forum of CPLP ministers with responsibility for gender equality. While there have been positive steps to build this forum of ministers, it is far from coordinated, funded and effective.

A particular constraint is the tension between this new institution building and the broader context of dominant patriarchal norms, which construct gender equality as a women's issue. There are also conflicting views on the best way to pursue gender equality in the NWPA-CPLP, with the better organised members from the South often at odds with the old established order. These distinct perspectives speak to the tensions between new and old institutions and norms, and how these are intensified by geopolitical power relationships within a community still trying to define itself.

Note

1 Despite Angola's status as Africa's second largest oil exporter and third largest economy, income inequality is high and poverty is widespread in rural areas (IMF, 2012). Human Rights Watch (2017) has raised concerns over the continued repression of human rights and pro-democracy activism, as well as corruption and the mismanagement of Angola's public funds.

6 Administrative data and their potential for gender analysis in the education sector

Since its first unexpected appearance in Timor-Leste's 2008 budget papers, GRB has expanded into a political and institutional narrative, and materialised as a political strategy for gender activists. To support this expanding gender equality agenda the government has sponsored a variety of research initiatives including a study on the link between school dropout rates and teenage pregnancy (MoE et al., 2010). This research has led to a debate on the policy options for enhancing the experience of the education system for teenage mothers. Such studies illustrate the value that is increasingly ascribed to knowledge about gender relations in Timor-Leste.

GRB has provided impetus for the development of gender-relevant indicators. The role of indicators as conduits for GRB and gender-sensitive policy was outlined in the first gender statement enclosed in the 2008 budget: 'Gender equality will also be integrated into Ministry Annual Action Plans and performance indicators' (Timor-Leste Ministry of Finance 2008: p. 34).

The significant footprint of international organisations built a demand for indicators. The emphasis on indicators also saw a renewed interest in administrative data. This chapter explores the potential of using administrative data to identify the differential impact of the budget on men and women. It explores how gender analysis, using administrative data, can contribute to an understanding of policy impacts and assist in fostering budgetary changes. To explore this problem, I developed indicators relevant to gender equality in education using administrative data collected and managed by the MoE, the EMIS. These indicators focus on measuring and comparing intra- and inter-district school performance in the delivery of education services. Information on students was used to devise indicators on the share of total enrolment that is female and the share of students that are in a school grade that is age-appropriate or higher. This was complemented by data on teachers, which I used to develop an indicator that deals with women's representation in the teaching workforce.

The relevance of the gender analysis of the EMIS data to policy and budget decisions was enhanced by linking this data to household survey data, the Timor-Leste Living Standards Survey (TLLSS). The TLLSS adds social and economic data that help to explain the gender gaps in education identified through the EMIS analysis. Ultimately, my aim is to provide further policy directions on how Timor-Leste can improve its gender equality outcomes in education. Chapter 7 extends this analysis by exploring the circumstances that hinder or enhance the policy potential of this gender analysis. It reflects on the reaction of policy makers in the MoE to the indicators developed here, and discusses their views on how gender analysis can contribute to positive budgetary and policy change.

Five rationales explain my choice to focus on education administrative data in this study. First, I drew on principles of social justice and women's rights. Girls' right to education gained renewed international attention when, in 2012, Taliban gunmen attempted to assassinate young Pakistani Malala Yousafzai for her activism supporting girls' right to be educated (Husain, 2013). The global recognition that women's empowerment and gender equality are development objectives in their own right has a long tradition in the MDGs and CEDAW. Second, empirical literature has found that education of girls has been associated with social and economic progress (see Hanushek, 2008; Herz & Sperling, 2004). A 2004 study into the cost of missing the target of gender equity in primary and secondary education in 45 countries suggests that these countries will see a reduction in economic growth and have less impact in reducing fertility rates, child mortality and undernutrition. It suggests that investing in the education of girls is an effective public investment (Abu-Ghaida & Klasen, 2004). Third, education has in some contexts strengthened the bond between state and society, establishing social normalcy and consolidating the territory. The 2011 Education for All Global Monitoring Report *The hidden crisis: armed conflict and education* (UNESCO, 2011a) concludes that success in education can help underpin the peace process, strengthen government legitimacy and set a country back on a path to recovery. In practical terms, providing effective and accessible education services sends a strong signal of normalcy to communities in a fragile state. Fourth, there is some evidence that investment in quality education is a concern for the population, and the women's movement in particular, in Timor-Leste. Of particular importance in this study was the fact that education was identified by 70 per cent of the population in Timor-Leste as the top priority for public expenditure (Timor-Leste Planning Commission, 2001). Gender equality and gender mainstreaming have gained traction in Timor-Leste's policy context, having been identified as guiding principles in the law governing the education system and its 2007–2012 associated education policy (Soares & Lauvigne, 2009). An initial political commitment to adopt GRB in the 2008 pledge to invest in gender equality, the Deklarasaun Kompromisu Dili, linked equality in education with improvements in women's status and the national economy. This pledge strengthens the case for education being a critical area for the technical and political development of GRB.

This chapter is structured around four sections. The first section provides a detailed background analysis of the EMIS. The second section examines its potential to deliver gender-relevant indicators of school performance with respect, first, to student outcomes (indicators 1 and 2) and, second, the teaching workforce (indicator 3). The third section investigates the potential of the

TLLSS to develop socio-economic indicators that illuminate gender gaps and inequalities in school performance. The chapter concludes with a discussion of the policy implications of such indicators.

The Education Management Information System (EMIS)

Administrative data refer to statistical information regularly collected by government agencies as part of their assessment of service delivery. EMIS is one such source of administrative data. EMIS refers broadly to the set of structures and procedures that generate, manage and disseminate data and statistics for the management of service delivery in education (see Cassidy, 2005; Sultana, 2003; Wako, 2003). While there is a degree of variation from country to country, most EMISs cover a range of education-related input variables including those on students, teachers, school infrastructure and materials (see Amin & Chaudhury, 2008; Cambridge Education, 2006b). EMISs do not typically collect data on finances and cost accounting (Amin & Chaudhury, 2008).

EMIS was popularised in developing countries during more than three decades of international assistance. UNESCO, together with bilateral donor support, played a crucial role in its dissemination (Amin & Chaudhury, 2008). As early as the 1990s, US bilateral support to this sector was estimated to reach more than US$2–3 million per year (Crouch, 1997). Between 2002 and 2006 more than 40 World Bank education projects were recorded as having elements related to EMIS (see Powell, 2006). The consequence of such international efforts is that similar approaches and structures of EMIS have emerged across a number of developing countries. Information systems in education have mobilised significant resources.

Support for EMIS was reinforced by international development goals, and efforts to record progress against these goals. In particular, the MDGs and the EFA emphasise quality in education and indicators of success in schooling, including improvements in gender parity. Notions of educational entitlement and the accountability of the state to its citizens have provided the impetus for this shift (Sultana, 2003). Improvements in computer technology provided further support for this expansion. The effect of these institutional, financial and technical forces is that some form of EMIS has been used in almost all developing countries (Hua, 2011).

There is a body of empirical evidence on the development of EMIS in a diversity of contexts. These reports have focused on the technical elements of the EMIS system in a variety of development contexts, for example Kosovo (Sommers & Buckland, 2004), West Bank and Gaza Strip (Sultana, 2003), Mozambique (Cambridge Education, 2006b; Powell, 2006), Namibia (Voigts, 1999), Ghana (Cambridge Education, 2006a; Powell, 2006), Nigeria (Cambridge Education, 2006c; Powell, 2006) and Bangladesh (Powell, 2006). These reports have focused on the 'supply side' of the data issue, exploring the mechanics of establishing and developing an EMIS including institutional arrangements, management and operations for data collection and organisation, software used, structure of the data collected and approaches to dissemination of EMIS outputs and analysis. The particular challenges and opportunities of establishing and developing an EMIS in fragile contexts are elucidated by Sommers and Buckland (2004) and Sultana (2003).

Support for EMIS has its roots in the assumption that better data will bring about better policy decisions, and improve resource allocations and service delivery. The education strategy of the World Bank (2011d: p. 43), for example, sets out these links, arguing that information and research can play a critical role in service delivery in fragile situations:

> Knowledge tools and information are perhaps even more critical in fragile states, where broken communication links between governments, providers, and beneficiaries are one of the effects of conflict, reflecting both the destruction of communication infrastructure and deep social fractures . . . In fragile contexts, where the needs are great and families may have to assume the cost of restoring basic services, doing enough analysis to identify the interventions with the highest value-added is imperative.

In this report, the World Bank (2011d) advocates for an emphasis on information that can shed light on performance as an avenue to repair damage in service delivery. These issues have been echoed in research by Sultana (2003), who illuminated the role of establishing an EMIS in the state-building effort with his account of the development of an EMIS in the West Bank and Gaza Strip:

> Those involved in the technical aspects of EMIS are clearly aware of the educational aspects of the work they are doing – they are not just crunching numbers, but are thinking of educational processes and the implications that decisions based on statistical information can have on the real lives of real pupils.
>
> (Sultana, 2003: p. 87)

Sultana provided a positive assessment of the impact of EMIS in policy making and the emergence of evidence-based education planning and management. Notwithstanding this, evidence of a role for EMIS in informing policy has been mixed. A few accounts suggest a positive role for EMIS data in education budgeting and planning. One such positive account is the case of Guinea where, in 1997, an interdepartmental government team commenced a dialogue with teachers, inspectors, public officials and parent associations to devise indicators of school quality. This data was used in 1999 and 2000 to inform decisions on teacher recruitment and school construction (Amin & Chaudhury, 2008; Crouch & Spratt, 2001). Positive evidence from Ghana suggests that EMIS has played a role in assisting district offices in the formulation of their annual operational budgets (Powell, 2006: p. 18). There are also some references to school report cards, and district and school-specific composite indices developed in low-income countries in West Africa (Brossard, 2011, cited in

Attfield & Vu, 2013). However, whether EMIS can make a contribution to improve policy and budgetary decision making in fragile contexts is far from established.

Another area that has received limited attention is the link between EMIS and gender equality. In Mozambique, it has been suggested that the existing gender unit within the Ministry of Education had an ambiguous role and the extent to which it used EMIS for planning was unclear (Cambridge Education, 2006b: p. 19). In Palestine, gender issues have been described as marginal to the data design and implementation and only haphazardly analysed (Sultana, 2003). This paucity of references suggests that gender equality remains marginal in the preparation, collection, compilation and analysis of EMIS data. Despite the wealth of data collected and compiled, the potential of EMIS to develop and use indicators to guide GRB has yet to be considered. Even less is known of what can be expected in a fragile context.

Examining the potential to use EMIS to achieve indicators relevant to gender-responsive budgeting in education

Using the EMIS datasets for 2010 and 2008–2009, in this chapter I investigate what sorts of gender-relevant indicators could be developed to measure school performance and identify the poorest and best performing districts and sub-districts. My aim with the approach devised here is to provide directions for a policy conversation on what kinds of policies and projects could improve education outcomes for girls and promote equality. The Timor-Leste EMIS collects information on characteristics of individual students (name, school, grade and class, status, sex, date of birth, parent qualification), teachers (name, school, sex, qualifications, date of birth, contract type, grade and classes he/she teaches) and schools (public and non-public school, level, location and date of construction). In 2010 EMIS collected information on characteristics of 409,452 students, 11,247 teachers and 1456 schools across 13 districts.[1]

The education policy emphasis in Timor-Leste has been on a basic nine years of compulsory education, or 'basic education'. Basic education is comprised of a mixture of education in primary, pre-secondary (or junior high) and basic schools. This emphasis on basic education is reflected in the distribution of schools. As shown in Figure 6.1, in 2010 primary schools (grades 1 to 6) represented 71.5 per cent of the school infrastructure. Basic schools (grades 1 to 9) represented the second largest group of schools at 18.9 per cent of all schools. Timor-Leste's education is in transition towards the implementation of a nine-year free education model. As a result, there is an overlap between grades in primary schools (grades 1–6) and those in basic schools (grades 1–9). Secondary schools (grades 10 to 12) represented a mere 5.5 per cent of the school infrastructure, with 75 schools.

EMIS collects information on school sector (private and public schools) and the year in which the school was built. The data suggests that close to one in

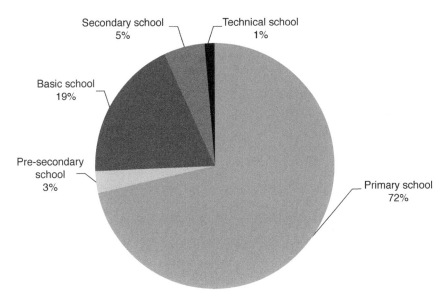

Figure 6.1   Percentage of school infrastructure by school level, 2010

Source: EMIS data, 2010.[2]

Notes: Schools = 1,356; Min. = 0 (pre-primary schools); Max. = 970 (72 per cent, primary schools)

six schools, at 16.1 per cent, are classified as private. Forty-three per cent of the school infrastructure was built between 2000 and 2010. This indicates that Timor-Leste has seen a significant investment in education since the withdrawal in 1999 of the Indonesian forces, which left the education system in ruins. Close to 90 per cent of its infrastructure was destroyed and 80 per cent of its teachers and administrators departed (Asian Development Bank, 2005).

The following sections explore the potential of EMIS to deliver gender-relevant indicators of school performance with respect to, first, student outcomes (indicators 1 and 2) and, second, the teaching workforce (indicator 3). The analysis focuses largely on primary schools for a number of practical and theoretical reasons. First, as noted above, primary schools represent the largest group of schools in Timor-Leste, with a presence throughout the territory. As a result, the data on primary schools offer the greatest opportunity to demonstrate the value of EMIS for insights into policy-relevant issues of access to and quality of education. Second, primary education is a basic need of children and, in the context of fragility and crisis, an important avenue to bring normalcy to their lives and to promote their rights and responsibilities. Third, there is a link between state fragility and poor access to, and participation in, primary school, with approximately half the primary school-age children who are not in school located in contexts of conflict and fragility (Chandy & Gertz, 2011; Kirk, 2008). Gender inequality issues are significant to understanding these connections, with the *2011*

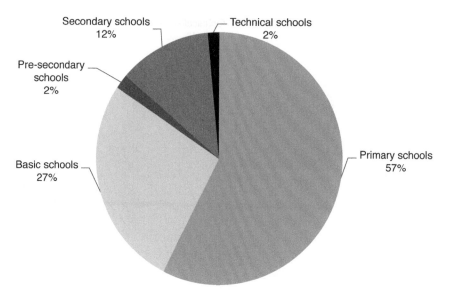

Figure 6.2   Percentage of students enrolled by school level, 2010

Source: EMIS data, 2010.

Notes: Students = 361,115; Min. = 1.5 per cent (technical-professional secondary schools); Max. = 56.9 per cent (primary schools).

education for all global monitoring report (UNESCO, 2011a: p. 40) observing that being female and poor further aggravates the disadvantage of those in contexts of conflict. Despite the focus in this chapter on primary schools (grades 1 to 6), the empirical approach detailed in this chapter could easily be replicated for other school groups and could be conducted separately for public and private schools.

Indicators on student outcomes

The EMIS datasets hold a wealth of information on the characteristics of students enrolled, enabling investigations of patterns in student enrolment. For example, the data can be used to show how student enrolment varies across school levels. As shown in Figure 6.2, enrolments in primary schools represent more than half of the total enrolment number. Enrolments drop dramatically at the secondary school level, with enrolments at this level comprising only 12 per cent of the total.

It is possible to use the information collected on students to investigate parity issues, including gender differences in enrolment shares. Figure 6.3 shows girls' share of enrolment at each school level. Girls comprise less than half the total enrolment at each level. In the technical-professional level this shortfall is pronounced, with a 13.4 percentage points' difference between girls' share of the total enrolment and that of boys.

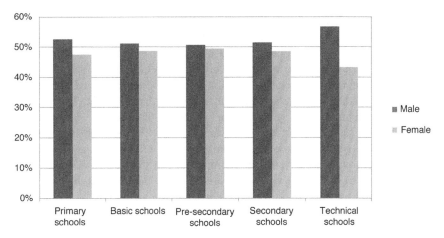

Figure 6.3 Proportion of boys and girls enrolled by school level, 2010

Source: EMIS data, 2010.

Notes: Students = 361,115; Min. = 43.30 per cent (female, technical schools); Max. = 56.7 per cent (male, technical schools).

Indicator 1: share of total enrolment that is female

In fragile and post-conflict states, girls are on the margins of the education system. In times of conflict and crisis and when resources are scarce, the education of boys tends to be favoured. Factors such as safety and security, accessibility, additional care work, early marriage and motherhood all marginalise girls from the education system. Violence against women places girls at particularly serious risk (Kirk, 2008).

Gender inequality in education has been an area of interest for the MoE, with indicators relevant to gender parity featuring in the *Education statistical yearbook 2008/2009* (henceforth yearbook). The yearbook provides evidence of persistent gender inequality, with nine girls for every ten boys enrolled in public primary schools. It also shows disparity across districts; with 86 girls enrolled in primary school for every 100 boys in the district of Liquiça. This pattern is in contrast to the Oecussi enclave, where for every 100 boys there are 99 girls enrolled in primary school (Timor-Leste Ministry of Education and Culture, 2011). The yearbook provides an insight into issues relevant to accessibility and progression throughout the education system. However, its use to guide policy decisions and improve gender equality outcomes in the sector has, to date, been limited. An indicator that explores the experience of the education system for boys and girls in Timor-Leste, and identifies gaps in school performance across the different districts and regions of Timor-Leste, could be a catalyst for a conversation about policy options to improve education outcomes for vulnerable groups of girls.

I developed an indicator of gender parity using the share of total enrolment that is female. I then compared schools' performance across districts and sub-districts and identified districts and sub-districts that are underperforming. Seven steps were involved in this approach. I calculated the share of total enrolment that is female for each school. To avoid distortion in the results, I excluded all single-sex schools from the population of schools. The second step involved identifying the national median for the share of total enrolment that is female. The median provides a benchmark of a typical primary school in Timor-Leste. In 2010, the typical primary school had a female enrolment rate of 47.7 per cent. In step three I compared the performance of each primary school in Timor-Leste against this median. To provide an inter-district comparison, in step four I calculated the median school in each district and compared it to the national benchmark.

One of the ways this data can be presented for an easy comparison of school performance between districts is to calculate, in percentage points, the extent of the difference between a typical primary school performance in a particular district and that of a typical national primary school. This comparison is presented in Figure 6.4. It suggests, for example, that in a typical primary school in the northern coast Liquiça district, the share of total enrolment that is female is 1.4 percentage points below the share of total enrolment that is female in the typical (median) national primary school. The analysis helps to identify the particular districts where issues associated with gender inequality in education might be largest.

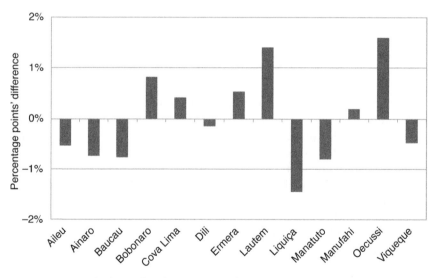

Figure 6.4   Female share of total primary enrolment: district median school performance relative to national median school performance, 2010

Source: Author's calculation from EMIS data, 2010.

Notes: Schools = 970; Min. = -1.45 per cent (Liquiça district); Max. = 1.6 per cent (Oecussi district).

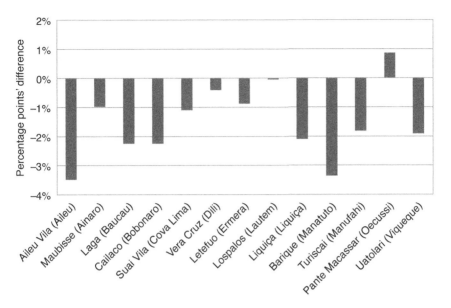

Figure 6.5   Female share of total primary enrolment: sub-district median school performance relative to national median school performance, 2010

Source: Author's calculation from EMIS data, 2010.

Notes: Schools = 970; Min. = -3.49 per cent (Aileu Vila); Max. = 6.71 per cent (Tutuala).[3]

One way to identify the schools where girls might be particularly at risk is to produce an intra-district comparison on the share of total enrolment that is female. In step five I identified the worst performing sub-districts in each district. Figure 6.5 compares the typical schools in these sub-districts against the national benchmark. This shows that the poorest performing sub-district in the coffee growing district of Aileu is Aileu Vila, where a typical primary school underperforms the typical national primary school on the indicator of share of total enrolment that is female by 3.5 percentage points.

An alternative path to identify the sub-districts where girls might be at risk is to produce an indicator of the prevalence of underperforming schools in each sub-district. To achieve this, in step 6 I identified the lowest quartile (25 per cent) of primary schools across all sub-districts. Then, in step 7, I calculated the proportion of primary schools in each sub-district that fall into this lowest quartile. Figure 6.6 identifies the worst performing sub-districts in each district on this gender parity indicator. It reveals, for example, that seven out of fourteen (50 per cent) primary schools in the sub-district of Cailaco (western district of Bobonaro) are among the lowest quartile of primary schools, as ranked on the basis of share of total enrolment that is female.

In summary, there appears to be significant potential to use EMIS to achieve indicators of the performance of individual schools, districts and sub-districts in

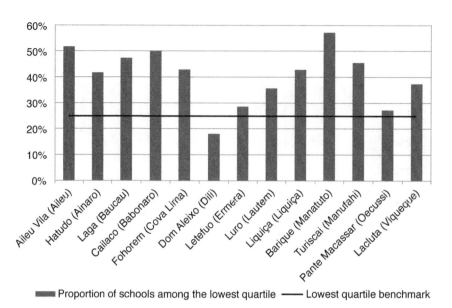

Figure 6.6   Proportion of primary schools in the lowest quartile of schools based on female enrolment share, by sub-district, 2010

Source: Author's calculation from EMIS data, 2010.

Notes: Schools = 970; Min. = 0 per cent (Atsabe, Metinaro, Passabe, Soibada, Tutuala and Vera Cruz);[4] Max. = 57.14 per cent (Barique).

relation to girls' enrolment in primary education. Policy makers interested in improving gender equity can potentially make use of these indicators to target further research efforts, budget allocations and programmes.

Indicator 2: Share of students that are in a grade that is age-appropriate or higher

In the pursuit of indicators relevant to a conversation on policies that can improve gender equality and gender parity, it is also important to take account of the age at which students enrol and progress through primary school. Of particular concern are delays in enrolment. In Timor-Leste, concerns with safety and beliefs that children are too young to enrol in primary school at six have led parents to enrol children in school at an older age. These concerns have been further aggravated by unsafe school infrastructure and the use of severe physical and verbal punishment by teachers (Timor-Leste Secretary of State for the Promotion of Equality, 2007). The Timor-Leste government's CEDAW report described this problem of over-aged students as a 'considerable financial burden on the education system' (Timor-Leste Secretary of State for the Promotion of Equality, 2007: p. 229) not the least for its relationship with school dropout and retention. Despite this, the problem of the mismatch between the grade the student is enrolled in and the grade the student *should* be enrolled in – based on his or her date of birth – has been granted little attention in the EMIS data analysis in Timor-Leste (see Timor-Leste Ministry of Education and Culture, 2011).

To address this, I developed an indicator to capture the mismatch between the grade the student is enrolled in and the grade the student should be in based on his or her date of birth. Significant preliminary work was required; the first step was to calculate the age of each student using the student's date of birth. Students who were recorded as having dropped out or died were excluded from the population of students. I also excluded students who appeared to be aged under five or over twenty. Decisions about the age-appropriate grade (that is, the grade the student should be in considering his/her age) were made in consultation with the EMIS team in the MoE.

Comparing the students' actual and age-appropriate grade revealed that, in 2010, 48.7 per cent were enrolled in a grade below the grade they should be in. Boys represented 55.5 per cent of these students. A measure of the magnitude of the difference between the students' actual and age-appropriate grade revealed that 21.1 per cent of boys and 18.4 per cent of girls were enrolled in a grade that was two to three years below the grade they should be enrolled in, considering their date of birth.

To develop this indicator, I reproduced the approach I used for indicator 1. First, for each school I calculated the share of students that are in the age-appropriate or higher grade and the national median. The median revealed that in the typical national primary school 53.8 per cent of students were in the age-appropriate grade or higher. Then I compared schools in each district and sub-district against this national benchmark. Figure 6.7 provides an illustration of this inter-district comparison. It suggests that the share of students enrolled at an age-appropriate level in a typical primary school in the district of Dili is 19.3 percentage points above the national median. In a typical primary school in the northern coast district of Liquiça, however, this share is 6.5 percentage points below the national typical primary school. It is also significant that Liquiça's neighbouring districts, Aileu and Ermera, performed poorly on this measure.

It is also possible to produce an intra-district comparison. Figure 6.8 compares a typical national primary school and a typical primary school in the worst performing sub-district based on this measure. It suggests that the share of students enrolled in a grade that is equal or higher than the grade they should be enrolled in, in a typical primary school in the sub-district of Iliomar (in the eastern district of Lautem), is 9.5 percentage points below the national typical primary school.

As detailed above, an alternative approach to identifying the worst perform-ing sub-districts is to measure the prevalence of underperforming schools in each sub-district with reference to the mismatch between the grade in which students are enrolled and their appropriate grade. Figure 6.9 illustrates the results. It suggests that in the sub-district of Laga, in the eastern district of

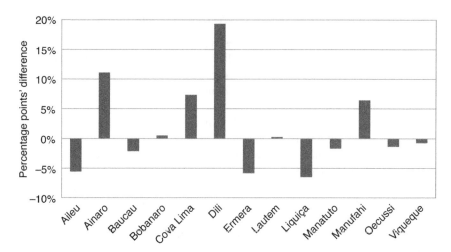

Figure 6.7 Share of students enrolled in age-appropriate grades or above: district median school performance relative to national median school performance, 2010

Source: Author's calculation from EMIS data, 2010.

Notes: Schools = 970; Min. = −6.49 per cent (Liquiça); Max. = 19.29 per cent (Dili).

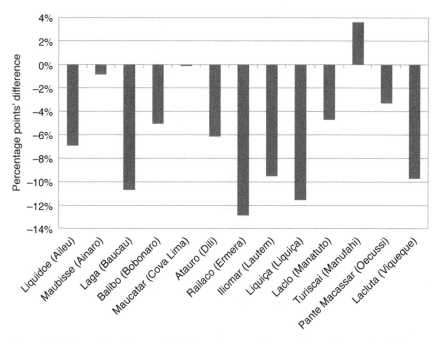

Figure 6.8 Share of students enrolled in age-appropriate grades or above: sub-district median school performance relative to national median school performance, 2010

Source: Author's calculation from EMIS data, 2010.

Notes: Schools = 970; Min. = −12.86 per cent (Railaco); Max. = 26.25 per cent (Dom Aleixo).[5]

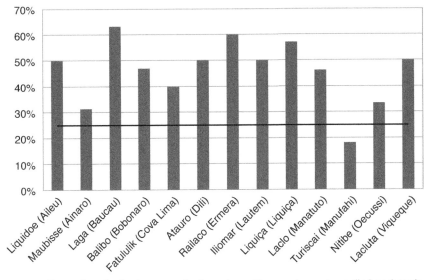

Proportion of schools among the lowest quartile ——— Lowest quartile benchmark

Figure 6.9　Proportion of primary schools in the lowest quartile of schools based on the share of students enrolled in age-appropriate grades or above, by sub-district, 2010

Source: Author's calculation from EMIS data, 2010.

Notes: Schools = 970; Min. = 0 per cent (Alas, Dom Aleixo, Fohorem, Laleia, Maliana, Metinaro, Soibada, Tutuala);[6] Max. = 63.16 per cent (Laga).

Baucau, 63.2 per cent of all primary schools (or 12 out of 19) were in the lowest quartile of schools in Timor-Leste on this measure of school performance. With few exceptions, there is a broad consistency between this measure and that illustrated in Figure 6.8.

The present section thus demonstrates the potential to use EMIS data to create measures of age-appropriate enrolment and indicates how these measures can be used to evaluate the performance of particular districts, sub-districts and schools against national benchmarks. This indicator offers information to governmental policy makers and gender activists interested in devising targeted budget allocations and programmes to improve student outcomes. The measure could be especially useful in guiding the targeting of programmes aimed at improving the educational outcomes of girls and boys who have joined school at a relatively late age. Such programmes might be especially important in reducing dropout rates associated with teenage motherhood and early marriage. Ensuring that girls are enrolled in school at an appropriate age will increase the likelihood that they will complete their education.

Indicators on the teaching workforce

Information collected by EMIS on the characteristics of teachers makes it possible to explore indicators related to gender equality in the teaching workforce and thus contribute to the debate over equal opportunity policies and budgetary allocations. Women are poorly represented in the Timor-Leste teaching workforce; in 2010, a mere 35.2 per cent of all teachers were female. Women's under-representation in the leadership of schools is confirmed by the EMIS data, with women representing 9.3 per cent of all head teachers. As Figure 6.10 shows, the EMIS data suggests that women's presence in the teaching workforce decreases with school level; in primary schools in 2010, women made up 38.5 per cent of all teachers, whereas in secondary schools women represented a little over one in four teachers.

Another important predictor of quality of education services delivered across the country is the qualification level of the teachers. Teachers' qualification levels are a constraint on improvements in quality in the education system in Timor-Leste, where only 49 per cent of all teachers hold a secondary education certificate. Employment arrangements and conditions of service are important to attract and retain qualified teachers. The data suggest that the majority of teachers face job insecurity, given that only 42.5 per cent of all teachers hold permanent positions.

Indicator 3: share of teaching workforce that is female

The literature on GRB suggests that improvements in equal employment indicators impact on the prospects of women, on their economic empowerment,

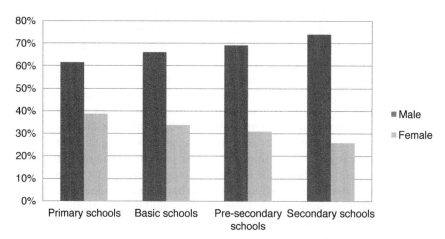

Figure 6.10   Proportion of male and female teachers by school level, 2010

Source: EMIS data, 2010.

Notes: Teachers = 10,998; Min. = 25.92 per cent (women teachers in secondary schools); Max. = 74.08 per cent (male teachers in secondary schools).

and their opportunities to progress and to have a fulfilled life engaging with their family and their community (see Budlender & Sharp, 1998). The vulnerability to violence in fragile states has been linked to restrictions on the professional and physical mobility of women teachers. These restrictions can undermine professional progress for women in the education sector.

Relevant literature on fragile states suggests that in these contexts there is a link between the presence of female teachers and improvements in girls' enrolment, retention and education outcomes. In some contexts, the lack of women teachers may hinder girls' opportunity to access education; this barrier may be particularly severe for older girls in upper primary and secondary classes (Kirk, 2006, 2008).

In Timor-Leste, women's mobility restrictions and their unpaid care responsibilities have been linked to their poor representation in the teaching workforce (Asian Development Bank, 2005). The government's CEDAW report observed that many voluntary women teachers provided critical education services during the 1999 emergency. However, many of these women failed to make it through the formal and competitive recruitment process a year later under the UNTAET administration, in which only those with the highest marks were recruited. It appears that no consideration was given to the particular professional and physical barriers that women have faced in terms of access to education and professional opportunities. Women represented a third of all candidates, and of these female candidates only half were selected (Timor-Leste Secretary of State for the Promotion of Equality, 2007). An outcome of these failings in recruiting female teachers was that girls' vulnerability was aggravated. Some girls report feeling intimidated by male teachers and being dissuaded from attending school (Timor-Leste Secretary of State for the Promotion of Equality, 2007).

Women's representation in the teaching workforce featured in the MoE yearbook. It provided evidence that women represent a moderate 35 per cent of the total teaching workforce. Further, it suggested that women's views remain underrepresented in decision-making positions with a mere 10 per cent of women among the 1,017 director positions (Timor-Leste Ministry of Education and Culture, 2011). The EMIS dataset can be used to further expand this conversation by comparing school performance on issues relating to equal opportunities in the teaching workforce.

I extended the approach I used to develop indicators 1 and 2 to calculate and compare school performance on the share of the teaching workforce that is female across districts and sub-districts. The first step was to calculate the share of the teaching workforce that is female for each school. This was followed by estimating the national median for the share of the teaching workforce. In a typical national primary school one in three teachers is a woman. Figure 6.11 shows that a typical primary school in the south-eastern district of Viqueque has a female share of its teaching workforce that is 16.7 percentage points below the national median. This poor showing may offer some insights into Viqueque's poor performance on students' performance, as measured by indicator 1.

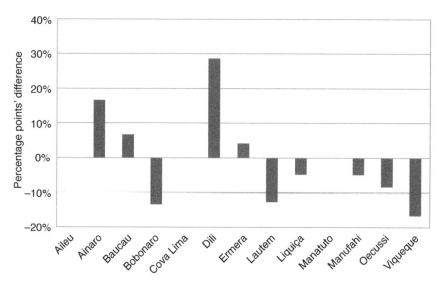

Figure 6.11 Female share of teaching workforce: district median school performance
relative to national median school performance, 2010

Source: Author's calculation from EMIS data, 2010.

Notes: Schools = 954; Min. = -16.67 per cent (Viqueque); Max. = 28.57 per cent (Dili).

As demonstrated with previous indicators, it is also possible to produce intra-district comparisons. Figure 6.12 provides a comparison between the typical school in the worst performing sub-district in each district against the national benchmark; it shows that on the indicator of share of teaching workforce that is female, a typical primary school on the island of Atauro (Dili district) is performing 33.3 percentage points below the national median. This poor showing is all the more significant as a typical primary school in the Dili district is performing 28.5 percentage points above the national benchmark.

Another approach to investigating intra- and inter-district inequality is to focus on the poorest performing schools across the country. Figure 6.13 displays the worst performing sub-district in each district. It shows that 69.2 per cent, or nine of the total thirteen, primary schools in the sub-district of Lolotoe (in the western district of Bobonaro) were in the lowest quartile of schools in Timor-Leste based on the female share of the teaching workforce. Of potential relevance for the aspirations of girls is the fact that both primary schools in the sub-district of Tutuala (in the eastern district of Lautem) are in the lowest quartile of primary schools in Timor-Leste on this indicator.

This section demonstrates the potential of an indicator on the share of teaching workforce that is female. This measure provides useful information for policy makers and gender activists as to where to target resources to improve performance on measures of equal opportunities in the public service, and

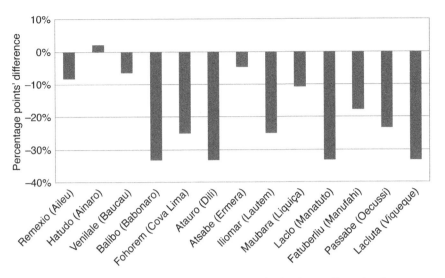

Figure 6.12 Female share of teaching workforce: sub-district median school performance relative to national median school performance, 2010

Source: Author's calculation from EMIS data, 2010.

Notes: Schools = 954; Min. = -33.33 per cent (Lolotoe, Lacluta, Laclo, Balibo, Atauro); Max. = 55.02 per cent (Nain Feto).[7]

thereby construct a positive and empowering education environment for girls. The findings reported in the section, together with those on indicators 1 and 2, demonstrate that EMIS data can be used to measure school performance on a range of gender-relevant indicators, compare school performance across districts and sub-districts, and identify schools that are performing particular poorly. An analogous approach can be used to identify the strongest performing schools, districts and sub-districts.

Quantitative analysis of the Timor-Leste Living Standards Survey to expand the use of EMIS for GRB

While the EMIS data can be used on their own to provide useful insights into the distribution and extent of problems with gender inequality in Timor-Leste, they do not provide a deep understanding of the social and economic context that frames these outcomes. To address this drawback of the EMIS data, information from other sources is required.

This section explores the potential to use the national household survey, the TLLSS, first to develop a set of indicators on household socio-economic characteristics in each area, and then to link these to the EMIS indicators. The objective of this investigation is to assess whether the TLLSS can be used to develop socio-economic indicators that are likely to be relevant to understanding poor or strong

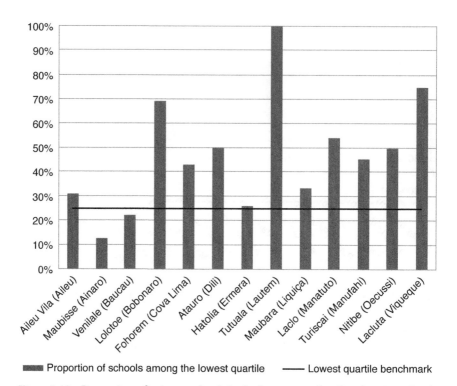

Proportion of schools among the lowest quartile ━━━━ Lowest quartile benchmark

Figure 6.13   Proportion of primary schools in the lowest quartile of performing schools based on female share of teaching workforce, by sub-district, 2010

Source: Author's calculation from EMIS data, 2010.

Notes: Schools = 970; Min. = 0 per cent (Fatululik, Fatumean, Laleia, Nain Feto, Railaco, Soibada, Tilomar, Vera Cruz);[8] Max. = 100 per cent (Tutuala).

school performance in particular districts, as identified by the EMIS indicators. This approach places schools and their performance into a broader social and economic context.

While a range of indicators can be derived from the TLLSS data, to illustrate the potential of the TLLSS data in this section I will focus on indicators that relate to poverty and ill health. I selected these indicators after considering the views of decision makers in the MoE regarding the sorts of issues that might influence household decisions about education, and also issues that have dominated the policy debate in Timor-Leste.

Research into girls' education in Timor-Leste provided ideas about likely relevant socio-economic indicators; specifically, a 2009 study found a link between household characteristics and girls' education in Timor-Leste. Factors highlighted in that study included household location, food consumption, educational background of household members, language background and age

(Austen et al., 2013). Also influential in the choice of indicators to be pursued was the growing literature on gender equality in education in fragile and developing contexts, which has highlighted the impact of particular household characteristics on education outcomes, namely wealth, language and geography (Anastasia & Teklemariam, 2011; Annin, 2009; Brock & Cammish, 1997; Herz & Sperling, 2004; Kirk, 2008). Next, I will provide a description of the TLLSS data used in this study, before moving attention to their potential to generate measures addressing poverty and ill health at the sub-district level.

The TLLSS data

The 2007 TLLSS, managed by the General Directorate of Statistics in the MoF, collected information on a range of household and individual characteristics including demography, housing conditions, access to facilities (e.g. transport, postal, and veterinary services), durable goods for household consumption (e.g. household appliances and vehicles), educational outcomes and access to services, health status and performance of the health system, employment conditions and the labour market, social capital (e.g. reach of existing groups and networks), and self-reported perceptions of welfare (e.g. adequacy of household income, satisfaction of basic needs, food security, and a comparison with the household's living conditions in 2001). Rolled out in March 2006, the TLLSS reached a cross-sectional sample of 2 per cent of the total households (around 4,500 households) over a period of significant political and security crisis in the mid-2000s. The approach presented here could be extended to the census or any other survey data.

Significantly, TLLSS identifies district and sub-district; with this information it was possible to link the TLLSS and EMIS data. Making this link was not, however, without challenges as there was no consistency between the coding attributed to sub-districts in the two datasets. I consulted the General Directorate of Statistics to make the link between sub-districts in the EMIS and TLLSS possible.[9]

Poverty

Poverty at the household level has been linked to low school enrolment, attendance and learning. Poverty has also been presented as an explanatory variable of gender gaps and inequalities in education outcomes (Annin, 2009; Filmer, 2008; Herz, 2006; World Bank, 2011b, 2011a). For many poor children and families, education may involve a range of direct and indirect costs as well as a trade-off between labour – either in the formal labour market or in the home and community – and going to school (Colclough et al., 2000; Herz & Sperling, 2004; World Bank, 2011a). In developing contexts such as Uganda, Bangladesh, Zambia and Nepal, education expenditure is on average the second or third major household expenditure (Herz & Sperling, 2004). Investigating whether the money was actually spent as planned complemented existing efforts to monitor how services were responding to women's needs and interests by reporting on CEDAW and the Platform for Action.

The interaction between poverty and gender gaps in education outcomes has gained profile in policy debates in Timor-Leste. Prime Minister Gusmão acknowledged these interactions in the 2013 budget when he stated that 'education costs the parents of the students a lot of money. These parents are making sacrifices to try and provide better futures for their children' (Timor-Leste Ministry of Finance, 2013a: p. 17).

The Timor-Leste Household Income and Expenditure Survey 2011 showed that there is a disparity in the cost of education, with the mean household expenditure on schools per month in rural contexts estimated at US$7.22 compared with US$26.51 in urban areas (Timor-Leste National Statistics Directorate, 2013). The government's CEDAW report suggested that hidden costs associated with education, particularly school uniforms, deter girls from schooling (Timor-Leste Secretary of State for the Promotion of Equality, 2007). It has been estimated that in 2011 urban and rural households allocated around 30 per cent of their total spending to education (Timor-Leste Secretary of State for the Promotion of Equality, 2014). A 2009 study investigated the link between girls living in households with consumption levels below the poverty line and non-attendance at school. It found that the link between poverty and girls' school attendance was particularly significant for pre-secondary school-age girls (Austen et al., 2013). Related reporting has uncovered a link between dropout rates among pupils in grades 4–6 and the cost of education and the role of children in supplementing household income (Creative Associates International, 2012).

The TLLSS collects data on the value of food, personal care items, durable goods, clothing and expenses related to festivities and cultural ceremonies. This data has been aggregated by the General Directorate of Statistics, MoF, to produce a measure of the total value of food and goods held by each household. The national average of food and goods held per household was estimated at US$116.45; however, the data suggests a great deal of disparity among districts. The mean value of food and goods held by a household in the district of Dili, the capital, was estimated at US$206.29. In Oecussi it was a mere US$40.36. This result is consistent with data in the Timor-Leste Household Income and Expenditure Survey 2011, which found that Oecussi, an enclave in the western and Indonesian part of the Timor island, was the poorest of Timor-Leste's districts with a per capita daily expenditure level of US$0.8 (Timor-Leste National Statistics Directorate, 2013). The next step was to develop an indicator of the prevalence of the poorest households in each sub-district. Households with goods and food valued below US$40 are among the poorest quartile in the country. Figure 6.14 shows the sub-district, in each district, with the highest proportion of households with less than US$40 in goods and food; in other words, it shows the sub-district in each district with the highest proportion of the poorest households. It suggests that in the sub-district of Nitibe, in the Oecussi district, poverty is widespread, with 94.4 per cent of all households among the nation's poorest.

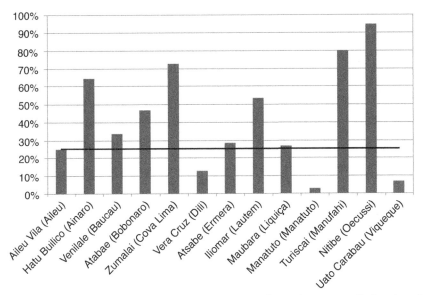

Figure 6.14 Proportion of households in the lowest quartile of households in terms of goods and food consumption level, by sub-district, 2007

Source: Author' calculation from TLLSS, 2007.[10]

Notes: Households = 4,477; Min. = 0 per cent (Baguia, Luro, Tutuala, Lacluta, Uatolari, Alas, Fatuberliu, Barique, Laclo, Laclubar, Laleia, Soibada, Laulara, Liquidoe, Remexio);[11] Max. = 94.38 per cent (Nitibe).

Subsequently I calculated the correlation coefficient to investigate the relationship between school performance on gender parity indicators and poverty. The data suggest that there is no significant correlation between the proportion of primary schools in the lowest quartile of primary schools based on female enrolment and the proportion of households in the poorest quartile. I estimated this correlation at -0.03. This near-to-zero correlation is illustrated through a scatter plot in Figure 6.15. It shows that there is no discernible relationship between school performance on gender parity indicators and poverty. These results are consistent with the research results published by Austen et al. (2013), who found that, at the household level, the link between school attendance of primary school-age girls and poverty was not statistically significant. Poverty had only a marginal impact on the probability of school attendance of girls in primary schools.

While there is no clear pattern of association between the level of poverty at the district level and the rate at which girls are involved in primary schooling, the indicators of poverty drawn from the TLLSS could have value to education policy makers. For example, they could assist policy makers by identifying districts where educational risks for girls might be compounded by high rates

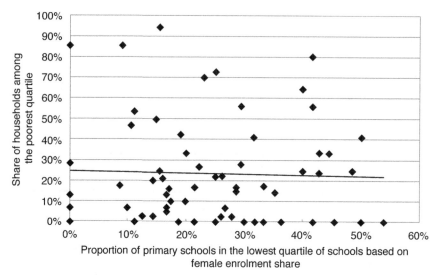

Figure 6.15   Comparison of the share of households among the lowest quartile
(TLLSS, 2007) and proportion of schools in the lowest quartile of
schools based on female enrolment share (EMIS, 2010), by sub-district

Source: Author's calculation from TLLSS, 2007 and EMIS, 2010.

Notes: Households = 4,477; Sub-districts = 64.

of poverty. In the Aileu Vila sub-district, for example, girls' share of enrolment
is relatively low, with a typical primary school underperforming the national
typical primary school by 3.5 percentage points (see indicator 1), and poverty
is prevalent. Targeting policy to reduce education costs to achieve better
educational outcomes is likely to be especially important in this district.

Ill health

Ill health can have a significant impact on education enrolment, attendance
and learning. Enduring cultural norms around the feminine nature of care work
ensure that girls play a significant role in care work within the household and
the community. These cultural norms have often resulted in poor school
performance and high dropout rates at mid-secondary school levels (Secretary
of State for the Promotion of Equality, 2014). The negative impact of poor
health services on girls' education outcomes can be aggravated by the lack of
adequate school infrastructure. This link between education infrastructure and
girls' education enrolment, participation and learning has been raised by the
women's movement in Timor-Leste, which observed that infrastructure remains
inadequate including access to toilets, clean water and safety.

Data collected in the 2007 TLLSS suggest that ill-health can be a barrier to
improvements in school attendance; when asked for reasons for absence from

school 73.1 per cent of students advanced their health problems and that of relatives as justification. There are further reasons to be concerned about the link between health and education, with the Demographic and Health Survey (2009–2010) indicating that 58 per cent of all children under five were stunted, of whom 33 per cent were severely stunted (Timor-Leste National Statistics Directorate & ICF Macro, 2010).

Social and cultural views about girls' experiences of menstruation and puberty can further undermine girls' enrolment, attendance and learning. In Tanzania, views about menstruation have been found to contribute to a gender gap in enrolment rates in primary and secondary school (Sommer, 2010). These cultural practices are further aggravated by the poor public health services common in many low-income and fragile contexts.

For this analysis I drew on individual records of health complaints in the previous 30 days to explore the link between school performance on gender parity in enrolment and health complaints. These TLLSS records include complaints such as cough, diarrhoea, malaria, dengue fever and accidents. I developed a measure of the distribution of health problems across districts. Figure 6.16 suggests a high incidence of health complaints across the country; it shows that three in ten people in the central district of Manatuto and close to one in five individuals in the district of Bobonaro reported health problems. Women represent 52 per cent of all individuals who reported health complaints. The effect of these health complaints on education and economic activities is significant, with 60.7 per cent of those who reported health complaints missing more than

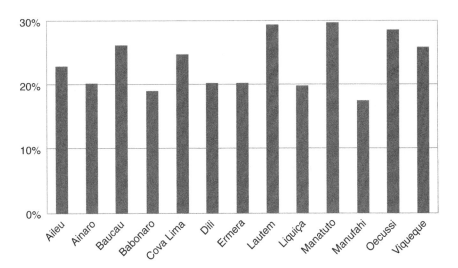

Figure 6.16 Proportion of individuals with health problems in the last 30 days, by district, 2007

Source: Author's calculation from TLLSS, 2007.

Notes: Individuals = 25,000; Min. = 17.5 per cent (Manufahi); Max. = 29.7 per cent (Manatuto).

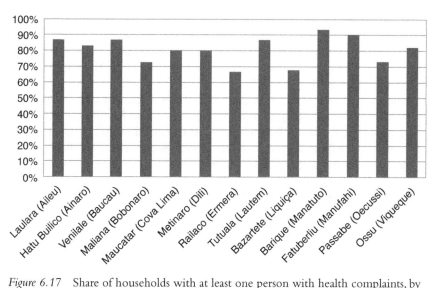

Figure 6.17 Share of households with at least one person with health complaints, by sub-district, 2007

Source: Author's calculation from TLLSS, 2007.

Notes: Sub-districts = 66; Min. = 13.33 per cent (Luro); Max. = 93.33 per cent (Barique, Laclubar).[12]

3 of the previous 30 days of their principal activity for health reasons, of whom 32.2 per cent missed more than 5 days.

A measure of the incidence of health issues at the household level was developed by identifying whether a household had at least one person with health complaints in the previous 30 days. With this information it is possible to calculate the share of households with at least one person with health complaints in the previous 30 days and to compare district and sub-district performance on this measure. I estimated that close to 68.5 per cent of all households had at least one person with health complaints. Figure 6.17 presents the sub-district in each district that exhibited the highest share of households with at least one person who had health problems. This figure illustrates the disruptive nature of health issues for families; for example, 93.3 per cent of all households in the sub-district of Barique, Manatuto district, had at least one person with health complaints in the previous 30 days.

My next step was to explore whether there is a correlation between the incidence of health complaints in the household and school performance on gender parity in enrolment at the sub-district level. The data suggests that there is a negative correlation between the proportion of primary schools in the lowest quartile based on female enrolment and the proportion of households with at least one person with health complaints in the previous 30 days.

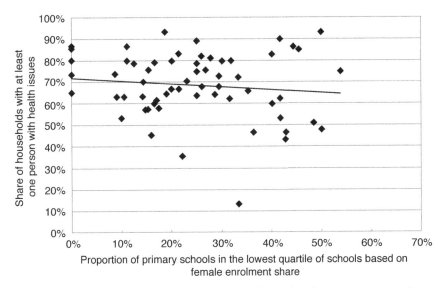

Figure 6.18   Comparison of the share of households with at least one person with
health complaints (TLLSS, 2007) and proportion of schools in the
lowest quartile of schools based on female enrolment share (EMIS,
2010), by sub-district

Source: Author's calculation from TLLSS, 2007 and EMIS, 2010.

Notes: Households = 4,477; Sub-districts = 64.

This correlation was estimated at -0.12. This near to zero correlation is
illustrated through a scatter plot in Figure 6.18. This plot shows that there is a
slight negative association between school performance on gender parity
indicators and health issues. Austen et al. (2013) found that the presence in the
household of adults in poor health had a marginal negative effect on girls'
chances of attending primary school.

While there is no clear association between school performance on gender
parity indicators and health issues, the indicators of incidence of health issues
derived from the TLLSS could have value to education policy makers. For
example, they can assist policy makers by identifying districts where educational
risks for girls might be compounded by a high incidence of health issues. In the
sub-district of Barique, Manatuto district, where girls' share of enrolment is
relatively low (see indicator 1) and the incidence of health complaints in the
household relatively high, targeting health policies is likely to be particularly
significant in achieving better educational outcomes.

In summary, this section illustrates how the TLLSS can be used to develop
socio-economic measures that can contribute to an explanation of poor (or
strong) school performance on the gender-relevant indicators devised using the
EMIS data. Through this approach schools' performance on gender parity

indicators is placed into a broader social and economic context. This illustrates that school performance can be affected by location characteristics.

Implications of this gender analysis using administrative data for gender-responsive policy and funding

The previous sections have illustrated how EMIS data can be used to measure school performance on three gender-relevant indicators focused on (1) student outcomes (share of total enrolment that is female and share of students that are in a grade that is age-appropriate or higher) and (2) teaching workforce (share of teaching workforce that is female). It is possible with these measures to compare intra- and inter-district school performance and identify schools that are underperforming. It also demonstrates how the TLLSS can be used to develop socio-economic measures that can provide explanations for the links between school performance and location characteristics. The TLLSS complements the EMIS by providing insights into gender deficits in education indicators and contributes to alternative proposals for policy and budgetary changes.

There has been an effort to set up an education system with new schools, a meal programme and a new career structure for teachers. However, no positive measures have been adopted to improve gender parity indicators. International research suggests that there is a wide range of initiatives that can have a positive effect on gender parity indicators, including provision of sanitary materials and facilities and proactively recruiting women teachers (see Kirk, 2006). This section explores how the indicators devised in this chapter could be useful to further current policy and budgetary debates.

With concerns over safety and security, a range of measures to improve school accessibility may have a positive impact on gender parity and the mismatch between the grade the student should be in and the grade the student is in. A particular area of investment is school infrastructure which, in the 2014 budget, involved the allocation of US$25 million for the rehabilitation of school infrastructure, including water, sanitation and school equipment (Timor-Leste Ministry of Finance, 2013a). While such investments are important to improve accessibility, this study points to the need to devise targeted programmes. Such infrastructure investments are likely to be more effective if combined with more substantive programmes addressing the particular challenges faced by girls in education including early marriage, teenage pregnancy, gender-based violence, violence in schools, and cultural stereotypes that surround what is expected and possible for girls and boys. It has been suggested that poorer families tend to invest in male education, as men hold a higher likelihood of becoming the bread-winner and improving economic returns to the family (Timor-Leste National Commission for Research and Development, 2008).

A 2013 report produced by Rede Feto claimed that 79 per cent of girl survivors of abuse abandon school (da Silva, 2013). The Committee on the Elimination of Discrimination against Women (2009) raised concern over the high level of girls abused and harassed by teachers and on their way to school. The wide use of corporal punishment in schools further undermines girls' enrolment and attendance in education. A 2013 study found that one-quarter of girls believe that teachers treat boys better than girls and think the boys are smarter. Cultural stereotypes were also prevalent, with 30 per cent of girls thinking that boys should stay longer in school and a similar proportion believing that boys are smarter than girls (Secretary of State for the Promotion of Equality, 2014).

The government has made some commitments to improving the quality of the education experience with a particular emphasis on qualifications and management of teachers. In 2010, this involved an allocation of US$2.6 million for a salary increase to teachers, and a new career regime. The argument for this measure was laid out in the overview of the 2010 budget documents:

> Apart from the quantity of schooling opportunities available, the Government is also concerned to assure that schooling quality is improved. Many teachers, through no fault of their own, are unqualified or underqualified for their positions. The Government will put in place a qualification driven career structure for teachers, thereby ensuring that teachers are given the opportunity to excel and to improve themselves and are assured of a defined career path, while the students receive a higher quality education than previously available.
>
> (Timor-Leste Ministry of Finance, 2009a: p. 59)

In this explanation, the government establishes a link between improved qualifications of current teachers and the development of a career structure, and the quality of the education services provided to boys and girls across Timor-Leste. In the 2014 budget, the government has committed US$9.5 million to provide salaries to 4,220 voluntary teachers (Timor-Leste Ministry of Finance, 2013a). This measure will potentially benefit many women in the education sector, in particular those at lower career levels. These new opportunities were positioned as an avenue to realise the commitment to '[i]ncrease the number of female teachers until [we] achieve parity in 2025' (Timor-Leste Ministry of Finance, 2009a: p. 210).

Investments in the teaching workforce have been an area of public debate. An NGO, La'o Hamutuk, for example, has been outspoken in defending the allocation of resources for teachers' qualifications and quality education:

> the Ministries which directly interact with our population, especially health and education, are understaffed, underfunded, and provide a level of service far below what we should accept . . . Our population of school-age children goes up by 6,000 every year, and we are working hard to increase the number of girls and boys who stay in school, but we do not increase the number of teachers. We need to invest in human capital – not just buildings and infrastructure. Timor-Leste will need qualified, educated workers and managers in our future multi-sectoral economy, the only way

to lift ourselves out of poverty and prepare for the day when oil revenues can no longer pay for our necessities or cover a huge balance of payments deficit.

(La'o Hamutuk, 2009)

These concerns with the quality of the teaching workforce were shared by members of parliament who have recommended, in their commentary on the 2010 budget, that the status of all temporary staff in the MoE be addressed and that incentives be created to attract teachers to rural communities, for example by providing for adequate homes for rural teachers (Parlamento de Timor-Leste Comissão de Economia Finanças e Anti-Corrupção, 2009). Such measures could be particularly significant for women teachers. This gender analysis of the EMIS data demonstrates how data on teachers can be used to produce an indicator on equal opportunities. This analysis provides support for these broad initiatives and provides information on which schools and sub-districts to target in order to improve performance on equal opportunities and to construct a positive and empowering education environment for girls.

The socio-economic measures derived from the TLLSS can contribute to an explanation of poor (or strong) school performance on the gender-relevant indicators devised using the EMIS data. The indicators identify that there are several sub-districts facing multiple challenges in improving educational outcomes. The Timor-Leste government has made significant headway in addressing the issue of poverty and food scarcity through the school system. It has removed school fees, established a school meals programme and initiated assistance for the purchase of school uniforms. The 2014 budget documents committed US$26.9 million to a school meals programme, increasing the amount spent on this programme from $0.15 to $0.25 per student per day (Timor-Leste Ministry of Finance, 2013a).

The implementation of these measures, however, has raised concerns. In 2009 the Parliamentary Committee reviewing the 2010 budget proposal commented that they had received complaints regarding the school meals programme. These concerns referred to the quality and the timely distribution of the meals. The Parliamentary Commission on Health, Education and Culture recommended that the government ensure the distribution of school meals to all students and its expansion to years 7, 8 and 9 (Parlamento de Timor-Leste Comissão de Economia Finanças e Anti-Corrupção, 2009). Some of these concerns have resurfaced in 2013 budget debates (National Parliament Committee on Public Finances, 2013). Beyond this, this study highlights the need for specific interventions in poorly performing schools and sub-districts to address economic barriers to access to education.

The 2010 budget speech sets out a collection of ambitious initiatives to improve health services and outcomes, including allocating US$10.3 million to the construction and refurbishment of hospitals and health clinics, US$6 million to medical drugs for the health system, and rolling out programmes to increase immunisation rates against measles, polio, tuberculosis and other diseases.

In parallel, US$11 million was allocated for clean water projects (Timor-Leste Ministry of Finance, 2009a: p. 16). These projects and initiatives are likely to have a positive effect on gender parity outcomes in primary schools in Timor-Leste by both reducing the incidence of health issues among school-age boys and girls, and decreasing girls' care work. Cultural stereotypes that place men as the breadwinner and the most able to improve the economic outcomes of the family are additional targets for policy action (Timor-Leste National Commission for Research and Development, 2008).

This section has explored the potential of a gender analysis using EMIS data to improve current policies and budgets and to assist in developing new policy and budget initiatives. It provides backing to existing programmes and policies that invest in teacher qualifications, school meals and health services. These are all important steps towards improving boys' and girls' enrolment, attendance and overall educational outcomes. It highlights that such interventions would be more effective if complemented by additional projects and budgetary support to improve pedagogy and education practices and address cultural stereotypes and practices in the community, families and schools. This gender analysis has provided important information to improve governance in Timor-Leste by targeting projects and budgets. A World Bank survey found that teacher–parent associations covered 90.2 per cent of all primary schools (World Bank, 2013: p. 26). This analysis can provide impetus for a national (and local) conversation with parents and teachers on the accessibility and quality of the education services that the government is delivering to boys and girls across Timor-Leste.

Conclusion

Since the 1990s, indicators have flourished in international development discourse as tools for assessing and supporting social justice and reform strategies. Indicators have come to reflect a political culture that demands more openness, and defends action against corruption, bias and the arbitrary development of the power of elites. Indicators are a powerful tool to shed light on state failures by emphasising areas of deficit or inequality. Indicators have also become a significant governance tool for allocation of resources and to frame policy decisions. From this vantage point, statistical information and indicators have become symbols of a modern state (Merry, 2011; Porter, 1996). This study shows how indicators can be used to improve service delivery, accountability between citizens and the state, and state resilience.

The political power of numbers has not been lost in the fragile state of Timor-Leste where statistical information and indicators have been an area of governance focus. Since 2002 Timor-Leste has invested significant resources in two censuses, and has developed mechanisms for administrative data collection, compilation and analysis.

The GRB initiative in Timor-Leste has sparked an additional interest in the use and potential of statistical information and indicators to support and assess

Timor-Leste's growing gender equality agenda. This chapter has explored how administrative data could be used to raise an understanding among policy makers and gender activists in Timor-Leste of the impact of the budget on boys and girls, men and women. This could contribute to a debate over how expenditure is allocated and spent in Timor-Leste with key political actors raising concern over the government's priorities. In a letter President Ruak voiced his concerns:

> that, on the one hand, in the structure of expenditure in this State Budget, 46% is allocated to the construction of infrastructure, prioritizing spending on electrification of the country, road reconstruction . . . On the other hand, there is much less spending in key areas of human development – education receives only 5.6%, health receives 3.7% – and agriculture, which involves about 80% of the population, gets only 1.5% of the total budget.
>
> (Ruak, cited in La'o Hamutuk, 2013)

He went on to call for a public debate on this emphasis on infrastructure 'in particular when compared with other expenses with obvious social utility' (cited in La'o Hamutuk, 2013).

This chapter makes a contribution to this policy debate. I have investigated the potential of using EMIS data to develop gender-relevant indicators that measure school performance and compare them across districts and sub-districts. This analysis was illustrative and focused on three indicators: share of enrolment that is female, share of students that are in a grade that is age-appropriate or higher, and share of teachers who are female. These indicators provide some insights into the failure by the state to address gender inequality.

I have demonstrated that the potential of EMIS can be extended using social and economic indicators from a household survey dataset, the TLLSS, to explain the gender deficits identified through EMIS-based indicators. Indicators covered here include poverty, and health. I have illustrated how the link between these two sources of statistical information can polish and deepen the conversation on how Timor-Leste can improve its gender equality outcomes in education and thus educational outcomes in general. This contribution can further calls from non-governmental organisations for better programme design and targeting. In an analysis of the 2017 budget, La'o Hamutuk (2016b: p. 13) called for investment in services such as education, and argued for a 'serious analysis of the needs of the majority of Timorese people, which can then be used to design and channel funding to specific projects with the highest social impact and the best economic'.

These indicators provide some insights into the nature of the schooling experience and the particular social and economic challenges faced by girls in schools across districts and sub-districts. This, however, is only a partial picture without a conversation with teachers, school administrators, parents and students. This study offers a framework for a conversation on education services and outcomes with those engaged in the implementation of the government's education policy and those using the services. These can enhance the government's accountability and transparency to women and girls and play a role in promoting 'self-governance' among school and regional administrators (Merry, 2011: p. 89).

This study makes a contribution to international debates about the sorts of data that are being collected and how they can inform governance and government policy. International benchmarks through the MDGs and Education for All have been extremely successful in establishing a standard to which the poorest countries should aspire and provide the impetus for actions to improve international positioning (Merry, 2011). Part of the criticism of these benchmarks has been their failure to deliver better policy. Understandings of patterns of inequality in education, in particular education levels in regional areas, remain unchanged (Lewin, 2015a) as does tracking of change, its factors and context (Subrahmanian, 2005). Another issue is the link between information analysis and local planning competence, which has been largely ignored with attention directed towards international assessments and the aid community (Unterhalter, 2013; Lewin, 2015a). While some of the deficiencies of the MDGs and EFA were addressed in a broad and ambitious agenda in the 2030 SDGs (see special 2016 issue of *Gender & Development* 24 (1)), concerns have been raised about the economic model that underpins these goals, the weak connections with policy and the lack of consideration of the local context (see Lewin, 2015b; Razavi, 2016). Also important is the adoption of a weak, voluntary follow-up and review system, which may lead to weakening of and selectivity in the implementation of the SDG (Razavi, 2016).

Demand is growing for a different way of thinking about how gender inequality is measured. These calls have emphasised how measures and indicators can contribute to a deeper understanding of an increasingly complex experience of inequality. These debates have seen the development of an alternative in the Individual Deprivation Measure, a multidimensional measure of poverty that highlights the characteristics, depth and patterns in inequality between men and women and draws on participatory approaches to offer an insight into their real lived experiences (Bessell, 2010, 2015). Studies on this measure have shown that measuring inequality is not the same as understanding patterns of exclusion, its causes and impacts. Studying these patterns has the potential to improve policy responses (Bessell, 2015, 2010).

Comparable issues could be derived from the research on EMIS, which has focused on its technical elements, with only limited analysis of how it could be and is being used to offer a deeper understanding of patterns of inequality in education, inform policy and foster accountability. This chapter has illustrated how EMIS data can be used to identify and understand patterns of district and sub-district inequality in education outcomes. It has also highlighted the role of these understandings in policy making.

Notes

1 The Timor-Leste territory is divided into 13 districts and 67 sub-districts. There are some gaps in the EMIS data.

2 Education Management Information System data, Timor-Leste Ministry of Education, 2010.

3 Tutuala sub-district (Lautem district) is not shown in Figure 6.5 because its median school is not the worst performing in the Lautem district.

4 Atsabe (Ermera district), Passabe (Oecussi district), Soibada (Manatuto district), Tutuala (Lautem district), Metinaro and Vera Cruz (Dili district) do not have schools amongst the lowest quartile of primary schools as ranked on the basis of the share of total enrolment that is female.

5 Dom Aleixo (Dili district) is not shown in Figure 6.8 because its median school is not the worst performing among sub-districts in the Dili district.

6 Alas (Manufahi district), Fohorem (Cova Lima district), Maliana (Bobonaro district), Tutuala (Lautem district), Laleia and Soibada (Manatuto district), Dom Aleixo and Metinaro (Dili district) do not have schools amongst the lowest quartile of primary schools as ranked on the basis of the share of students enrolled in age-appropriate grades or above.

7 Nain Feto (Dili district) does not appear in Figure 6.12 because a median school in this sub-district is not amongst the worst performing in this district in terms of the share of teaching workforce that is female.

8 Laleia and Soibada (Manatuto district), Nain Feto and Vera Cruz (Dili district), Railaco (Ermera district) and Fatululik, Fatumean and Tilomar (Cova Lima district) do not have schools amongst the lowest quartile of primary schools as ranked on the basis of the female share of the teaching workforce.

9 Two sub-districts did not have data in both datasets. These sub-districts were removed from the analysis.

10 Timor-Leste Living Standards Survey, published by the Timor-Leste National Statistics Directorate, 2007.

11 Luro and Tutuala (Lautem district), Lacluta and Uatolari (Viqueque district), Alas and Fatuberliu (Manufahi district), Barique, Laclo, Laclubar, Laleia and Soibada (Manatuto district), Baguia (Baucau district), Laulara, Liquidoe and Remexio (Aileu district) are not included because these were not among the sub-districts with the highest proportion of households in the poorest quartile.

12 Barique and Laclubar are both sub-districts in the district of Manatuto. I illustrate with data from Barique sub-district. Also note that the sub-district of Luro (Lautem district) was not included as only the sub-district with the highest share of households that had at least one person with health complaints was included.

7 The potential of gender analysis to improve policy and budgeting

Gender-relevant data are crucial to assessing the impact of the budget on groups of men and women and, ideally, to producing more effective and equitable policy, planning and budgeting. Given Timor-Leste's commitment to GRB it is likely that policy actors would see gender analysis as important. As meaningful steps have been taken to mainstream gender in the government's policy and budgeting processes, interest in indicators and administrative data has received a boost within the Timor-Leste government. The international literature on the interface between research and policy suggests that institutional, actor and knowledge-based factors shape this relationship. However, this research has yet to show that there is a case for pursuing gender analysis in fragile state contexts. Instead, it would be expected that little could be achieved in terms of positive policy and budget changes in a fragile state context.

This chapter explores the reactions of government officials in the education department to the analysis outlined in Chapter 6 and their views on the policy value of these findings. I use qualitative data to assess the value of gender analysis of administrative data to influence policy and budgetary decision making in the fragile state of Timor-Leste. I ran a focus group session in 2011 and another in 2013 with a total of five middle-level management officials in the MoE focused on the potential of the gender analysis of the EMIS data. Participants were selected for their role in policy and data collection. Despite attempts to expand the representation of women, all participants were male. This imbalance can be explained by women's poor representation in roles of middle management in the MoE. In economics, focus groups have had limited take-up and have been restricted to small-scale studies (see Van Staveren 1997). The literature on focus groups has demonstrated that they are well suited to unearthing local views and popular knowledge, placing the researchers' values and interests under the microscope and fostering actions for change (Cancian 1992; DeVault 1996; Montell 1999; Van Staveren 1997; Wilkinson 1998). Data collected from the focus groups were supplemented by interview data accumulated throughout the study.

The first section of this chapter reviews existing research to identify knowledge on the policy impacts of research, especially on issues related to gender equity and education. The following three sections are the main sections of the chapter. The second section discusses the institutional context of data collection and policy work in Timor-Leste, focusing on key political factors. The remainder of the chapter investigates the values and behaviour of actors both inside and outside government and their views about credible and legitimate knowledge as critical factors in framing what knowledge influences policy.

Literature at the interface between research and policy development and budget decisions

While the specific literature on the interface between research and policy making is sparse, a number of works suggest that the interface is often weak, and that greater efforts are needed to improve it. Margaret Shields, a former New Zealand politician and founder of the Society for Research on Women, emphasised this point when she commented that the availability and accessibility of research, while crucial, is only a part of the process of incorporating gender into policy and budgeting:

> I had somewhat naively thought . . . that if you did some research and showed a clear path of action was needed, politicians would leap to attention and do it . . . [Instead] People [politicians] patted us [women] on the head metaphorically and said, 'Aren't you clever little things?' and that was that, really.
>
> (Shields, quoted in Welch, 2009: p. 97)

Shields argues that, rather than providing impetus for change in the conservative cultural and political context of New Zealand in the 1960s, research with a gender focus produced little more than a condescending pat on the head from policy makers. Research is only one of many inputs into policy and budgeting decision making. In this section I examine what other influences can frame the interface between gender-relevant research and policy. I draw on two bodies of literature: (1) scholarship covering the links between research and policy making; and (2) research into policy change aimed at increasing gender equality.

A further important section of literature on the links between research and policy making examines the role of research in developing countries. This literature includes Aberman et al. (2009) on the national fertiliser policy in Nigeria; Keeley and Scoones (1999) on environmental policy; Young (2005) on the link between research and policy; Ryan (1999) on rice policy in Vietnam; Ryan (2002) on the impact of policy-oriented social science; and Lindquist (2001) on the policy influence of projects sponsored by the Canadian International Development Research Centre. The complexity of the interaction between data, research and policy making in transition contexts is illustrated in post-apartheid South Africa. In this context, the highly competitive political environment played a critical role in encouraging a demand for analysis and data, and in framing discourses and the political debate (Crouch, 1997; Crouch & Spratt, 2001). This research highlights the gap between research and policy in developing contexts and links these patterns to low levels of capacity and poor education in science amongst the general public. Evidence-based policy is an unfamiliar paradigm in such contexts. Creating bridges between research and policy requires a degree of 'sensitivity to culture, power structures and local knowledge' (Jones et al., 2008: p. 37). Given the few exceptions of research conducted in fragile states (see Ouattara et al., 2007), the current understanding of how research contributes to policy in fragile contexts is limited. This research suggests that in such contexts the gap between evidence and policy making is likely to be more pronounced.

The particular effect of the EMIS data collection, compilation and analysis is to date undetermined, with most analysis focused primarily on its technical elements (including who is responsible for the data collection and what and how data is collected and organised) and available in dispersed reporting and planning documents. While EMIS has been adopted in most developing countries (see Hua, 2011), reporting on its implementation has focused on the 'supply side' of the data issue. EMIS has been touted as a tool for efficiency in resource allocation that can highlight areas for resource targeting. However, the potential of the EMIS data analysis to improve that education policy and its funding (the 'demand side' for data) have not been considered explicitly (Amin & Chaudhury, 2008). In a World Bank report, Samin Amin and Nazmul Chaudhury (2008: p. 78) argue focusing on the supply side of data has failed to produce a demand for quality data on education. Instead, these authors advocate making the system user-friendly, increasing scrutiny over the quality of the data, and analysing data output.

Studies that have attempted to theorise the determinants of the quality of the interface between research and policy in developing country contexts (Austen et al., 2013; Crewe & Young, 2002; Jones et al., 2013) identify three groups of factors: first, the political and cultural contexts framing the knowledge–policy interaction. The second group is the interest, values and beliefs of policy actors and the interaction between them. The third group of factors is the types of knowledge that compete to influence the course of policy decision making, including knowledge based on research, citizens' experiences, and knowledge about policy implementation.

Institutional and actor-centred explanations have also surfaced in related scholarship on policy change for gender equality. This literature points to a host of political and economic factors affecting the prospect for positive change and it sheds light on the relationship between economic indicators and gender equality policy (Annesley & Gains, 2013), the agency of critical actors in the executive (Annesley & Gains, 2010), in parliament (Franceschet, 2011; Piscopo, 2011; Sawer, 2011b, 2012) and in government (Goetz, 2007; McBride & Mazur, 2011; Sawer, 2011a; Staudt, 2007), and the contribution of, and interaction with, the women's movement (Franceschet, 2004; Weldon, 2002; Weldon & Htun, 2013). Scholarship is expanding to cover the challenges faced by activists in government and their strategic actions to produce changes to policies, agendas and discourses (see Eyben, 2004).

Both research into the interface between research and policy and studies into the processes of policy change for gender equality have contributed to a framework for analysing the interface between gender-relevant research and positive policy change. However, this scholarship has primarily focused on developed and resilient developing contexts. How these determinants and interactions unfold to produce positive policy and budgetary changes in a fragile context remains relatively unknown. The remainder of this chapter pursues themes that frame the interaction between research and policy – paying some attention to its funding – with the aim of uncovering the circumstances that render analysis using EMIS data as an effective tool to make policy and budgeting processes and decisions more gender-sensitive.

Political and institutional context frames the research–policy interaction in Timor-Leste

The fragile nature of the young state of Timor-Leste has made data collection, research and policy development difficult. This is apparent in the introduction to the 2010 census published on the website of the General Directorate of Statistics (previously known as National Statistics Directorate). As shown below, the statement highlights how the nation's recent experience of conflict has caused demographic changes and upset data collection. It suggests that the analysis derived from the previous data collection exercises, such as the 2004 census, would be 'misleading for planning' given the changes that the crisis had produced. It also points to scepticism about the government's ability to conduct a successful census:

> During and after independence substantial transformations took place, including demographic changes. Previously available data would have been misleading for planning in a new country. Nevertheless, many stakeholders were skeptical about the possibility of conducting a successful census. In spite of the doubts and reservations, the [Timor-Leste government] National Statistics Directorate and the United Nations Population Fund (UNFPA) took the challenge.
>
> (Timor-Leste Direcção Nacional de Estatística, 2007)

The political and security crisis of the mid-2000s created particular difficulties for the collection and analysis of educational data in Timor-Leste, given, among other things, the destruction of education records in the MoE. The crisis also made the task of collecting the EMIS data potentially more complex because of the displacement of approximately 150,000 people (United Nations, 2006).

It is also possible that the social and regional divisions associated with the crisis caused data collection to become highly politicised as it may have been seen as a basis for apportioning power (see Fernández-Castilla, 2011). The belief that the state is failing the community can worsen these divisions. The 2006 UNDP report *Timor-Leste human development report 2006. The path out of poverty:*

integrated rural development observed that there was a perception in rural communities that the Dili-based bureaucracy was not serving rural interests: 'The lion's share of CFET [Consolidated Fund for East Timor] expenditures continues to go to Dili; only one-third of the total public expenditure and one-fifth of goods and services are going to the districts' (United Nations Development Programme, 2006: p. 4). In a context such as Timor-Leste, opportunities for data collection can be undercut by mistrust of the administration and the perception that the state and its agencies lack legitimacy. The quality of the data collected in such a context is likely to be significantly impaired.

The political environment is important to understand the value of research. First, international bodies laid some important foundations for data collection. Data collection for the education sector, for example, was initiated under the UN administration in the 2000s (UNICEF, 2000). Second, the political context has framed distinct demands for data and research. There are some important contradictory moves at play. The 2012 elections resulted in a loss of some experienced parliamentarians and 'outspoken' *deputadas* such as Fernanda Borges and a reduction of political parties represented in parliament (Roughneen, 2012). The coalition government that followed brought together parties with distinct agendas and constituencies and amplified internal demands for more clarity in policy and budgetary processes. Further, the largest opposition party in parliament had significant executive and policy experience, having been in government until the 2006 crisis. This placed the government led by Prime Minister Gusmão under some political scrutiny and is likely to have contributed to furthering changes in policy and budgeting, including improvements in transparency on the budget.

New impetus for research has been given by the Office of the President, under President Ruak. The current president appears to be carving a role in the research and policy debate, having established a Department of Research and Analysis. In March 2013 the Office of the President held the first of a series of public policy discussions. This new development needs to be understood in the context of President Ruak's reframing of the presidential role. In late 2015 President Ruak gained a more prominent role in Timor-Leste's political competition having exercised his veto of the budget, challenging the military command and disapproving changes to the National Electoral Commission. These positions show a president who is focused on keeping a disproportionately strong government in check (Feijo, 2016). The president's investment in research fits well into a narrative for a more prominent monitoring role for the president in Timor-Leste's competitive political environment. It also suggests that there is a growing demand for indigenous research on themes and with methodologies that matter and make sense to Timor-Leste. The relative silence of such institutions on gender-relevant research speaks to the difficulty of planting gender issues in mainstream political institutions.

The alignment of gender equality with broad social and democratic policy currents was a further positive contextual factor for the interaction of research and gender-responsive policy change in Timor-Leste. As discussed in Chapter 2, gender equality has been embedded in the broader ideological consensus on social democratic and human rights goals in Timor-Leste. Critical to this was the agreement reached in the 1998 landmark conference of the East Timorese diaspora in Portugal (Hill, 2006). International norms and global targets such as the SDGs have been important conduits for the EMIS and gender analysis in Timor-Leste. At the time the Minister of Education and Culture, João Câncio Freitas, outlined the influence of these international norms and global targets in the first analysis of the EMIS data published by the MoE, the *Educational Statistical Yearbook 2008/2009* (Freitas, cited in Timor-Leste Ministry of Education and Culture, 2011). In the foreword to this yearbook he suggested that these international norms have had a significant influence on the way EMIS data should be used, the standards aimed for, and the type of indicators likely to be considered useful in policy and budget decision making on education. Similarly, international treaties such as CEDAW and its reporting mechanism can play an important role in inspiring changes in behaviour and promoting the use of gender analysis in policy decision making.

The value of research for policy development and budget decisions in Timor-Leste was undermined by the destruction of statistical resources and the displacement of people during conflict, and limited administrative territorial presence with poorly standardised systems. This was further compromised by the substantial role of international actors in producing research and framing its policy value. New institutional arrangements, however, have suggested that there is a strong symbolic value attributed to research and an understanding of its use in setting political agendas, shaping policy and budgeting, and ultimately improving service delivery. These positive forces are likely to be enhanced by political competition and a broad agreement around social democratic and human rights goals, which have built-in gender equality norms.

The interests and values of actors engaged in gender equality, education policy and budgeting processes in Timor-Leste

Gender activists and gender-focused institutions in government, together with non-government actors, have had a significant role in raising awareness of the meaningfulness of gender analysis. The following sections draw on a suite of research on Timor-Leste and data collected in interviews and focus groups to analyse the political and institutional circumstances that could render gender analysis an effective political tool for change in policy decisions and processes. The contribution of policy actors and their values and interests are also investigated. The next section describes the reaction in the MoE to the gender analysis, and discusses how statistics have been used as a political tool within the MoE to demonstrate the particular tensions around the credibility and legitimacy of the EMIS data. This is followed by an assessment of the role of the researcher in bridging research and policy in fragile states.

State actors and the value they attach to gender-relevant research

A number of policy actors have played a critical role in gender mainstreaming in the education sector. Their interests and values have framed what research is considered relevant for policy and budgeting in Timor-Leste. The focus in this section is on the MoE as the ministry responsible for the use and development of data and research for education policy and budgeting. Earlier chapters have discussed the role of parliament and women's organisations in gender research and policy. A previous section has highlighted the role of new players, such as the Office of the President, in fostering the use of research for policy. For these actors, however, gender-relevant research is not a priority at this stage.

The MoE has played a contradictory role in promoting gender-relevant data and research. There have been strong signs that the ministry has recognised the need for improved research to guide the government's allocation of resources, to assist in achieving its policy commitments and to deliver effective and quality services (see UNESCO, 2011b). Despite these words of support, political leadership within the MoE on EMIS has been patchy, partly because its value in informing education planning and budget decision making is far from established within the MoE.

Initially there were reasons to be positive about the potential for the research generated from this project to promote change, with the ministry establishing a gender unit. The unit undertook an assessment of the representation of boys, girls, men and women in the sector (Soares & Lauvigne, 2009) and the senior management in the MoE had committed to improve the representation of women in senior positions within the ministry. Combined, these measures suggested a policy commitment to gender equality in the MoE. The establishment of the gender unit within the MoE added to the body of gender-focused institutions within the government, including the Office of SEPI. As I argued in Chapter 2, these institutions have played a critical role in furthering gender-responsive policy and budgeting and have garnered ample political and institutional support. They have contributed to a degree of institutionalisation of feminist knowledge with an emphasis on qualitative and quantitative data that highlight gender gaps and inequalities.

The role of these gender-focused units, however, has not always been well understood in Timor-Leste. A critical factor has been that among senior policy makers the Office of SEPI is seen as responsible for the promotion of gender equality with women as the only legitimate voices of gender equality. A senior male public official in the MoE argued:

> for this Ministry [MoE] I think there has to be . . . a director, a woman director to promote this [gender equality] . . . if you are a male, a man, you cannot promote [gender equality] . . . You need to have a female director, not a male director.
>
> (Male policy maker, Interview, 2009)

This male public official found the idea of a male advocate for gender equality comical. These comments are not unusual; rather they point to a common form of contestation and resistance to the mainstreaming of a gender perspective within ministries. Another form of contesting gender mainstreaming is the view that the Office of SEPI is best placed to know how gender equality should be reflected in the budget.

Gender activists in Timor-Leste have exploited these institutional contradictions to carve a role for gender in the planning and budgeting processes across the public sector. Two particular areas suggest some positive progress: the codification of gender equality in the budget call circular issued by the MoF, and the involvement of the SEPI and her office in the budget review committees. This was a significant achievement and represented the recognition of the differential impacts of the budget on men and women. A male senior policy maker observed that such progress was not achieved 'automatically'. It was in his view the result of a lengthy advocacy effort from gender activists inside government: 'we have to be inside the system . . . [from inside the system] you have more influence and decision [power]' (Male policy maker, Interview, 2013). Such victories have however been short lived. The 2017 budget review committee, for example, failed to include a representative of the gender machinery.

Over the years, different incarnations of gender-focused institutions in the Timor-Leste government have trained public servants and raised awareness about gender issues, establishing networks with actors in parliament, international institutions and the women's movement (see Chapter 2). Data collection and analysis including, for example, the government's CEDAW report, have been prominent features of this advocacy work. Gaining a role in the budget review process was seen as the corollary of this advocacy work to get gender equality recognised as important in budgeting and policy making.

Positive changes to the budget procedures, such as the call circular and the budget review committee, suggest a commitment within MoF and the Office of the Prime Minister to integrate gender equality into the budget. However, a male senior public official commented that the Office of SEPI was instrumental in keeping gender in the policy agenda:

> without SEPI, GRB will not be implemented . . . [the MoF] wanted to add one more column [to the budget format for gender] but [the Office of SEPI] told them that this is not the way, gender is integrated in their programmes and activities and not separated.
>
> (Male policy maker, Interview, 2013)

This observation suggests a contestation over how to integrate gender equality in the budget and points to a broader context of traditional gender politics within which gender-focused institutions have had to operate. One such traditional view is that gender is solely a women's issue.

Interaction between state actors and non-government actors around research for policy and budgeting

Related literature suggests that pressure from organisations outside government has been critical in promoting gender-disaggregated analysis within the Timor-Leste government (see Austen et al., 2013). Outside government, women's organisations have provided the impetus for the production and use of gender-relevant research. An area where the women's movement has been particularly effective in using gender-relevant research has been the issue of violence against women, where the movement has been able to mobilise an agenda for change and support for legislation and its implementation. Women's organisations have collected data on the nature of assaults, and the relationship of the perpetrator to the victim, for inclusion in the government's CEDAW report (Timor-Leste Secretary of State for the Promotion of Equality, 2007). This information and analysis have proven to be important in supporting political agendas pursued by *deputadas* in parliament. Their activism in parliament has carved a more prominent monitoring role and generated some demand for information and research on the impact of policy and budgeting on men and women (see Chapter 3).

International actors have played an instrumental role in preparing, collecting, compiling, analysing and publishing gender-relevant research in Timor-Leste, including EMIS data. The United Nations Population Fund (UNFPA) provided technical, human resource and financial support to carry out the census with bilateral support from Indonesia and Japan (Timor-Leste Direcção Nacional de Estatística, 2007). International organisations are widely regarded as having an unprecedented influence over the policy process and, as a male researcher described it, have contributed to the marginalisation of 'universities as an army of the pens' (Male researcher, Interview, 2013).

Through active support of data collection, reporting on progress and a significant advisory role, international actors have become a constitutive element of the policy process and have framed the tools that matter for policy decision making (see Stone, 2004). A male senior policy maker in the MoE observed that data collection and analysis depended on international bodies and advisers: 'I don't want us to be dependent on internationals. I can see that Timorese have capacity . . . what I see is that internationals take advantage of the system' (Male policy maker, Interview, 2011). His particular concern was that EMIS was a captive of international actors. Concerns about the undue influence of international actors have been voiced in a range of ways; a senior public official confessed his frustration with the apparent mismatch between the views and priorities of the government and those of international actors with regards to gender equality. These views point to a concern that international influences obscure local views and marginalise alternative types of knowledge (see Alatas, 2000; Jones et al., 2013). The views have also been exploited as part of a strategy to undermine claims for gender equality from Timorese activists by branding them as international influences (see Chapter 1).

The value of research in the budgetary context

The value of gender analysis of the EMIS data in planning and budgeting is not yet established. A male public official from the MoE observed that in practice budgeting remains informed primarily by past budgeting exercises: 'so far [the data] we use is just EMIS . . . the total money . . . that we put for 2009 gender budget, is in accordance with the last year data, plus new . . . data that [were] provided by EMIS' (Male policy maker, Interview, 2009).

This male public official from the MoE confirmed a preference for the ministry's own dataset, which the ministry controls and trusts. However, he hinted at a partial use of the EMIS data and unfamiliarity with the full potential of the EMIS data. Despite an important investment in data collection, interest in using data and research has been slow to gain pace. This point was further illustrated by a female international commentator, who observed: [MoE] 'has access to that data but that data never feeds in to any of the discussions that they're having. It feeds into UNICEF discussions, World Bank discussions, our [advisors'] discussions' (Female international commentator, Interview, 2009). This commentator highlighted that international actors are the primary users of the EMIS data. This link was well illustrated by the indicators used in the MoE's first yearbook. The yearbook invokes international debates over inequality in access to and through education, but failed to provide context-appropriate and practical measures for policy, planning and budget decision making.

A particular characteristic of the policy environment in Timor-Leste has been the secrecy around decision making and the centralised nature of executive power, with most ministers resistant to divulging information beyond a small group of advisers. Policy decisions are made without significant public consultation or information sharing, and there are tensions within the government. These patterns have been aggravated by the lack of strong political institutions that can challenge the government and hold it accountable (see Kaltenborn-Stachau, 2008; Shah, 2012). This is not a new problem, as a centralised, militarised and masculine administration has a long legacy in Timor-Leste's history (see Chapter 2).

A male senior official highlighted the centralised nature of power, commenting that the inclusion of gender equality in budget processes and decision making depended on the Council of Ministers and on whether gender equality is chosen as a 'political message of the government' (Male policy maker, Interview, 2011). His view was that change needs to be driven by politicians. Significantly, he did not see a role for himself as a senior bureaucrat setting a pathway to integrate gender equality in the budget process. An international female commentator observed that 'only the minister makes policy, and policy is approved through the councillors, ministers and the parliament' (Female international commentator, Interview, 2009). In this context gaining the endorsement of gender equality by the executive was critical to its success. A senior male policy maker observed that only with such support would gender equality be considered 'a serious issue' (Male policy maker, Interview, 2013).

When Indonesia retreated from Timor-Leste in 1999 so did an estimated 20 to 25 per cent of civil servants, including the Indonesian civil servants who held leadership, skilled and technical positions (Cliffe, 2003). Since then international advisers have maintained key positions in the administration and their views and experiences have influenced decisions on the budget. In parallel new knowledge networks are emerging with the MoF investing in its Timorese civil servants and funding scholarships to universities in Indonesia and Australia. An additional illustration of the significant international tone to the knowledge networks that have influenced policy in Timor-Leste is the visit of the prominent American economist Jeffrey Sachs to Dili in 2010 on an invitation by the Minister of Finance, Emilia Pires.

The budget was first designed to operate as a report card; with the budget used by the donor community as leverage to pursue their agendas and with the Timor-Leste government using the budget to demonstrate how these agendas were being reflected. A female international commentator noted that this strong international watermark has constrained progress on budget reforms. It was her view that the budget format and process, while responsive to international standards, was inadequate for Timor-Leste:

> not necessarily what Timor needs right now . . . It's running before people can walk, it's producing massive tables where people don't understand what the numbers in it are, so how are they meant to produce a quality product when they don't really understand.
> (Female international commentator, Interview, 2009)

The budget has had significant shortcomings including a line item budget system, weak links between policy objectives, planning and the budget, and little consistency in the budget calendar (see Van Eden et al., 2010). Many have raised concerns that the budget system was not adequate to ensure transparency and accountability. The *Open Budget Survey* of 2012 argued for the need for the Timor-Leste government to produce more comprehensive and better-classified expenditures for the current and prior budget years. The report recommended the use of functional classification of data and detailed impact analysis (International Budget Partnership, 2012). The availability of this large and 'quality' information, however, has been significant to encourage the active engagement of non-governmental organisations in the budget debate (see Chapter 4).

The budget became instrumental to Timor-Leste's peace and political stability, with spending an important focus. Between 2008 and the supplementary 2016 budget the budget increased more than five times, from US$348 million to US$1,953 million. The rate of this increase has been nothing short of remarkable with five budgets between August 2007 and the 2009 supplementary budget, with each budget approximately doubling the expenditure of the previous one. Larger spending commitments involved substantial infrastructure projects and a sizeable social protection programme (Porter & Rab, 2010; Akmeemana &

Porter, 2015). Specialists associated with the World Bank Saku Akmeemana and Douglas Porter (2015: p. 123) argued that these projects could be seen as the government signalling change, and a time of more inclusion at that, by showing that benefits would be derived from the resource wealth.

Spending became a priority for the government, which assigned spending powers to line ministries and encouraged spending on goods and services (Porter & Rab, 2010; Akmeemana & Porter, 2015). One particular disenfranchised group benefited from these changes, the veterans of the resistance and their families (Akmeemana & Porter, 2015). The female international commentator described how, in this new political context, the preparation of the budget was perceived to be bothersome step: 'the budget was just seen as a really frustrating and annoying administrative step we have to go through to spend a lot of money' (Female international commentator, interview, 2009). This boost in spending sheds light on the flaws of the procurement system, which was devised by the World Bank in the early 2000s (World Bank Group & Independent Evaluation Group, 2011). The effect of these challenges in the budgetary system and process were significant for the delivery of quality and effective services in education, with a 2010 IMF report suggesting that the government, and the MoE, lacked capacity to effectively disburse its entire budget (IMF, 2010; Timor-Leste Ministry of Education, 2011). These challenges have meaningful implications for the policy and budgetary potential of EMIS-based research, as it suggests that policy makers may be under some pressure to disburse expenditure. While attempts to significantly rein in expenditure have failed, there is a growing political demand for careful and targeted expenditure. This suggests that the time may be ripe to have a conversation on expenditure targeting and to position gender research in devising more effective policies.

In summary, actors in the executive, parliament, women's movement and international community have all been engaged in the production of data (qualitative and quantitative) and research relevant to education and gender equality in Timor-Leste. In different ways these various actors have contributed to raising the political relevance and use of research, and have provided impetus to the demand for context-relevant research. Gender-focused institutions in government and parliament have played a critical role in placing gender equality issues in the budget and policy agenda. In parallel, women's organisations have provided alternative sources of gender-relevant research and policy advice. In a context that values research, it is likely that EMIS data would attract renewed interest and may be meaningful for policy and budget decision making in a period of intense scrutiny.

Credibility and legitimacy of the gender analysis using EMIS data

Many participants saw the need and relevance of the gender analysis to guide and monitor the budget. Despite the fact that their reaction was enthusiastic, they were concerned that doubts about the credibility and legitimacy of the EMIS data and its management would render any effort to expand the use of the EMIS data unsuccessful. A particular concern was a lack of standardised systems and procedures within the government, with alternative data collection systems undermining the legitimacy of EMIS.

Reaction to my gender analysis of the EMIS data

The response to my gender analysis developed using EMIS data (see Chapter 6) was positive, with a male official in the MoE remarking that the analysis arrived 'at the right time! We have much data, but analysis of the data . . . remains a challenge' (Male public official, Focus group, 2011). His point was that the study demonstrated the usefulness of the EMIS data beyond its current use primarily as a source of simple descriptive statistics for budgeting and reporting against international commitments. He found that the analysis demonstrated how EMIS could be translated into policy-relevant measures. Another male official found that this analysis was in alignment with what the 'government wants' (Male public official, Focus group, 2013), meaning that the analysis illustrated how EMIS could be used to identify the gaps in service delivery and where to target additional resources.

The implication of such comments is that the approach employed in EMIS data analysis is failing to provide the MoE with effective policy advice. The focus on schools and the schooling experience appeared to provide a more direct framework for the analysis of service delivery in Timor-Leste. This, combined with the analysis of context-relevant factors, provided policy makers and gender activists with information on the link between school performance and social and economic context. It was a departure from the analysis included in the MoE yearbook, with its focus on traditional indicators. These indicators failed to provide information on school-based gender gaps and inequality or insights into how resources might be better allocated at the school level. It is noteworthy that a male public official saw in this study an opportunity to challenge traditional views over gender equality and to increase transparency and accountability in the MoE by engaging with local leadership and parents around the quality of the education services delivered by the schools. Such engagement with local leadership and parents would, in effect, enhance the potential of this analysis in mitigating existing conditions of fragility.

The emphasis on gender equality and schools was well received. The views of a senior male public official on the role of data in decision making illuminated this point:

> [Let's say we find that] more males are in schools compared to females, for example, then we can do something for the next year's budget. Maybe we have to allocate a special budget, to encourage females. However . . . by

having that [policy commitment to providing a nine-year basic education], indirectly we have encouraged females to get the same opportunity.

(Senior policy maker, Interview, 2009)

He suggested that an analysis that highlights gender gaps and inequality would be useful to identify what 'special treatment' would be effective to 'encourage girls to go to school'. This is significant, for it suggests that public officials in the MoE may welcome targeted expenditures. This view, however, was contradicted by the suggestion that the implementation of a nine-year basic education policy places the MoE in a strong position to achieve parity: 'we have encouraged females to get the same opportunity'. He resisted the view that the way services are being delivered may produce gender gaps and inequality. This view was further illustrated by observations from a female international commentator: 'people [in the MoE] don't see that the rules . . . may favour men and disadvantage women' (Female international commentator, Interview, 2009). This commentator suggested that there is a wide view that the MoE policies and budgets are gender neutral. Instead, she argued that MoE officials are unaware of the different impacts that education policy and budget have on the lives and empowerment of boys and girls.

Given men's and women's distinct roles, socio-economic positions and responsibilities in the paid and unpaid economy it is unlikely that policy and budgeting will have the same effect on the lives of men and women, boys and girls. Research by Austen et al. (2013) makes an important contribution to this discussion. Using attendance data, their study shows that spending on education in Timor-Leste was not equally distributed between rural boys and girls, with rural girls in particular poorly served by spending on pre-secondary and secondary schooling. This research suggests that expansion in basic education to nine years will not produce gender parity in school attendance, without a comprehensive and targeted effort to address the socio-economic and cultural factors that affect girls' school attendance.

Resistance to the use of EMIS data

The political resistance to EMIS and its policy use has taken a variety of forms. First, questions about the qualifications of the team behind EMIS have marred their confidence and perceived legitimacy. Second, competing data collection systems have survived. Growing high-level demand for the consolidation of these systems under EMIS has met with significant political resistance to EMIS and its use in policy making.

The qualifications and skills of those engaged in data planning, collection and compilation have been under scrutiny. Those engaged in EMIS believed that others in the MoE did not recognise their expertise, gained primarily through experience on the job. As a result, they believed, the credibility of the EMIS data was seriously undermined. A male official expressed this sentiment: 'maybe it is not the quality of the data [that has generated resistance to the use of EMIS], it is not EMIS equipment but capacity' (Male policy maker, Focus group, 2013). EMIS was perceived by some as being under threat. The impact of these questions about the legitimacy of the team behind EMIS has been significant to the confidence of the team and, ultimately, to EMIS's policy potential. This official has also drawn attention to the lack of standardised systems and procedures within the government and its effect in undermining the legitimacy of EMIS. The emergent Timorese administration has been characterised by highly centralised decision making and multiple and patchy administrative systems and procedures. This has made it possible for competing data collection systems on schools to survive. A broader implication of these internal debates is that EMIS has failed to demonstrate its potential to contribute to policy making, leaving a void that has allowed alternative data systems to survive.

The role of the external researcher in the interface between research and policy

The role of international organisations in EMIS was an issue that divided participants in this study. With EMIS data collection reaching close to a decade in Timor-Leste, some are asking when EMIS can be fully prepared, implemented and analysed by the MoE national staff. An international consultant, for example, developed the yearbook, and a new consultant has been deployed to produce the next yearbook. The large volume of international aid has contributed to further undermining the legitimacy of the EMIS data and their use within the MoE.

Timor-Leste has been a welcoming territory for researchers from across the world. There are some signs that Timorese are questioning what they are gaining from the wealth of research that has been generated around their lives, their efforts, their successes and failures. A male public official summarised this growing frustration with the MoE's partial access to international academic research. His argument was that it is not possible to talk about the interactions between research and policy without addressing the only limited access to the multiple academic studies that have focused on Timor-Leste over the years: 'We [can't] talk about how to use it [research for policy and budgeting] – [the problem is] that we don't get it, we don't have the research' (Male policy maker, Interview, 2013). He suggested that many researchers have failed to deliver on their part of the bargain by neglecting a more meaningful and long-term commitment to change in Timor-Leste. In this reflection he hints at the tension between their interests and that of international researcher and suggests that limited access to quality research is widening the gap between research and policy making.

The participants were clear on what sorts of indicators would capture the attention of policy makers. It was their view that indicators on school dropout rates, repetition and patterns of enrolment across schools would advance policy debate within the MoE. Of note was the relative lack of interest in the use of the national household survey dataset, the 2007 TLLSS, for education policy analysis.

In part, this resistance can be explained by the battle to reclaim the credibility of EMIS; however, the cost of such resistance is high. It has resulted in limited understanding of the factors that produce significant and persistent inequalities in education outcomes and, consequently, an incomplete range of policy options can be identified to produce positive changes.

Despite the positive response to this study, the approach adopted for the analysis of the data was contested. The focus on the worst performing schools, while pragmatic, was considered as providing only a limited view of the status of school performance across the country. The participants agreed that identifying the best performing schools against each indicator was important to provide a more comprehensive picture of the delivery of education services. Such an approach could provide a framework for transferring pedagogies from leading to lagging schools. For another male senior public official this focus on the schools that were lagging behind was reminiscent of what he perceived to be the problem of the way gender activists in Timor-Leste communicate their concerns, as they place the focus on 'everything [that] is negative' (Male policy maker, Interview, 2013). His particular concern reveals the continued resistance to the significant transformation that gender activists are demanding in Timor-Leste.

With experience being the primary source of influence in the policy and budget process in Timor-Leste, administrative data appear to be a secondary positive force for change. Characteristics of Timor-Leste's fragile state, such as poor standardised systems, have enabled multiple data collection systems to coexist, and undermined the legitimacy and credibility of EMIS. The debate over the type of data that can effectively influence policy and budgeting has frequently focused on the capacity of the team responsible and on the significant role of the international community in the collection, compilation and analysis of the EMIS dataset. Finally, those engaged in the EMIS dataset collection and compilation believed that there was a role for this study in reclaiming a place for the EMIS dataset in policy and budget decision making.

Conclusion

This study of the policy value of the gender analysis outlined in Chapter 6 explored the circumstances that could bring about policy and budget decisions and processes that are more gender sensitive. Policy actors in the MoE welcomed the development of gender-relevant indicators on school performance using Timor-Leste's administrative data. However, several aspects of Timor-Leste's fragile status contributed to undermining its potential policy and budgetary influence. With statistical resources destroyed, limited available staff with qualifications, a state administration with a limited territorial presence and poor standardised systems, the Timor-Leste MoE had seen the emergence of a multiplicity of data collection systems and the erosion of the legitimacy and credibility of the EMIS dataset. The highly centralised policy and budget processes emphasised experience as the principal source of influence and positioned administrative data as a secondary force for change. This was further compromised by the significant role that international bodies have played, and continue to play, in the collection, compilation and analysis of the EMIS data.

Positive influences for a greater use of research more generally were also evident. Timor-Leste's diverse political environment and the broad agreement around social democratic and human rights goals, backed by international norms, created opportunities for the demand and use of gender research. This demand has been furthered by the actions of activists in the executive, gender-focused institutions in the bureaucracy and in parliament, the women's movement and the international community. The emergence of new sources of research, such as the creation of a research body under the Office of the President, suggests that a strong symbolic value is attributed to research and that there is an understanding of its use in setting political agendas, shaping policy and budgeting, and ultimately improving service delivery. It also suggests the complexity of such contexts where multiple institutions are claiming a role in setting the policy agenda and building a resilient state.

Despite such tensions, the interaction between policy actors has developed productive relationships around research development; with the women's movement providing the impetus for policy debate in parliament through their community-based data collection exercises. The Office of SEPI has established positive relationships with other ministries around research development and has engaged in a conversation about its significance for the way services are being delivered. An example of this is the research conducted around teenage pregnancy and its implications for education policy. While new institutions and norms have presented opportunities to codify gender in budgetary processes, traditional gender politics and ways of prioritising and allocating resources have continued to undermine positive change.

This study shows that a sustained interaction between researchers, decision makers and activists is critical for effective meditation between analysis and policy. My role and my interest in the analysis of EMIS data was subject to debate. This was in part related to the particular tension posed by my insider and outsider position. I was an insider due to my long and continued relationship with Timor-Leste, and specifically with feminist and gender equality activists in Timor-Leste. I was also an outsider. First and foremost, I was an educated and Western feminist researcher. Despite these tensions, an important outcome of my research was that those engaged in EMIS data collection and the gender analysis recognised that they had a significant role to play in claiming a role for EMIS in policy and budget decision making and in engaging those implementing the policy (including parents and the community) in a conversation about service delivery.

For GRB to reach its full potential in practice, gender analysis needs to be integrated into policy and budget decision-making processes. In this chapter I have emphasised that GRB is a political process as much as a technical exercise. For a productive analysis–policy interface to eventuate, the political and cultural context, the values and behaviour of policy actors, and their interactions and views over what constitutes legitimate and credible knowledge, need to be considered. Finally, I argue that significant investment in data collection, compilation and analysis in developing countries needs to be understood as part of a state-building effort.

8 Conclusion

I have shown in this book that GRB can work in fragile state contexts such as that of Timor-Leste. Timor-Leste offered an exceptional opportunity to observe closely the politics and practice that underpin GRB. Its government had committed to the implementation of a gender agenda in its economic policy as part of its broader strategy to improve gender equality outcomes. Budget and political processes have changed as a result of this strategy. However, such positive signals have yet to filter through to women and children in measurable outcomes. Women and their dependent children have borne much of the impact of Timor-Leste's low-income status and poor development performance, with gender inequality featuring as a social, economic and political issue. The 2014 MDG report found that Timor-Leste remains incapable of achieving some of its gender equality targets. For example, it reports that it is unlikely that the MDG targets in relation to gender parity in primary school and maternal mortality will be achieved by 2015 (Timor-Leste Ministry of Finance, 2014). Having experienced numerous instances of violence and political instability, Timor-Leste has gained the status of fragile state among the international community. This concept has also surfaced in internal political conversations where the idea of fragile has been used as a descriptor of the country's development status.

I argue that GRB can work in a fragile state context such as that of Timor-Leste. In particular, I have shown in this book that in such contexts GRB can make a positive contribution to improvements in policy and budgeting processes and decision making, and strengthen the state's accountability and transparency to women. The experience in Timor-Leste suggests that the potential of GRB is shaped by a range of political and technical factors including political context, economic agenda and policy, the actions and interactions of gender-focused institutions, access and use of gender-relevant data and research, and the contribution of experts outside the state.

Whether GRB has anything to offer fragile states is a pressing question; there is mounting evidence that elements of GRB are being adopted in various fragile contexts, including Afghanistan, Bangladesh, Egypt, Uganda, Zimbabwe and Sri Lanka, and substantial resources are being poured into supporting these initiatives. Timor-Leste's GRB initiative has gained some international prominence after being identified as one of the few advanced efforts in fragile state contexts (see Stotsky, 2016).

The experience of Timor-Leste illustrates a path for the adoption of GRB in a fragile context. There is much that can be learned from this experience that would have relevance to GRB initiatives in similar contexts, not the least that gender-focused institutions matter. A particular set of contextual, normative, institutional and social circumstances has enabled the emergence and the adoption of GRB in Timor-Leste. The groundwork of building a broad positive climate for gender equality was significant. It included a broad commitment to gender equality latterly endorsed by political parties and the government and a context of institution building that saw the emergence of a gender architecture in the new political institutions. The gender machinery in government, women's organisations, and women's cross-party caucuses in parliament and in international parliamentary networks have all played a crucial role in ushering in positive changes to the budget, bolstering the GRB agenda and ensuring accountability for commitments to gender equality. Activists have found in these institutions alternative routes for women to represent a gender equality agenda; and they took advantage of the expansion of the budget and the administration to generate support for this agenda.

Other factors have undermined progress, not least the crisis that Timor-Leste has experienced leading to population displacement and the destruction of data. Resistance to such new politics has taken a range of shapes including the contestation of gender mainstreaming as a strategy for achieving equality. Expectations that better gender knowledge could leapfrog the process of change have been frustrated. This case study shows that gender-relevant data and research gain meaning through the political process. The budget and policy context, views about the credibility and legitimacy of the knowledge generated, and the values and behaviour of critical actors play an important role in influencing gender analysis in the budget process. The implications of this study are significant for other fragile states, pointing to the need for a deeper understanding of actors, knowledge and policy to translate gender analysis effectively into improvements in educational opportunities for women and girls. Despite some success, including success in financing the implementation of the law against domestic violence, this study shows that political practice, cultural values and old gender norms have hampered attempts to embed a gender agenda in economic policy.

Implications of the study for economic debates

Through this research I have sought to make a contribution to economic policy debate about whether GRB can deter or enhance institution-building and state-building efforts in fragile contexts. Some economists have argued that GRB worsens the competition for a limited pool of resources and skills, and ultimately detracts from state-building and peace-building efforts (Joshi & Naidu, 2007). This study challenges these views. I argue that GRB does not proceed in a linear and organised fashion, building upon 'basics first' in economic policy. I have drawn attention to the institutional legacies, norms and ideas that may undermine efforts to change economic policy. I have shown that social actors are taking up any political and institutional opportunities to change rules and institutions to produce more equal and effective economic outcomes. The experience of Timor-Leste shows that the process of institution and state building has generated enclaves of reform (see Andrews, 2006) and critical political junctures that provide fertile ground to embed a gender agenda in economic policy (through, for example, standardisation of internal procedures and legislation). Cognizant of this, gender activists in Timor-Leste have acted strategically, organised themselves, collaborated, produced data and research, and drawn on the broad direction of the women's movement to build an agenda and narrative for GRB. In these ways the adoption of GRB can help improve outcomes for women and girls, grow the economy and contribute to peace building.

Most analyses of the link between GRB and fragile states have focused on providing a rationale for its adoption in such contexts. Included in this rationale is the potential of GRB to improve policy processes and decision making, citizen–state relationships, state accountability and transparency, gender equality, and to curb corruption (Harcourt, 2009a; Khan, 2009). These arguments reflect a wealth of scholarship on the impact of GRB, covering a range of developed and developing contexts. Scholarship on GRB offers an insight into the array of political, institutional and technical circumstances that are significant in making GRB effective. There is less clarity about what can be expected from these initiatives in fragile states and the circumstances that make these initiatives effective and sustainable. Fragile contexts pose particular political and institutional challenges for GRB and policy development, due to their vulnerability to conflict and state breakdown, weak institutions and control over the budget, lack of standardised procedures and poor service delivery.

This study engages with these debates from a new perspective by exploring the particular circumstances that make GRB effective in improving gender equality in fragile contexts. To explore these circumstances I have drawn inspiration from the work of Walby (2005), who argued that GRB invokes a successful complementarity between participatory-democratic and expert-bureaucratic strategies. How these two streams of strategies evolved and interacted is discussed below in the second and third sections of this concluding chapter. The second section highlights the political elements of the GRB project in Timor-Leste. It draws attention to the narrative and practice that has framed GRB in Timor-Leste, the broader political and economic context, and the role of gender-focused institutions. This is followed by an assessment of circumstances that may render gender-relevant analysis an effective tool to influence policy, planning and budgeting (third section). This study of the Timor-Leste experience shows that GRB can make a significant contribution to economic policy and help to build state resilience by increasing accountability and transparency, improving the representation of diverse voices in decision making, producing better policy and budgeting processes, and contributing to more effective and equitable economic and social decisions. This study has countered the criticisms of economists who have failed to recognise Timor-Leste's political, institutional and historical contexts, and gender politics. This construction can lead such economists to misjudge the potential of GRB as a strategy for equity and economic efficiency.

Through this research I have sought to contribute to feminist perspectives on fragile contexts. Feminist contributions to fragile state research have had a strong emphasis on service delivery, governance and citizenship issues. This study provides a novel perspective to these feminist contributions by focusing on economic policy. Economics has been featured in debates over fragile state contexts, with the politics of taxation, macroeconomic policy and the degree of participation in the budget process being linked to state legitimacy and resilience (Putzel & Di John, 2012). This study has bolstered feminist scholarship on fragile state contexts by showing that, in Timor-Leste, the inclusion of a gender agenda in economic policy has increased demand for the government's accountability and transparency to women and their agendas, and improved the representation of women in budget decision making. This study has shown how activists have mobilised to ensure that the priorities of the women's movement are appropriately funded. An example of this is state funding for the implementation of the law against domestic violence. Such moves have strengthened the state's legitimacy from Timorese women's perspective and have prompted the emergence of a coalition of policy actors interested in a development agenda that considers equality. This emerging political conversation has included a demand for transparency, accountability, and a more sustainable and considered spending strategy of Timor-Leste's natural resources. The gender and economic policy agenda has made a contribution to these aspirations by placing gender equity in the development and budget debate.

Gender-responsive budgeting as a political and democratic project: the role of gender-focused institutions

The experience of GRB in Timor-Leste illustrates its potential to improve the impact of economic policy on women by holding the government accountable for its commitments to women and gender equality. This transformative potential has been enhanced by the political framing of GRB and the support it has garnered. Impetus for GRB in Timor-Leste has been bolstered by the specific characteristics of the political and institutional context, and by critical actors such as gender-focused institutions.

This study has sought to contribute to understandings of the role of gender-focused institutions, and the interaction between them, in the pursuit of positive changes in budget processes, priorities and policy development. The contribution that these institutional arrangements and processes potentially make to GRB in fragile contexts has rarely been examined. It was to be expected that in a context such as Timor-Leste gender-focused institutions would find it problematic to make a positive contribution to change. What the experience of Timor-Leste has shown is that gender-focused institutions can take advantage of critical junctures, draw on international bodies and norms, and act collaboratively and strategically to translate policy commitments into budget change. From this vantage point, gender-focused institutions in Timor-Leste have positioned GRB as a political and democratic project. This study focuses on the particular role of gender-focused institutions in the executive (covered in Chapters 2 and 7), in parliament and in an international parliamentary network (Chapters 3 and 5), and in the women's movement (Chapter 4).

The gender-focused institutions in the executive, embodied in the Secretary of State for the Promotion of Equality and her office, have been a catalyst for GRB narratives and practice. A network of gender units in ministries has underpinned their work. Despite the sophistication of the gender policy machinery, the role of the Office of SEPI has often been misunderstood; with the office seen as responsible for the promotion of gender equality, and with women seen as the only legitimate voices on gender equality. Gender activists in Timor-Leste have contested such views, and have exploited existing institutional contradictions to carve a role for gender in the planning and budgeting processes. Two notable successes have been the codification of gender equality in the budget call circular and the involvement of the Secretary of State for the Promotion of Equality and her Office in the budget review committees. These novel institutional arrangements in a fragile state represent the recognition of the differential impacts of the budget on men and women and attest to the political influence of the Secretary of State and her Office. These positive changes have emerged amidst a weak policy process in which executive power is centralised and immersed in secrecy. Together with the undue influence of the executive and the overwhelming power of (male) political elites, this has undermined the space for fiscal democracy for women.

While there is a wealth of literature on gender-focused institutions in the executive, such as women's policy agencies, the role of gender-focused parliamentary institutions in bringing about positive change has rarely been examined. This study found that the presence of the women's caucus in parliament, with a mandate to focus on gender equality, proved a significant enabling factor for GRB in Timor-Leste. A substantive example of the contribution of the women's caucus was the introduction of a parliamentary resolution on GRB. This resolution provided a comprehensive framework for GRB, emphasised gender as an integral part of policy development and budget decision making, and paved the way for fiscal democracy by making the budget process transparent, accountable and open to women. This resolution had a significant influence; for example the Secretary of State for the Promotion of Equality referred to it when urging line ministries to show their commitment to implementing the domestic violence law. It demonstrated that *deputadas* were able to act collectively and strategically to pursue particular elements of the gender agenda. It has been suggested that the recent emergence of a government of national unity has resulted in reduced scrutiny of the budget including a closed-door ad-hoc committee to consider budget amendments and limited hearings with advocacy organisations. The opportunity and impetus for *deputadas* to engage with women's organisations may have been significantly abbreviated. An additional point that can be derived from this is the lack of well-established procedures and practices (such as changes to the budget calendar), which undermines active participation and debate over the government's priorities.

Timor-Leste *deputadas* have also drawn on gender-focused institutions in international parliamentary networks, specifically the fledgling NWPA-CPLP. This study has shown that *deputadas* have drawn on the NWPA-CPLP to strengthen their national agendas, using the legitimacy of the Parliamentary Assembly of the CPLP to advocate and, to a degree, educate for change. The NWPA-CPLP has provided support to the GRB agenda by endorsing GRB in its documentation and by creating opportunities to strengthen capacity to implement GRB.

Another source of institutional support for GRB has been women's organisations. This research found that the peak body of the Timorese women's movement, Rede Feto, has played an important role in influencing public policy and its budgeting. Specifically, its national congresses and a political agenda in the Platform for Action have established Rede Feto as an important political voice and an effective actor in politics in Timor-Leste. One of its most recent areas of attention is economic policy. The women's movement working group with a GRB focus has campaigned for more open access to budget documents, more equal outcomes and adequate resourcing for its agenda. Since it was first established in the late 2000s this group has lobbied the parliament through their budget committee debates, monitored budget spending and raised awareness within the community around budget monitoring and its impact on men and women. Through their active engagement, Rede Feto has construed action on a gender agenda as a less risky political endeavour.

Particularly critical to the apparent success of embedding a gender agenda in economic policy has been the interaction between these social actors. Gender-focused institutions in Timor-Leste in the national parliament, the executive, in international institutions and the women's movement have contributed to the impetus behind the GRB agenda, produced changes to the budget and offered an alternative route for women to represent women. Despite the positive impact of these new institutional arrangements, these gender-focused institutions are nested in the traditional way of doing politics. This study has shown that political practice and cultural values continue to significantly hamper attempts to embed a gender agenda in economic policy, and that gender politics frames much of the conversation on gender equality in policy and budgeting. A particular issue is the masculinisation and militarisation of Timor-Leste's state administration. For women, these characteristics of the state have further undermined the recognition of women as legitimate voices, constrained women's engagement with the state, with political life and with public services. One of the ways these patterns have become evident is through the budget. The budget of the government of Timor-Leste reflects militarisation and masculinisation, with defence and security representing the second largest budget allocation in the 2006–2007 budget. The significant weight of defence has been retained; these sectors represented the fifth largest budget allocation, with 4 per cent of the budget, in 2013 (Timor-Leste Ministry of Finance, 2013a). The realisation of the militarisation and masculinisation of the state in Timor-Leste has brought home the centrality of the debate over budget decision making and economic policy and the need to reclaim the development agenda and recast the relationship between the state and its citizens. Women and gender-focused institutions in Timor-Leste have been part of this process of changing the developing state.

Gender-responsive budgeting as a technical and economic project: exploring the interface between gender analysis and policy and budget change

Feminist economists have mounted a strong argument for gender-relevant data and research for its crucial role in assessing the impact of budgets and policies on men and women, boys and girls and thus guiding more equitable and effective policy development and budget decisions. However, the circumstances that assist in the translation of gender analysis to influence policy in developing contexts remain broadly unknown. Chapters 6 and 7 explored whether the potential of gender analysis of administrative data can be realised and investigated its use in policy, planning and budgeting changes. This study demonstrated that a gender analysis, using administrative data, can contribute to understanding the impact of the budget on the education of boys and girls. I argue, though, that linear links between gender analysis and policy development and budget change should not be assumed in contexts of political instability, a lack of standardised systems and procedures, poor institutionalisation of evidence-based policy and low capacity. Instead, the extent to which gender-relevant data and research influences policy and budgeting is directly related to the broader budget and policy context, the values and behaviour of critical actors inside and outside government, and views about credible and legitimate knowledge.

The Timor-Leste government is under some pressure to prioritise resources, deliver better services and improve the nation's economic and development outcomes. Through this study I have sought to make a particular contribution to this debate. I produced a report card on the performance of primary schools using indicators relevant to gender equality, and examining the barriers to and enablers of the use of gender research in Timor-Leste. Using MoE administrative data, EMIS, this report card showed how to target resources in order to achieve the government's education policy agenda. In Chapter 6 I argued that drawing on a diversity of data sources expands the potential of this administrative data to promote education and gender equality. I offered a new approach that expands the insights derived from an analysis of EMIS data by developing social and economic indicators using the TLLSS survey data. These social and economic indicators provided policy directions for how Timor-Leste can improve its gender equality outcomes in education.

This study was well received by policy actors in the MoE. Several features of the approach adopted explained this positive reception, not the least being the emphasis on schools, the schooling experience and the identification of context-relevant factors that explain gender gaps and inequality. Overall, this approach provided a framework for the use of gender analysis in a conversation on education service delivery and outcomes between those engaged in implementing the government's education policy and those using the services. The enthusiasm with which this study was received uncovered the failure of existing analysis and limited use of the EMIS data to provide policy-relevant information on how resources might be better allocated at the school level. This study confirmed that indicators derived from administrative data can improve understandings of the impact of the budget and contribute to enhancing service delivery by placing the focus on where resources are needed to improve effectiveness and equality. Such indicators have the potential to further accountability between citizens and the state by providing relevant and focused information on school performance to key actors in the education sector, enabling a conversation on the way forward, and ultimately helping to mitigate existing conditions of fragility.

While policy actors in the MoE welcomed gender analysis using the EMIS data, this study shows that this alone was not sufficient to produce budget changes and policy developments. Without a deeper understanding of the critical actors, institutions and dynamics that underpin budget changes, it would be hard for gender analysis of EMIS data to improve education opportunities for women and girls in Timor-Leste. Chapter 7 explored these processes and their interaction.

The characteristics of Timor-Leste's political context appeared to be a particularly prominent factor in the potential of research to influence policies and budgets. During the mid-2000s crisis data collected by the MoE were destroyed and a large section of the population was displaced. The potential use of information by MoE was further undermined given limited staff with the necessary knowledge to conduct analysis and mediate its translation into policy and budgeting. A particular result of this political instability was the emergence of multiple data collection systems within the MoE. This resulted in competition over the credibility of data sources for decision making, which placed EMIS under enormous scrutiny and eroded its legitimacy and credibility. It is also possible that such political instability produced a degree of mistrust of the administration and consequentially undermined the nature of the relationship between communities and officials engaged in data collection.

Timor-Leste's diverse political environment has had an ambiguous impact on the interface between research and policy. The broad agreement around social democratic and human rights, backed by international norms, has created a positive context for the demand for and use of feminist knowledge. In this context, statistical information and indicators have become a symbol of a modern state capable of self-governance. In parallel, President Ruak's more prominent role in Timor-Leste's political competition has increased engagement in research. Monitoring of the budget has gained some support with the work of an independent auditor.

A variety of policy actors have participated in efforts to collect, analyse and use data to develop gender policy and influence budget decisions. Significant to the institutionalisation of feminist knowledge (Goetz, 1994) was the role of gender-focused institutions. Over the years, different incarnations of gender-focused institutions in government have built demand for gender-relevant data, produced knowledge on gender issues and established strategic networks. Positive changes to budget procedures, such as the codification of gender equality in the call circular and the engagement of the Secretary of State for the Promotion of Equality and her office in the budget review processes, have created a demand for gender-disaggregated data. *Deputadas*, for example, have been vocal on concerns over the lack of gender-relevant data and analysis for assessing the gender impacts of the budget. They have drawn on the views of women, through women's groups, to fill gaps in knowledge. From this vantage point a range of gender research is being used as an alternative mechanism for boosting scrutiny of the executive and fostering an inclusive policy agenda.

While Timor-Leste's political and economic context have presented opportunities to codify gender in budget processes, traditional gender politics and ways of prioritising and allocating resources have undercut positive changes. One of the ways this traditional gender politics has expressed itself is through contestation over how to integrate gender equality in the budget, with a strong view emerging that gender-focused institutions are the motors for gender equality. The unprecedented influence of international organisations in data collection, compilation and analysis, combined with the highly centralised nature of policy and budget processes, has undermined the use of gender analysis in Timor-Leste. EMIS analysis has been informed by international organisations, and their interests have determined the sort of indicators that are developed. This significant influence has undermined the emergence of alternative research agendas; instead, it is likely that international priorities have overridden local voices. Notwithstanding this, the experience of Timor-Leste confirms that international indicators and bodies have a positive political role in instigating action to improve service delivery to meet internationally established standards.

References

ABC/Reuters (2008) Ramos Horta wounded, Reinado dead in Timor attack. *ABC News*, 11 February. Available from: www.abc.net.au/news/2008-02-11/ramos-horta-wounded-reinado-dead-in-timor-attack/1038982 [accessed 27 October 2014].

Aberman, N.-L., Schiffer, E., Johnson, M. & Oboh, V. (2009) *Mapping the policy process in Nigeria: examining linkages between research and policy*. Washington, DC, International Food Policy Research Institute. NSSP Background Paper 12.

Abrantes, L. (2011) *Movimentos sociais de mulheres no Timor-Leste: a Rede Feto, suas interrelacoes e o papel das suas liderancas*. Dili, Asia Pacific Support Collective Timor-Leste and Gabinete do Primeiro Ministro da RDTL, Assessoria para a Sociedade Civil.

Abu-Ghaida, D. & Klasen, S. (2004) The costs of missing the Millennium Development Goal on gender equity. *World Development*, 32 (7), 1075–1107.

Adebanjo, D. (2009) Gender budgeting: case study of the Zimbabwe experience. *Open Space*, 2 (4), 80–84.

Agencia Angola Press. (2013) Deputadas da CPLP abordam direitos da mulher. Available from: www.portalangop.co.ao/angola/pt_pt/noticias/politica/2013/10/44/Deputadas-CPLP-abordam-direitos-mulher,3e767f1f-5376-43b8-8b39-869dbe4d6c8c.html [accessed 30 November 2015].

Akmeemana, S. & Porter, D. (2015) Securing a new ordering of power in Timor-Leste: the role of sub-national spending. In Kent, L., Ingram, S. & McWilliam, A. (eds) *A new era? Timor-Leste after the UN*. Canberra, ANU Press, pp. 117–140.

Alatas, S.H. (2000) Intellectual imperialism: definition, traits, and problems. *Southeast Asian Journal of Social Science*, 28 (1), 23–45.

Alldén, S. (2009) *How do international norms travel? Women's political rights in Cambodia and Timor-Leste*. Doctoral thesis, Department of Political Science, Umea Universitet, Umea.

Allen, R. (2009) *The challenge of reforming budgetary institutions in developing countries*. Fiscal Affairs Department, International Monetary Fund.

Amin, S. & Chaudhury, N. (2008) An introduction to methodologies for measuring service delivery in education. In Amin, S., Das, J. & Goldstein, M. (eds) *Are you being served? New tools for measuring service delivery*. World Bank, Washington, pp. 67–109.

Anastasia, N. & Teklemariam, A. (2011) Socio-cultural and economic factors affecting primary education of Masaai girls in Loitokitok District, Kenya. *Western Journal of Black Studies*, 35 (4), 268–280.

Anderson, T. (2003) Self-determination after independence: East Timor and the World Bank. *Portuguese Studies Review*, 11 (1), 169–185.

Anderson, T. (2012) Development strategy. In Leach, M. & Kingsbury, D. (eds) *The politics of Timor-Leste: democratic consolidation after intervention*. Ithaca, NY, Cornell Southeast Asia Program Publications, pp. 215–238.

Andrew, M. (2008) Questioning women's movement 'strategies': Australian activism on work and care. *Social Politics*, 15 (3), 369–395.

Andrews, M. (2006) Beyond 'best practice' and 'basics first' in adopting performance budgeting reform. *Public Administration and Development*, 26 (2), 147–161.

Annesley, C. (2012) Campaigning against cuts: gender equality movements in tough times. *Political Quarterly*, 83 (1), 19–23.

Annesley, C., Engeli, I., Gains, F. & Resodihardjo, S. (2014) Policy advocacy in hard times: the impact of economic performance on gendering executive attention. *West European Politics*, 37 (5), 886–902.

Annesley, C. & Gains, F. (2010) The core executive: gender, power and change. *Political Studies*, 58 (5), 909–929.

Annesley, C. & Gains, F. (2013) Investigating the economic determinants of the UK gender equality policy agenda. *British Journal of Politics and International Relations*, 15 (1), 125–146.

Annin, C. (2009) *From messages to voices: understanding girls' educational experiences in selected communities in the Akuapim South District, Ghana*. Doctoral thesis, Department of Educational Studies and the College of Education, Ohio University.

Asian Development Bank (ADB) (2005) *Gender and nation building in Timor-Leste: country gender assessment*. Philippines, Asian Development Bank.

Asian Development Bank (ADB) (2014) *Timor-Leste country gender assessment*. Manila, ADB, UN Women and SEPI.

Assembleia Parlamentar da Comunidade dos Países de Lingua Portuguesa (2009) *Estatutos da Assembleia Parlamentar da Comunidade dos Países de Lingua Portuguesa*. São Tomé e Príncipe, Assembleia Parlamentar da Comunidade dos Países de Lingua Portuguesa.

Attfield, I. & Vu, B.T. (2013) A rising tide of primary school standards: the role of data systems in improving equitable access for all to quality education in Vietnam. *International Journal of Educational Development*, 33, 74–87.

Austen, S., Costa, M., Sharp, R. & Elson, D. (2013) Expenditure incidence analysis: a gender-responsive budgeting tool for educational expenditure in Timor-Leste? *Feminist Economics*, 19 (4), 1–24.

Bakker, I. (2002) *Fiscal policy, accountability and voice: the example of gender responsive budget initiatives*. Human Development Report Office, United Nations Development Programme.

Bakker, I. (2003) Neo-liberal governance and the reprivatization of social reproduction: social provisioning and shifting gender orders. In Bakker, I. & Gill, S. (eds) *Power, production and social reproduction*. Chippenham and Eastborne, Great Britain, Palgrave Macmillan, pp. 66–82.

Bakker, I. (2007) *Financing for gender equality and the empowerment of women: paradoxes and possibilities*. Background paper prepared for United Nations Division for the Advancement of Women, Expert Group Meeting on financing for gender equality and the empowerment of women. Oslo, 4–7 September.

Bakker, I. (2011) Changing macroeconomic governance and gender orders: the case of Canada. In Young, B., Bakker, I. & Elson, D. (eds) *Questioning financial governance from a feminist perspective*. Oxon, Routledge, pp. 38–50.

Bakker, I. & Gill, S. (2003) Global economy and social reproduction. In Bakker, I. & Gill, S. (eds) *Power, production and social reproduction.* Chippenham and Eastborne, Palgrave Macmillan, pp. 3–16.

Ballington, J. (2008) *Equality in politics: a survey of women and men in parliaments.* Geneva, Inter-Parliamentary Union.

Baranyi, S. & Powell, K. (2005a) *Bringing gender back into Canada's engagement in fragile states: options for CIDA in a whole-of-government approach.* Ottawa, Canada, North–South Institute.

Baranyi, S. & Powell, K. (2005b) *Fragile states, gender equality and aid effectiveness: a review of donor perspectives.* Ottawa, Canada, North–South Institute.

Barnett, K. & Grown, C. (2004) *Gender impacts of government revenue collection: the case of taxation.* London, Commonwealth Secretariat.

BBC (2002) East Timor declares state of alert. *BBC News World Edition,* 4 December. Available from: http://news.bbc.co.uk/2/hi/asia-pacific/2541609.stm [accessed 30 June 2013].

Beckwith, K. (2007) Mapping strategic engagements: women's movements and the state. *International Feminist Journal of Politics,* 9 (3), 312–338.

Bell, C. & O'Rourke, C. (2010) Peace agreements or pieces of paper? The impact of UNSC Resolution 1325 on Peace Processes and their Agreements. *International and Comparative Law Quarterly,* 59 (4), 941–980.

Benequista, N. (2010) Putting citizens at the centre: linking states and societies for responsive governance: a policy-maker's guide to the research of the Development Research Centre on Citizenship, Participation and Accountability. Paper prepared for 'The Politics of Poverty, Elites, Citizens and States' Conference sponsored by the Department for International Development, 21–3 June.

Berik, G., Meulen Rodgers, Y. & Seguino, S. (2009) Feminist economics of inequality, development, and growth. *Feminist Economics,* 15 (3), 1–33.

Bertoli, S. & Ticci, E. (2011) *A fragile guideline to development assistance.* Siena, Dipartimento di Politica Economica, Finanza e Svillupo, Universita di Siena.

Bessell, S. (2010) Methodologies for gender-sensitive and pro-poor poverty measures. In Chant, S. (ed.) *The international handbook of gender and poverty: concepts, research and policy.* Cheltenham, Edward Elgar, pp. 59–64.

Bessell, S. (2015) The Individual Deprivation Measure: measuring poverty as if gender and inequality matter. *Gender and Development,* 23 (2), 223–240.

Brock, C. & Cammish, N. (1997) *Factors affecting female participation in education in seven developing countries.* London, Department for International Development.

Budlender, D. (2002a) Gender budgets: what's in it for NGOs? *Gender & Development,* 10 (3), 82–87.

Budlender, D. (2002b) A profile of country activities. In Budlender, D. et al. (eds) *Gender budgets make cents: understanding gender-responsive budgets.* London, Commonwealth Secretariat, pp. 131–164.

Budlender, D. (2004) *Budgeting to fulfill international gender and human rights commitments.* Harare, UNIFEM.

Budlender, D. (2009) *Ten-country overview report: integrating gender-responsive budgeting into the aid effectiveness agenda.* Harare, UNIFEM.

Budlender, D. (2015) *Budget call circulars and gender budget statements in the Asia Pacific: a review.* UN Women.

Budlender, D., Fitzgerald, M.-A., Viniqi, L. & Whittington, S. (2010) *Price of peace: financing for gender equality in post-conflict reconstruction (synthesis report).* New York, United Nations Development Programme.

Budlender, D. & Hewitt, G. (2003) *Engendering budgets: a practitioner's guide to understanding and implementing gender-responsive budgets*. London, Commonwealth Secretariat.

Budlender, D. & Sharp, R. (1998) *How to do a gender-sensitive budget analysis: contemporary research and practice*. Underdale, South Australia, Australian Agency for International Development and Commonwealth Secretariat.

Byanyima, W. (2002) Strengthening parliamentary governance through gender budgeting: the experience of three African countries. Paper presented at the Policy Dialogue on Legislative Development, Brussels, 20–22 November.

Cambridge Education (2006a) *Education Management Information System: a short case study of Ghana. info*Dev.

Cambridge Education (2006b) *Education Management Information System: a short case study of Mozambique. info*Dev.

Cambridge Education (2006c) *Education Management Information System: a short case study of Nigeria. info*Dev.

Cammack, D., McLeod, D., Menocal, A.R. & Christiansen, K. (2006) *Donors and the 'fragile states' agenda: a survey of current thinking and practice*. London, Poverty and Public Policy Group, Overseas Development Institute.

Cancian, F.M. (1992) Feminist science: methodologies that challenge inequality. *Gender & Society*, 6 (4), 623–642.

Carey, P. (2001) Challenging tradition, changing society: the role of women in East Timor's transition to independence. *Revue Lusotopie*, 2001, 255–267.

Casale, D.M. (2012) Indirect taxation and gender equity: evidence from South Africa. *Feminist Economics*, 18 (3), 25–54.

Cassidy, T. (2005) *Education Management Information System (EMIS) development in Latin America and the Caribbean: lessons and challenges*. Washington, DC, Inter-American Development Bank.

Castillejo, C. (2008) *Strengthening women's citizenship in the context of state-building: the experience of Sierra Leone*. Madrid, Fundacion para las relaciones Internacionales y el dialogo exterior (FRIDE).

Castillejo, C. (2011) *Building a state that works for women: integrating gender into post-conflict state building*. Madrid, FRIDE.

CAVR (2005) *Chega! The report of the Commission for Reception, Truth, and Reconciliation Timor-Leste*. Dili, Commission for Reception, Truth, and Reconciliation in Timor-Leste (CAVR).

Celis, K. & Childs, S. (2008) Introduction: the descriptive and substantive representation of women: new directions. *Parliamentary Affairs*, 61 (3), 419–425.

Chandy, L. & Gertz, G. (2011) *Poverty in numbers: the changing state of global poverty from 2005 to 2015*. Washington, DC, Brookings Institution.

Chakraborty, L. (2016) *Asia: a survey of gender budgeting efforts*. Washington, DC, International Monetary Fund. Working Paper WP/16/150.

Charlesworth, H. & Wood, M. (2002) Women and human rights in the rebuilding of East Timor. *Nordic Journal of International Law*, 71 (2), 325–348.

Chinaud, J. (2007) *A gender perspective audit of the 2007 Parliamentary Elections of Timor-Leste*. Dili, UNMIT. Available from: www.etan.org/etanpdf/2007/GENDERAUDITParl07.pdf [accessed 9 December 2016].

Chopra, J. (2002) Building state failure in East Timor. *Development and Change*, 33 (5), 979–1000.

Christie, T.A.L. & Thakur, D. (2016) *Caribbean and Pacific Islands: a survey of gender budgeting efforts*. Washington, DC, International Monetary Fund. Working Paper 16/154.

Cliffe, S. (2003) The Joint Assessment Mission and reconstruction in East Timor. In Fox, J.J. (ed.) *Out of the ashes: destruction and reconstruction of East Timor*. Canberra, ANU Press, pp. 234–242.

CNN (2002) Police patrol riot-hit Timor. CNN World, 4 December. Available from: http://edition.cnn.com/2002/WORLD/asiapcf/southeast/12/04/timor.violence/ [accessed 4 December 2002].

Cochrane, L. (2012) *Report on a program to teach East Timor's children in their mother tongue*. Australia Network. Available from: www.abc.net.au/australianetwork/focus/s3527521.htm [accessed 12 December 2016].

Colclough, C., Rose, P. & Tembon, M. (2000) Gender inequalities in primary schooling: the roles of poverty and adverse cultural practice. *International Journal of Educational Development*, 20, 5–27.

Committee on Economy, Finance and Anti-Corruption (2011) Report and opinion: proposed law no. 42/II: the State Budget for 2011. Dili, CEFAC.

Committee on the Elimination of Discrimination against Women (2009) Concluding observations of the Committee on the Elimination of Discrimination against Women, forty-fourth session, 20 July–7 August 2009 (CEDAW/C/TLS/CO/1).

Commonwealth Women Parliamentarians (2013) Outcomes document to 10th Commonwealth Women's Affairs Ministers' meeting. Parliamentary workshop on 'women's political party caucusing', hosted by the Parliament of Bangladesh, Dhaka, 16 June.

Comunidade dos Países de Lingua Portuguesa (CPLP) (2011) *Plano Estratégico Igualdade de Género e Empoderamento das Mulheres CPLP*. Comunidade dos Países de Lingua Portuguesa.

Conselho de Ministros da Comunidade dos Países de Lingua Portuguesa (2007) XII Reunião Ordinária do Conselho de Ministros da Comunidade dos Países de Lingua Portuguesa – Resolução sobre o Estabelecimento da Assembleia Parlamentar da CPLP, Lisboa, 2 de Novembro de 2007. Conselho de Ministros da Comunidade dos Países de Lingua Portuguesa.

Cooper, J. & Sharp, R. (2007) Engendering accountabilty in government budgets in Mexico. In Griffin-Cohen, M. & Brodie, J. (eds) *Remapping gender in the new global order*. London, Routledge, pp. 205–222.

Costa, M.P.D.J.D. (2009) The voice and experiences of women parliamentarians' caucus in promoting gender equality and women's empowerment in the National Parliament of Timor-Leste. Paper presented at the Second International Women for Peace Conference, Voice for Change, Dili, 5–6 March.

Costa, Monica (2016) Gender-focused institutions in international parliamentary bodies: the case of the women's caucus of the Parliamentary Assembly of the Portuguese-Speaking Countries. *Parliamentary Affairs*, 69 (4), 748–762.

Costa, M. & Sharp, R. (2011) *The Pacific Island countries: Fiji, Papua New Guinea (PNG), Samoa, Solomon Islands, Vanuatu and Tuvalu*. Adelaide, Australia, University of South Australia. Gender-responsive Budgeting in the Asia-Pacific Region Project country profile.

Costa, M. & Sharp, R. (2017) Budgetary policy, gender equality and the politics of change in Timor-Leste. In Niner, S. (ed.) *Women and the politics of gender in post-conflict Timor-Leste: between heaven and earth*. Oxon and New York, Routledge.

Costa, M., Sawer, M. & Sharp, R. (2013) Women acting for women: gender-responsive budgeting in Timor-Leste. *International Feminist Journal of Politics*, 15 (3), 333–352.

Costa, M., Sharp, R. & Austen, S. (2009) Unlocking the potential for gender-sensitive public finances in Timor-Leste. In Chester, L., Johnson, M. & Kriesler, P. (eds) *Heterodox economics' visions: proceedings of the 8th Australian Society of Heterodox Economists Conference 2009.* Sydney, University of New South Wales, Faculty of Commerce & Economics, pp. 151–168.

Costa, M., Sharp, R. & Elson, D. (2009) *Democratic Republic of Timor-Leste.* Adelaide, University of South Australia. Gender-Responsive Budgeting in the Asia-Pacific Region Project country profile.

Costa, M., Sharp, R. & Elson, D. (2010) *Indonesia.* Adelaide, University of South Australia. Gender-Responsive Budgeting in the Asia-Pacific Region Project country profile.

CPLP (2011) *Plano Estratégico Igualdade de Género e Empoderamento das Mulheres CPLP.* CPLP.

Creative Associates International (2012) *School dropout prevention pilot program, pilot design plan: Timor Leste.* Washington, DC, USAID.

Crewe, E. & Young, J. (2002) *Bridging research and policy: context, evidence and links.* London, Overseas Development Institute.

Cristalis, I. & Scott, C. (2005) *Independent women: the story of women's activism in East Timor.* London, Catholic Institute for International Relations.

Crouch, L. (1997) Sustainable EMIS: who is accountable? In Chapman, D., Mahlck, L. & Smulders, A. (eds) *From planning to action: government initiatives for improving school-level practice.* Paris, Pergamon, pp. 211–239.

Crouch, L. & Spratt, J. (2001) EMIS success in South Africa and Guinea: insights from practitioners. *TechKnowLogia*, 3 (1), 36–38.

Cunha, T. (2011) Karau Timor Inan ferik. O fado ou a furia da bufala velha? Um ensaio feminista sobre a poliracionalidade da emancipacao. In Silva, K. & Sousa, L. (eds) *Ita maun alin . . . O livro do irmao mais novo: afinidades antropologicas em torno de Timor-Leste, vol. Coleccao 'a IELTsar se vai ao longe' n. 35.* Lisboa, Instituto de Estudos de Literatura Tradicional, Faculdade de Ciencias Sociais e Humanas, Universidade Nova de Lisboa, pp. 257–275.

da Silva, J. (2013) Impact of sexual violence, 79% of underage girl victims dropout of school. *Jornal Independente*, 17 May. Available from: www.timorhauniandoben. com/2013/05/impact-of-sexual-violence-79-of.html?m=1 [accessed 27 October 2014].

Dahlerup, D. (1988) From a small to a large minority: women in Scandinavian politics. *Scandinavian Political Studies*, 11 (4), 275–298.

Dale, P., Lepuschuetz, L. & Umapathi, N. (2014) Peace, prosperity and safety nets in Timor-Leste: competing priorities or complementary investments? *Asia & the Pacific Policy Studies*, 1 (2), 287–296.

Daley, P. (1999) Gusmão wary of World Bank's policy push. *Sydney Morning Herald*, 10 November. Available from: http://etan.org/et99c/november/7-13/10gusma.htm [accessed 16 November 2014].

Davis, T. (2010) Reconstructing Timor-Leste: the World Bank's trust fund for East Timor. In Leach, M. et al. (eds) *Hatene kona ba/Compreender/Understanding/Mengerti Timor-Leste.* Hawthorn, Vic, Swinburne Press, pp. 196–201.

Department for International Development (2005) *Why we need to work more effectively in fragile states.* London, DFID.

DeVault, M. (1996) Talking back to sociology: distinctive contributions of feminist methodology. *Annual Review of Sociology*, 22, 29–50.

Di John, J. (2008) Conceptualising the causes and consequences of failed states: a critical review of the literature. London, Crisis States Research Centre. Working Paper no. 25.

Di John, J. & Putzel, J. (2009) *Political settlements: issues paper*. Birmingham, Governance and Social Development Resource Centre.

Disch, A., Bezerra, R., Gairdner, D. & Kuroda, K. (2007) *Review of post-crisis multi-donor trust funds country study annexes*. Scanteam/NORAD.

Dobell, G. (1999) World Bank release plan for rebuilding East Timor. *ABC Radio Australia*, 18 November. Available from: www.abc.net.au/pm/stories/s67245.htm [accessed 30 June 2013].

Drysdale, J. (2007) *Sustainable development or resource cursed? An exploration of Timor-Leste's institutional choices*. Doctoral thesis, Fenner School for Environment and Society, Australian National University, Canberra.

Dunn, J. (1996) *Timor: a people betrayed*. Sydney, ABC Books.

Durand, F. (2006) *East Timor: a country at the crossroads of Asia and the Pacific: a geo-historical atlas*. Chiang Mai, Thailand, Silkworm Books.

Earle, L. (2011) *Literature review on the dynamics of social movements in fragile and conflict-affected states*. Birmingham, GSDRC.

East Timor Legal Information Site (2008) Timor-Leste is not a failed nation. *Timor-Leste Legal News*, March (part 4). Available from: www.easttimorlegalinformation.org/Legal_News/March_2008_4.html [accessed 14 November 2010].

Ellis, E. (2009) Power women: Emilia Pires. *Forbes Asia Magazine*, 28 August. Available from: www.forbes.com/global/2009/0907/power-women-09-east-timor-finance-emilia-pires.html [accessed 5 May 2011].

Ellsberg, M., Bradley, C., Egan, A. & Haddad, A. (2008) *Violence against women in Melanesia and East Timor: building on global and regional promising approaches*. Canberra, AusAID.

Elson, D. (1994) Structural adjustment with gender awareness? *Indian Journal of Gender Studies*, 1 (2), 149–167.

Elson, D. (1995) *Male bias in the development process*. Manchester, Manchester University Press.

Elson, D. (2002) Integrating gender into government budgets within a context of economic reform. In Budlender, D. et al. (eds) *Gender budget make cents: understanding gender-responsive budgets*. London, Commonwealth Secretariat, pp. 23–48.

Elson, D. (2004) Engendering government budgets in the context of globalization(s). *International Feminist Journal of Politics*, 6 (4), 623–642.

Elson, D. (2006) *Budgeting for women's rights: monitoring government budgets for compliance with CEDAW*. New York, UNIFEM.

Elson, D., Sharp, R., Ichii, R., Vas Dev, S. & Costa, M. (2009) *The Republic of South Korea*. Adelaide, University of South Australia. Gender-Responsive Budgeting in the Asia-Pacific Region Project country profile.

Eyben, R. (2004) Battles over booklets: gender myths in the British Aid Programme. *IDS Bulletin*, 35 (4), 73–81.

Feijo, R.G. (2016) A long and winding road: a brief history of the idea of a 'Government of National Unity' in Timor-Leste and its current implications. Canberra, State, Society & Governance in Melanesia, ANU. SSGM Discussion Paper 2016/3.

Fernández-Castilla, R.E. (2011) Conducting censuses under challenging situations, crisis and post conflict. Paper presented at the 58th International Statistical Institute World Statistics Congress, Dublin, 21–26 August.

Filmer, D. (2008) Inequalities in education: effects of gender, poverty, orphanhood, and disability. In Tembon, M. & Fort, L. (eds) *Girls' education in the 21st century*. Washington, DC, World Bank, pp. 93–114.

Forum Komunikasi untuk Perempuan Timor Lorosae (Fokupers) (2009) *Women of Timor-Leste in political life: results of project on monitoring and documentation of the 2007 election campaign from a gender perspective*. Dili, Fokupers and UNIFEM.

Franceschet, S. (2004) Explaining social movement outcomes: collective action frames and strategic choices in first- and second-wave feminism in Chile. *Comparative Political Studies*, 37 (5), 499–530.

Franceschet, S. (2011) Gendered institutions and women's substantive representation: female legislators in Argentina and Chile. In Krook, M.L. & Mackay, F. (eds) *Gender, politics and institutions: towards a feminist institutionalism*. Chippenham, Palgrave Macmillan, pp. 58–78.

Franceschet, S. & Piscopo, J.M. (2008) Gender quotas and women's substantive representation: lessons from Argentina. *Politics & Gender*, 4 (3), 393–425.

Franks, E. (1996) Women and resistance in East Timor: 'the centre, as they say, knows itself by the margins'. *Women's Studies International Forum*, 19 (1/2), 155–168.

Fretilin (2007) Fretilin advances women's participation in politics. Media release, 23 June. Available from: http://fretilin-rdtl.blogspot.com.au/2007/06/media-release-fretilin-advances-womens.html [accessed 9 December 2016].

Friedemann-Sanchez, G. (2006) Assets in intrahousehold bargaining among women workers in Columbia's cut flower industry. *Feminist Economics*, 12 (1/2), 247–269.

g7+ (2013) *Note on the fragility spectrum launched in Kinshasa, Democratic Republic of Congo, 2013*. Kishasa, g7+. Available from www.g7plus.org/sites/default/files/resources/g7%2B%2BEnglish%2BFS%2BNote%2BDesign.pdf [accessed 31 March 2107].

Goetz, A.M. (1994) From feminist knowledge to data for development: The bureaucratic management of information on women and development. *IDS Bulletin*, 25 (2), 27–36.

Goetz, A.M. (2007) National women's machinery: state-based institutions to advocate for gender equality. In Rai, S. (ed.) *Mainstreaming gender, democratizing the state? Institutional mechanisms for the advancement of women*. Manchester, Manchester University Press, pp. 69–95.

Gonzalez, K. & Sample, K. (2010) *One size does not fit all: lessons learned from legislative gender commissions and caucuses*. Peru, National Democratic Institute (NDI) and Institute for Democracy and Electoral Assistance (IDEA).

Grace, J. (2011) Parliament with a purpose: holding the Canadian government accountable to women. Paper presented at the Second European Conference on Politics and Gender Central European, Budapest, Hungary, 13–15 January.

GREAT Initiative (2011) Interview of President Ellen Johnson Sirleaf by Mariella Frostrup. *The Great Initiative*, 8 October. Available from: www.thegreatinitiative.org.uk/interview-of-president-ellen-johnson-sirleaf-by-mariella-frostrup/ [accessed 16 November 2014].

Greenlees, D. & Garran, R. (2002) *Deliverance: the inside story of East Timor's fight for freedom*. Crows Nest, NSW, Allen & Unwin.

Grown, C. (2005) *What gender equality advocates should know about taxation*. Cape Town, Association for Women's Rights in Development.

Grown, C. & Valodia, I. (2010) *Taxation and gender equity: a comparative analysis of direct and indirect taxes in developing and developed countries.* London, Routledge.

Grown, C., Bahadur, C., Handbury, J. & Elson, D. (2008) The financial requirements of achieving gender equality and women's empowerment. In Buvinić, M. et al. (eds) *Equality for women: where do we stand on Millennium Development Goal 3?* Washington, DC, World Bank.

Gusmão, X. (2000) *New Year message.* Dili, 31 December. Available from: http://members.pcug.org.au/~wildwood/JanNewYear.htm [accessed 18 September 2013].

Gusmão, X. (2012) Address to g7+ High-Level Side Event of the United Nations General Assembly, New York, 23 September.

Gusmão, X. (2013) Keynote address to Leadership, Innovation and Partnership for Green/Blue Pacific Economies, Pacific Islands Development Forum, Nadi, Fiji, 5 August.

Hall, N. (2009) East Timorese women challenge domestic violence. *Australian Journal of Political Science,* 44 (2), 309–325.

Hall, N. & True, J. (2009) Gender mainstreaming in a post-conflict state: toward democratic peace in Timor-Leste? In D'Costa, B. & Lee-Koo, K. (eds) *Gender and global politics in the Asia-Pacific.* New York, Palgrave Macmillan, pp. 159–174.

Hanushek, E.A. (2008) Schooling, gender equity, and economic outcomes. In Tembon, M. & Fort, L. (eds), *Girls' education in the 21st century: gender equality, empowerment, and economic growth.* Washington, DC, World Bank, pp. 23–39.

Harcourt, W. (2009a) Gender and fragility: policy responses. Paper presented at the Moving Towards the European Report on Development Conference, Florence, Italy, 21–23 June.

Harcourt, W. (2009b) *Literature review on gender and fragility.* European Report on Development.

Hassim, S. (2005) Voices, hierarchies and spaces: reconfiguring the women's movement in democratic South Africa. *Politikon,* 32 (2), 175–193.

Heimans, J. (2002) *Strengthening participation in public expenditure management: policy recommendations for key stakeholders.* OECD Development Centre. Policy Brief 22.

Herz, B. (2006) *Educating girls in South Asia: promising approaches.* Kathamandu, United Nations Children' Fund and United Nations Girls' Education Initiative.

Herz, B. & Sperling, G.B. (2004) *What works in girls' education: evidence and policies from developing world.* New York, Council on Foreign Relations.

Hewitt, G. & Mukhopadhyay, T. (2002) Promoting gender equality through public expenditure. In Budlender, D. et al. (eds) *Gender budgets make cents: understanding gender budgets.* London, Commonwealth Secretariat, pp. 49–82.

Hill, H. (1978) *Fretilin: the origins, ideologies and strategies of a nationalist movement in East Timor.* Masters thesis, Monash University.

Hill, H. (2006) Stand up, the real Mr Alkatiri. *The Age,* 1 June. Available from: www.theage.com.au/news/opinion/stand-up-the-real-mr-alkatiri/2006/05/31/1148956413913.html?page=fullpage [accessed 29 March 2011].

Himmelweit, S. (2002) Making visible the hidden economy: the case for gender-impact analysis of economic policy. *Feminist Economics,* 8 (1), 49–70.

Himmelweit, S. (2008) Policy on care: a help or a hindrance to gender equality? In Scott, J., Dex, S. & Joshi, H. (eds), *Women and employment: changing lives and new challenges.* Cheltenham, Edward Elgar Publishing, pp. 347–368.

Hofbauer, H. (2002) Mexico: collaborating with a range of actors. In Budlender, D. & Hewitt, G. (eds) *Gender budgets make more cents: country studies and good practice.* London, Commonwealth Secretariat, pp. 84–97.

Hua, H. (2011) *EMIS development in a new era*. Available from: https://edutechdebate. org/education-management-information-systems/emis-development-in-a-new-era/ [accessed 13 October 2014].

Human Rights Watch (2017) *World Development Report 2017, Events of 2016*. New York, Human Rights Watch.

Hunt, J. (2008) *Local NGOs in national development: the case of East Timor*. Doctoral thesis, RMIT University, Melbourne.

Hunt, J. & Wigglesworth, A. (2014) Civil society in transition. In Loney, H., da Silva, A.B., Mendes, N.C., Ximenes, A.C. & Fernandes, C. (eds) Proceedings of the Understanding Timor-Leste 2013 Conference, National University of Timor-Lorosa'e (UNTL), Dili, Timor-Leste, 15–16 July 2013. Hawthorn, Vic, Swinburne Press, pp. 251–256.

Husain, M. (2013) *Malala: the girl who was shot for going to school. BBC News*, 7 October. Available from: www.bbc.co.uk/news/magazine-24379018 [accessed 26 November 2013].

IBP (2012) *Open budget survey 2012*. Washington, DC, International Budget Partnership.

IBP (2016) *Open budget survey 2015:* Timor-Leste, International Budget Partnership.

ICRC (2011) *A sixteen-country study: health care in danger*. Geneva, International Committee of the Red Cross.

IMF (2005) *Democratic Republic of Timor-Leste: 2005 Article IV Consultation – Staff Report; Public Information Notice on the Executive Board Discussion; and statement by the Executive Director for the Democratic Republic of Timor-Leste*. Country Report No. 05/245. International Monetary Fund.

IMF (2010) *Democratic Republic of Timor-Leste: public financial management performance report 10/341*. Dili, International Monetary Fund.

IMF (2012) *Angola: 2012 Article IV consultation and post-program monitoring*. Country Report No. 12/215. International Monetary Fund.

IMF (2013) *Guinea-Bissau staff report for the 2013 Article IV consultation: key issues*. International Monetary Fund.

IMF (2016) *2016 Article IV Consultation – Press Release Staff Report; and Statement by the Executive Director for Timor-Leste*. Country Report No. 16/183. International Monetary Fund.

Ingram, S. (2012) *Building the wrong peace: re-viewing the United Nations Transitional Administration in East Timor through a political settlement lens*. Canberra, State, Society and Governance in Melanesia Program, ANU College of Asia & the Pacific. SSGM Discussion Paper 2012/4.

Ingram, S. & Maia, H. (2015) *Timor-Leste's new way of 'doing politics' . . . and will it last?* Canberra, State, Society and Governance in Melanesia, ANU. In Brief 2015/41.

IPU (2015) 'Women in National Parliaments' (situation as of 1 January). Inter-Parliamentary Union. Available from: www.ipu.org/wmn-e/arc/classif010115.htm [accessed 14 October 2015].

IRIN News (2012) Analysis: Latest Coup another Setback for Guinea-Bissau. Available from: www.irinnews.org/report/95340/analysis-latest-coup-another-setback-for-guinea-bissau [accessed 19 December 2015].

Jennings, K.M. (2010) *Gender and post-conflict statebuilding*. New York, Ralph Bunche Institute for International Studies, City University of New York.

Jhamb, B. & Sinha, N. (2010) *Millennium Development Goals & gender budgeting: where does India stand?* New Delhi, Centre for Budget and Governance Accountability.

Joan B. Kroc Institute (2008) *Crafting human security in an insecure world*. San Diego, Joan B. Kroc Institute, University of San Diego.

Jolliffe, J. (1978) *East Timor, nationalism and colonialism.* Saint Lucia, Queensland, University of Queensland Press.

Jones, H., Jones, N., Shaxson, L. & Walker, D. (2013) *Knowledge, policy and power in international development: a practical framework for improving policy.* London, Overseas Development Institute.

Jones, N., Jones, H. & Walsh, C. (2008) *Political science? Strengthening science–policy dialogue in developing countries.* London, Overseas Development Institute.

Jornal São Tomé (2010) Jornadas da Rede das Mulheres da CPLP – São Tomé e Príncipe: Resolução apela a uma maior intervenção das mulheres. *Jornal São Tomé.* Available from: www.jornal.st/noticias.php?noticia=7758 [accessed 2 March 2014].

Joshi, S. & Naidu, S. (2007) Agenda item 4: Paper 12, Advancing the process of 'gender budgeting' in the Pacific, SPC/Women 10/Working Paper 12. Paper presented at the 10th Triennial Conference of Pacific Women, Pacific Women, Pacific Plan: Stepping Up the Pace to 2010, Noumea, New Caledonia, 27–31 May.

Joshi, V. (2005) *Building opportunities: women's organising, militarism and the United Nations Transitional Administration in East Timor.* Doctoral thesis, Department of Women's Studies, Clark University, Worcester, MA.

Justice System Monitoring Programme (2004) *Access to justice for women victims.* Dili, JSMP.

Kabeer, N. & Natali, L. (2013) *Gender equality and economic growth: is there a win–win?* Brighton, Institute of Development Studies. Working Paper 417/2013.

Kaltenborn-Stachau, H. von (2008) *The missing link: fostering positive citizen–state relations in post-conflict environments.* New York, Communication for Governance and Accountability Program, World Bank.

Kantola, J. (2010) *Gender and the European Union.* Hamphshire and New York, Palgrave Macmillan.

Karamessini, M. & Rubery, J. (eds) (2013) *Women and austerity: the economic crisis and the future for gender equality.* Oxon, Routledge.

Keck, M.E. & Sikkink, K. (1998) *Activists beyond borders: advocacy networks in international politics.* New York, Cornell University.

Keeley, J. & Scoones, I. (1999) *Understanding environmental policy processes: a review.* Brighton, Institute of Development Studies. Working paper 89.

Khan, Z. (2009) Gender responsive budgeting. Paper presented at the Financial Markets, Adverse Shocks and Policy Responses in Fragile Countries Conference, Accra, Ghana, 21–23 May.

Kingsbury, D. & Leach, M. (2007) Introduction. In Kingsbury, D. & Leach, M. (eds) *East Timor: beyond independence.* Melbourne, Monash University Press, pp. 1–18.

Kirk, J. (2006) *Education in emergencies: the gender implications. Advocacy brief.* Bangkok, UNESCO.

Kirk, J. (2008) Addressing gender disparities in education in contexts of crisis, postcrisis, and state fragility. In Tembon, M. & Fort, L. (eds) *Girls' education in the 21st century.* Washington, DC, World Bank, pp. 153–180.

Koch, J. (2008) *Does gender matter in fragile states?* Copenhagen, Denmark, Danish Institute for International Studies.

Kolovich, L. & Shibuya, S. (2016) *Middle East and Central Asia: a survey of gender budgeting efforts.* Washington, DC, IMF. Working Paper WP/16/151.

Langan, D. & Morton, M. (2009) Reflecting on community/academic 'collaboration': the challenge of 'doing' feminist participatory action research. *Action Research*, 7 (2), 165–184.

La'o Hamutuk (2008) Submission to Commission C: National Parliament Democratic Republic of Timor-Leste regarding tax reform law (25 March 2008). Dili, La'o Hamutuk (Timor-Leste Institute for Development Monitoring and Analysis). Available from: www.laohamutuk.org/misc/AMPGovt/tax/LHTaxEn.pdf [accessed 16 November 2014].

La'o Hamutuk (2009) Submission to Committee C, National Parliament, Democratic Republic of Timor-Leste from La'o Hamutuk regarding the proposed RDTL General State Budget for 2010, 4 November 2009. Dili, La'o Hamutuk (Timor-Leste Institute for Development Monitoring and Analysis). Available from: www. laohamutuk.org/econ/OGE10/sub/LHSubPNComCOGE10En.pdf [accessed 16 November 2014].

La'o Hamutuk (2013) Presidential concerns about the State Budget. *La'o Hamutuk blog*, 24 May. Available from: http://laohamutuk.blogspot.com.au/2013/05/presidential-concerns-about-state-budget.html [accessed 24 May 2013].

La'o Hamutuk (2014) 2013 General State Budget – Orsamentu Jeral Estadu 2013. *La'o Hamutuk*, updated 2 December. Available from: www.laohamutuk.org/econ/OGE13/12OGE13.htm [accessed 23 September 2016].

La'o Hamutuk (2016a) 2014 General State Budget – Orsamentu Jeral Estadu 2014. *La'o Hamutuk*, updated 2 February 2016. Available from: www.laohamutuk.org/econ/OGE14/13OGE14.htm [accessed 23 September 2016].

La'o Hamutuk (2016b) *Submission to Timor-Leste National Parliament on the Proposed General State Budget for 2017* (7 November 2016). Dili, La'o Hamutuk.

Leach, M. (2009) The 2007 presidential and parliamentary elections in Timor-Leste. *Australian Journal of Politics and History*, 55 (2), 219–232.

Lewin, K. (2015a) *Educational access, equity, and development: Planning to make rights realities, Fundamentals of Educational Planning*. Paris, UNESCO.

Lewin, K. (2015b) Are the Sustainable Development Goals sustainable? (13 September 2015). *The Education and Development Forum*. Available from: www.ukfiet.org/2015/are-the-sustainable-development-goals-sustainable/ [accessed 8 December 2016].

Lilja, N. & Bellon, M. (2008) Some common questions about participatory research: a review of the literature. *Development in Practice*, 18 (4/5), 479–488.

Lindquist, E.A. (2001) *Discerning policy influence: framework for a strategic evaluation of IDRC-supported research*. Ottawa, International Development Research Centre.

Lusa (2014) Portugal insiste na necessidade de braço executivo da CPLP para a Igualdade. *Notícias ao Minuto*, 13 February. Available from: http://noticias.sapo.tl/portugues/lusa/artigo/17302805.html [accessed 16 November 2014].

McBride, D. & Mazur, A. (2011) *Gender machineries worldwide (background paper prepared for the World Development Report 2012)*. Nordic Trust Fund for Human Rights of the World Bank. Available from http://econ.worldbank.org/WBSITE/EXTERNAL/EXTDEC/EXTRESEARCH/EXTWDRS/EXTWDR2012/0,,contentMDK:22999750~menuPK:8154981~pagePK:64167689~piPK:64167673~theSitePK:7778063,00.html [accessed 31 March 2017].

Mackay, F. (2009) Institutionalising 'new politics' in post devolution Scotland: 'nested newness' and the gendered limits of change. Paper presented at the Political Science Association Annual Conference (Panel: Feminist Institutionalism: The Way Forward?), Manchester, 7–9 April.

Mackay, F. (2014) Nested newness, institutional innovation, and the gendered limits of change *Politics & Gender*, 4 (10), 549–571.

McKechnie, A. (2013) *Managing natural resource revenues: the Timor-Leste Petroleum Fund*. London, ODI.

MacKinnon, I. (2008) East Timor president recounts assassination attempt. *The Guardian*, 19 March. Available from: www.guardian.co.uk/world/2008/mar/19/easttimor [accessed 30 June 2013].

Mcloughlin, C. (2009) *Topic guide on fragile states*. London, Department for International Development Governance and Social Development Resource Centre.

McMahon, C. (2014) Recasting Transnationalism through Performance – Theatre Festivals in Cape Verde, Mozambique and Brazil, New York and Houndmills, Palgrave Macmillan.

MacQueen, N. (2003) A community of illusions? Portugal, the CPLP and peacemaking in Guiné-Bissau. *International Peacekeeping*, 10 (2), 2–26.

Maddison, S. & Partridge, E. (2007) *How well does Australian democracy serve Australian women?* Canberra, Australian National University. Democratic Audit of Australia Report No. 8.

Martin, M. & Walker, J. (2015) *Financing the sustainable development goals: lessons from government spending on the MDGs 2015 Report*. Government Spending Watch, Development Finance International and Oxfam International.

Merry, S. (2011) Measuring the world: indicators, human rights, and global governance. *Current Anthropology*, 52 (3), 83–95.

Ministros Responsáveis pela Igualdade de Género da CPLP (2014) *Declaração de Maputo – III Reunião de Ministros/as Responsáveis pela Igualdade de Género da CPLP*. Available from: www.cplp.org/id-316.aspx?Action=1&NewsId=3123&M=NewsV2&PID=304 [accessed 16 November 2014].

Mirwobe, S.E. (2013) Macro, mezzo and micro-level analysis of gender responsive budgeting in Rwanda. *Journal of Development and Agricultural Economics*, 5 (3), 71–83.

MoE, MS, MSS, SEPI & UNTL (2010) *Feto foin sai/husik eskola tamba hetan isin rua/gravida, Resultado peskiza Outobru 2010, Dadus husi distritu 3 (Liquiça, Ainaro, Ermera)*. Dili, Timor-Leste Government.

Molas-Gallart, J., Tang, P. & Morrow, S. (2000) Grant funding. Assessing the non-academic impact of grant-funded socio-economic research: Results from a pilot study. *Research Evaluation*, 9(3), 171–182.

Montell, F. (1999) Focus group interviews: a new feminist method. *NWSA Journal*, 11 (1), 44–71.

Moser, A. (2007) *Gender and indicators – overview report*. Brighton, Institute of Development Studies.

Moxham, B. (2008) *State-making and the post-conflict city: integration in Dili, disintegration in Timor-Leste*. London, Development Studies Institute, London School of Economics and Political Science. Working Paper 32.

Mukunda, J. (2011) *Progress towards achieving gender responsive budget in Rwanda: a CSO response to sectoral GB statements for the FY 2011/12*. Rwanda Civil Society Platform. Available from www.rcsprwanda.org/IMG/pdf/Final_GB_statements_Asessment_Report_1_.pdf [accessed 31 March 2017].

Myrttinen, H. (2009) *Poster boys no more: gender and security sector reform in Timor-Leste*. Geneva, Geneva Centre for the Democratic Control of Armed Forces.

National Congress for the Reconstruction of East Timor (2007) CNRT defends women's rights. Media release, 21 June 2007. Available from: www.easttimorlegalinformation.org/Parliamentary_Election_2007/Page_2a.html [accessed 20 April 2011].

National Parliament Committee on Public Finances (2013) *Report and opinion of initial assessment of proposed law 2/III (1): general state budget for 2013*. Dili, Parlamento Nacional.

Nay, O. (2012) Fragile and failed states: critical perspectives on conceptual hybrids or fragile and failed state studies: recent perspectives on conceptual deficiencies and pitfalls. Paper presented at the International Political Science Association Madrid Conference, Reshaping Power, Shifting Boundaries, Madrid, 8–12 July.

Nelson, J. (1995) Feminism and economics. *Journal of Economic Perspectives*, 9 (2), 131–148.

Niner, S. (2009) *Xanana: leader of the struggle for independent Timor-Leste.* North Melbourne, Australian Scholarship Publishing.

Niner, S. (2011) Hakat klot, narrow steps: negotiating gender in post-conflict Timor-Leste. *International Feminist Journal of Politics*, 13 (3), 413–435.

Niner, S. (2016) Effects and affects: women in the post-conflict moment in Timor-Leste: an application of V. Spike Peterson's 'Gendering insecurities, informalization and war economies'. In Harcourt, W. (ed.) *The Palgrave handbook of gender and development: critical engagements in feminist theory and practice.* Houndmills, Palgrave Macmillan, pp. 495–512.

Nixon, R. (2011) Timor-Leste: change, stagnation, and questions of political economy. In Duncan, R. (ed.) *The political economy of economic reform in the Pacific.* Mandaluyong, The Philippines, ADB Pacific Studies Series, pp. 227–264.

Norris, P. (2006) Political protest in fragile states. Paper presented at the International Political Science Association World Congress, Fukuoka, Japan, 13 July.

O Pais Online (2011) Lei contra a violência doméstica já é um facto. *O Pais Online*, 27 June. Available from: www.opais.net/pt/opais/?det=21869&id=1929&mid= [accessed 4 April 2014].

O'Connell, H. (2011) What are the opportunities to promote gender equity and equality in conflict-affected and fragile states? Insights from a review of evidence. *Gender & Development*, 19 (3), 455–466.

OECD (2013) *Gender and statebuilding in fragile and conflict-affected states.* Paris, OECD Publishing.

OECD (2015) *States of fragility 2015: meeting post-2015 ambitions.* Paris, OECD Publishing.

O'Hagan, A. (2015) Favourable conditions for the adoption and implementation of gender budgeting: insights from comparative analysis. *Politica Economica/Journal of Economic Policy*, 31 (2), 233–252.

Okumu, P. (2011) *Democracy, aid and disenabling environment: motivation and impact of disenabling environment on development work in Africa, an analysis based on studies and discussions in 40 African countries.* Nairobi, Africa Civil Society Platform on Principled Partnership.

Oosterom, M. (2009) Fragility at the local level: challenges to building local state–citizen relations in fragile settings. Paper presented at the Local Governance in Fragile Settings Workshop, The Hague, November.

Ospina, S. (2006a) *Participation of women in politics and decision making in Timor-Leste: a recent history.* Dili, UNIFEM.

Ospina, S. (2006b) *A review and evaluation of gender-related activities of UN peacekeeping operations and their impact on gender relations in Timor-Leste.* New York, Department of Peacekeeping Operations of the United Nations.

Ouattara, M., Sylla, K., Diallo, S.S. & Ouattara, Y. (2007) A new research contract between economic research and decision-makers: lessons from Côte D'Ivoire. In Ayuk, E. & Marouani, M. (eds) *Policy paradox in Africa: strengthening links between economic research and policymaking.* Ottawa, International Development Research Centre, pp. 263–276.

Paantjens, M. (2009) *Establishing the linkages between gender and fragility.* The Hague, Clingendael (Netherlands Institute of International Relations). Working paper 1.3.

Paffenholz, T. (2009) *Summary of results for a comparative research project: civil society and peacebuilding.* Geneva, Centre on Conflict, Development and Peacebuilding. Working Paper 4.

Paffenholz, T. (2015) Inclusive politics: lessons from and for the New Deal. *Journal of Peacebuilding & Development,* 10 (1), 84–89.

Palmieri, S. (2012) *A global review of good practice: gender-sensitive parliaments.* Geneva, Inter-Parliamentary Union.

Parlamento de Timor-Leste (2006a) *Lei n. 6/2006 de 28 de Dezembro – Lei Eleitoral para o Parlamento Nacional (Law on the election of the National Parliament).* Dili, República Democrática de Timor-Leste.

Parlamento de Timor-Leste (2006b) *Resolução do Parlamento Nacional n. 6/2006 que Aprova a Constituição do Grupo das Mulheres Parlamentares Timorenses.* Dili, República Democrática de Timor-Leste.

Parlamento de Timor-Leste (2007) *Resolução do Parlamento Nacional No.16/2007 de 24 de Outubro Aprova a Criação do Grupo das Mulheres Parlamentares Timorenses.* Dili, República Democrática de Timor-Leste.

Parlamento de Timor-Leste (2009) *Agenda n. 223/II – Reuniaun Plenaria (14 de Julho de 2009).* Dili, Timor-Leste Parlamento Nacional.

Parlamento de Timor-Leste (2010) *Resolução do Parlamento Nacional n. 12/2010 de 19 de Maio relativa à Preparação de um Orçamento que tenha em consideração a Igualdade de Género.* Dili, República Democrática de Timor-Leste.

Parlamento de Timor-Leste (2011) *Segunda Alteracao a Lei n. 6/2006, de 28 de Dezembro (Lei Eleitoral para o Parlamento Nacional).* Dili, República Democrática de Timor-Leste.

Parlamento de Timor-Leste Comissão de Economia Finanças e Anti-Corrupção (2009) *Relatório e parecer proposta de lei n.o 29/II Orçamento Geral do Estado para 2010.* Dili, Timor-Leste National Parliament.

Peace Women Across the Globe (2011) Maria Domingas Fernandes. *Peace Women Across the Globe.* Available from: www.1000peacewomen.org/eng/friedensfrauen_biographien_gefunden.php?WomenID=496 [accessed 10 June 2011].

Pearce, J. (2007) *Violence, power and participation: building citizenship in contexts of chronic violence.* Brighton, Institute of Development Studies. Working Paper 274.

Pearson, R. & Sweetman, C. (2010) Introduction. *Gender & Development,* 18 (2), 165–177.

Pérez Fragoso, L. & Rodríguez Enríquez, C. (2016) *Western hemisphere: a survey of gender budgeting efforts.* Washington, DC, IMF. Working Paper 16/153.

Pires, M. (2004) *Enhancing women's participation in electoral processes in post conflict countries: experiences from East Timor.* Glen Cove, NY, United Nations.

Pires, M. & Scott, C. (1998) East Timorese women: the feminine face of resistance. In Retboll, T. (ed.) *East Timor: occupation and resistance.* Copenhagen, International Work Group for Indigenous Affairs, pp. 141–152.

Piscopo, J.M. (2011) Committed to changing gender policy: female elites' caucus formation and advocacy work in Mexico. Paper presented at the European Conference on Politics and Gender, Budapest, January.

Porter, D. & Rab, H. (2010) *Timor-Leste's recovery from the 2006 crisis: some lessons.* Washington, DC, World Bank.

Porter, E. (2007) *Peacebuilding: women in international perspective*. Abingdon, Oxon, Routledge.

Porter, E. (2013) Rethinking women's empowerment. *Journal of Peacebuilding & Development*, 8 (1), 1–14.

Porter, T. (1996) *Trust in numbers: the pursuit of objectivity in science and public life*. Princeton, NJ, Princeton University Press.

Powell, M. (2006) *Rethinking Education Management Information Systems: lessons from and options for less developed countries*. Washington, DC, *InfoDev*. Working Paper 6.

PST, UNDERTIM, Fretilin, CNRT, PD, PSD/ASDT, PR, PMD, PDC, PUN, PDRT & PNT (2007) Women's political platform of women's organizations in political parties for the Parliamentary Elections 2007. Available from: www.unifem.org/attachments/stories/200707_TimorLeste_WomensPoliticalPlatform.pdf [accessed 28 May 2007].

Putzel, J. & Di John, J. (2012) *Meeting the challenge of crisis states*. London, Crisis States Research Centre, London School of Economics and Political Science.

Rai, S.M. (1996) Women and the state in the third world: some issues for debate. In Rai, S.M. & Lievesley, G. (eds), *Women and the state: international perpectives*. Exeter, Taylor & Francis, pp. 5–22.

Razavi, S. (2016) The 2030 Agenda: challenges of implementation to attain gender equality and women's rights. *Gender & Development*, 24 (1), 25–41.

Rede das Mulheres da Assembleia Parlamentar da CPLP (2010) *Estatuto da Rede de Mulheres da Assembleia Parlamentar da CPLP*. Lisbon, Rede das Mulheres.

Rede das Mulheres da Assembleia Parlamentar da CPLP (2011) *Relatório Anual 2009–2010*. Paper presented by the Rede das Mulheres da Assembleia Parlamentar da CPLP at the III Assembleia Parlamentar da CPLP, Dili.

Rede Feto (2008) Commemoration of International Women's Day 2008. *Rede Feto*. Available from: http://redefeto.blogspot.com.au/2008/01/commemoration-of-international-womens.html [accessed 22 April 2014].

Rede Feto Timor-Leste (2008) *Advocacy programme activities 2006–2007*. Dili, Rede Feto. Available from: http://redefeto.blogspot.com/2009/10/advocacy-programme-activities-2006-2007.html [accessed 16 November 2014].

Redondo, J. (2008) A Importancia das aliancas assentes nas similitudes linguisticas: O caso da CPLP. Working Papers Europa, Seguranca e Migracoes. Porto, Centro de Estudos da Populacao, Economia e Sociedade (CEPESE).

Rees, S., Silove, D., Verdial, T., Tam, N., Savio, E., Fonseca, Z., Thorpe, R., Liddell, B., Zwi, A., Tay, K., Brooks, R. & Steel, Z. (2013) Intermittent explosive disorder amongst women in conflict-affected Timor-Leste: associations with human rights trauma, ongoing violence, poverty, and injustice. *PLOS ONE*, 8 (8), 1–7.

Reid, C. (2004) Advancing women's social justice agendas: a feminist action research framework. *International Journal of Qualitative Methods*, 3 (3), article 1.

República Democrática de Timor-Leste (2011) Resolução do governo n. 27/2011 de 14 de Setembro que aprova o estabelecimento do mecanismo de grupo de trabalho para o género a nivel nacional e distrital. *Jornal da Republica*, 1 (34), pp. 5142–4.

Reyes, C. (2002) Institutionalizing a gender and development initiative in the Philippines. In Judd, K. (ed.) *Gender budget initiatives: strategies, concepts and experiences*. New York, UNIFEM, pp. 140–146.

Rocha Menocal, A. & Sharma, B. (2008) *Joint evaluation of citizens' voice and accountability: synthesis report*. London, DFID.

Rodrigues, I.M. (2011) Statement: review of the implementation of the BPfA, sharing of experiences and good practices, with a view to overcoming remaining obstacles and new challenges. Paper presented at the 55th Session of the Commission on the Status of Women, United Nations, New York, 24 February.

Roque, R. (2010) The unruly island: colonialism's predicament in the late nintheenth-century East Timor. *Portuguese Literary and Cultural Studies*, 17 (18), 303–330.

Roque, R. (2011) Os Portuguese e os reinos de Timor no seculo XIX. *Oriente*, 20, 91–111.

Roughneen, S. (2012) Gusmao set to return as Timor-Leste PM. *The Irrawaddy*, 11 July. Available from: www.irrawaddy.com/news/asia/gusmao-set-to-return-as-timor-leste-pm.html [accessed 14 December 2016].

Roynestad, E. (2003) *Peace agreements as a means for promoting gender equality and ensuring participation of women*. Ottawa, UNDAW.

Ruak, T.M. (2012) The President's address on the inauguration of 5th Constitutional Government. *East Timor Law and Justice Bulletin*, 10 August. Available from: www.easttimorlawandjusticebulletin.com/2012/08/the-presidents-address-on-inauguration.html [accessed 27 October 2014].

Ruak, T.M. (2016) *Message to the national parliament on the promulgation of the amending general state budget for 2016*. Available from: https://www.laohamutuk.org/econ/OGE16/Ret/PresMsgPN8Aug2016En.pdf [accessed 8 December 2016].

Rugkhla, O. & Alvarado, M. (2016) *UN Women costing evidence improves essential services for women experiencing violence in Indonesia, Lao PDR, Timor-Leste and Viet Nam*. UN Women Asia and the Pacific. Available from: http://asiapacific.unwomen.org/en/news-and-events/stories/2016/06/un-women-costing-tools-have-led-to-improved-essential-services [accessed 25 September 2016].

Ryan, J. (1999) *Assessing the impact of rice policy changes in Viet Nam and the contribution of policy research*. Washington, DC, International Food Policy Research Institute. Impact Assessment Discussion Paper 8.

Ryan, J. (2002) Synthesis report of workshop on assessing the impact of policy-oriented social science research in Scheveningen, The Netherlands, 12–13 November, 2001. Washington, DC, International Food Policy Research Institute. Impact Assessment Discussion Paper 15.

SADC (2014) *SADC guidelines on gender-responsive budgeting*. Southern African Development Community. Available from https://www.sadc.int/files/8914/4681/2781/SADC_GUIDELINES_ON_GENDER_RESPONSIVE_BUDGETING.pdf [accessed 31 March 2017].

Saldanha, J.M. (2008) Anatomy of political parties in Timor-Leste. In Rich, R., Hambly, L. & Morgan, M. (eds), *Political parties in the Pacific Islands*. Canberra, ANU E Press, pp. 69–81.

São Tomé e Príncipe Assembleia National (2009) Assembleia Nacional – Resolução n. 74/VIII/2009: Medidas de Reforço da Participação Cívica e Política das Mulheres. *São Tomé e Príncipe Diário da República*, 62, 935–936.

Sawer, M. (1990) *Sisters in suits: women and public policy in Australia*. Sydney, Allen & Unwin.

Sawer, M. (2002) Australia: the mandarin approach to gender budgets. In Budlender, D. & Hewitt, G. (eds) *Gender budgets make more cents: country studies and good practice*. London, Commonwealth Secretariat, pp. 43–64.

Sawer, M. (2006) 'When women support women . . .' EMILY's list and the substantive representation of women in Australia. In Sawer, M., Tremblay, M. & Trimble, L. (eds) *Representing women in parliament: a comparative study*. London, Routledge, pp. 103–119.

Sawer, M. (2010) Women and elections. In LeDuc, L., Niemi, R. & Norris, P. (eds) *Comparing democracies 3: elections and voting in the 21st century*. Thousand Oaks, CA, Sage, pp. 202–221.

Sawer, M. (2011a) The political architecture of gender equality. Paper presented at the Gender Consortium, Flinders University, Adelaide, 7 October.

Sawer, M. (2011b) Women and representation revisited: institutional supports for the representation of women. Australian National University, unpublished.

Sawer, M. (2012) What makes the substantive representation of women possible in a Westminster parliament? The story of RU486 in Australia. *International Political Science Review*, 33 (3), 319–335.

Sawer, M. (2014) Beyond numbers: the role of specialised parliamentary bodies in promoting gender equality. Paper presented at the Australasian Study of Parliament Group Conference 2014, Sydney, 3 October 2014.

Sawer, M. and Turner, A. (2016) Specialised Parliamentary Bodies: Their Role and Relevance to Women's Movement Repertoire. *Parliamentary Affairs*, 69, 763–777.

Scambary, J. (2015) In search of white elephants: the political economy of resource income expenditure in East Timor. *Critical Asian Studies*, 47 (2), 283–308.

Semana (2015) Primeiro diário caboverdiano em linha, Mulheres Parlamentares de Cabo Verde capacitam colegas. Available from http://asemana.publ.cv/spip.php/ IMG/ spip.php?article109460&ak=1 [accessed 18 December 2015].

Shah, R. (2012) Goodbye conflict, hello development? Curriculum reform in Timor-Leste. *International Journal of Educational Development*, 32 (1), 31–38.

Sharp, R. (2000) *The economics and politics of auditing government budgets for their impacts*. Adelaide, Hawke Institute, University of South Australia. Working Paper No. 3.

Sharp, R. (2003a) *Budgeting for equity: gender budget initiatives within a framework of performance-oriented budgeting*. New York, UNIFEM.

Sharp, R. (2003b) Government budgets: integrating a gender perspective. In Argyrous, G. & Stilwell, F. (eds) *Economics as a social science*. 2nd edn. Annadale, Pluto Press, pp. 243–246.

Sharp, R. & Broomhill, R. (1990) Women and government budgets. *Australian Journal of Social Issues*, 25 (1), 1–14.

Sharp, R. & Broomhill, R. (1999) Australia's role in the development of gender-sensitive budgets. Paper presented at the UNDP and UNIFEM Workshop on Pro-Poor, Gender and Environment-Sensitive Budgets, New York, 28–30 June.

Sharp, R. & Broomhill, R. (2002) Budgeting for equality: the Australian experience. *Feminist Economics*, 8 (1), 25–47.

Sharp, R. & Broomhill, R. (2013) *A case study of Australia's gender budget statements*. London, Commonwealth Secretariat.

Sharp, R. & Costa, M. (2011) *Commonwealth of Australia*. Adelaide, University of South Australia. Gender-Responsive Budgeting in the Asia-Pacific Region Project country profile.

Sharp, R. & Elson, D. (2008) Improving budgets: a framework for assessing gender-responsive budget initiatives. In Mastuti, S. (ed), *Audit Gender Terhadap Anggaran*. Jakarta, CiBa.

Sharp, R., Elson, D. & Costa, M. (2010) *Islamic Republic of Pakistan*. Adelaide, University of South Australia. Gender-Responsive Budgeting in the Asia-Pacific Region Project country profile.

Sharp, R., Elson, D., Costa, M. & Vas Dev, S. (2009). *Federal Democratic Republic of Nepal.* Adelaide, University of South Australia. Gender-Responsive Budgeting in the Asia-Pacific Region Project country profile.

Sharp, R., Elson, D., Costa, M. & Vas Dev, S. (2011) *Republic of the Philippines.* Adelaide, University of South Australia. Gender-Responsive Budgeting in the Asia-Pacific Region Project country profile.

Sharp, R., Vas Dev, S., Elson, D. & Costa, M. (2009) *The Republic of the Marshall Islands.* Adelaide, University of South Australia. Gender-Responsive Budgeting in the Asia-Pacific Region Project country profile.

Siapno, J. (2006) Bitter taste of victory. *Inside Indonesia,* 8 (October–December).

Siapno, J. (2008) Whispered confidences: articulating the female in the PNTL (police) and the F-FDTL (military) in Timor Leste. *International Institute for Asian Studies Newsletter,* 48, 7–8.

Siddique, K. (2013) *A case study of gender responsive budgeting in Bangladesh, research report.* London, Commonwealth Secretariat.

Simão, Y. (2011) Ministra pede orçamento. *Observe,* 12 May. Available from: www. observe.ufba.br/noticias/exibir/263 [accessed 16 November 2014].

Smith, S. (2014) The continuum of women's activism in Timor-Leste in the context of UN peacebuilding. In Loney, H., Silva, A.B., Canas Mendes, N., Costa Ximenes, A. & Fernandes, C. (eds) *Understanding Timor-Leste 2013 Volume II.* Hawthorn, Vic, Swinburne Press, pp.87–93.

Soares, A. & Lauvigne, M. (2009) *Are girls and boys equally represented in education? A gender assessment.* Dili, Ministry of Education and UNIFEM.

Soetjipto, A (2014) *The role of the parliamentary women's caucus in promoting women's participation and representation: A case study in Indonesia and Timor-Leste.* Jakarta, Kemitraan Bagi Pembaruan Tata Pemerintahan.

Sommer, M. (2010) Where the education system and women's bodies collide: the social and health impact of girls' experiences of menstruation and schooling in Tanzania. *Journal of Adolescence,* 33 (4), 521–529.

Sommers, M. & Buckland, P. (2004) *Parallel worlds: rebuilding the education system in Kosovo.* Paris, International Institute for Educational Planning.

Spence, N. (2002) Foreword. In Budlender, D. et al. (eds) *Gender budgets make cents: understanding gender-responsive budgets.* London, Commonwealth Secretariat, pp. 7–10.

Staudt, K. (2007) Gender mainstreaming: conceptual links to institutional machineries. In Rai, S. (ed.) *Mainstreaming gender, democratizing the state? Institutional mechanisms for the advancement of women.* Manchester, Manchester University Press, pp. 40–66.

Steele, J.F.P. (2002) The Liberal women's caucus. *Canadian Parliamentary Review,* Summer 2002, 13–19.

Stewart, F. & Brown, G. (2009) *Fragile states.* Oxford, Centre for Research on Inequality, Human Security and Ethnicity, Oxford University. Working Paper 51.

Stone, D. (2004) Transfer agents and global networks in the 'transnationalization' of policy. *Journal of European Public Policy,* 11 (3), 545–566.

Stotsky, J. (1997) How tax systems treat men and women differently. *Finance & Development,* 34 (1), 30–33.

Stotsky, J. (2016) *Gender budgeting: fiscal context and current outcomes.* Washington, DC, IMF. Working Paper 16/149.

Stotsky, J.G., Kolovich, L. & Kebhaj, S. (2016) *Sub-Saharan Africa: a survey of gender budgeting efforts.* Washington, DC, IMF. Working Paper 16/152.

Subrahmanian, R. (2005) Gender equality in education: definitions and measurements. *International Journal of Educational Development*, 25 (4), 395–407.

Sultana, R. (2003) An EMIS for Palestine: the Education Management Information System in the West Bank and Gaza Strip. *Mediterranean Journal of Educational Studies*, 7 (2), 61–92.

Taft, A. & Watson, L. (2013) *Violence against women in Timor-Leste. Secondary analysis of the 2009–2010 Demographic and Health Survey: final report.* Japan International Cooperation Agency.

Timor-Leste Central Bank (2014) *Petroleum Fund of Timor-Leste, quarterly report, Volume 10, Number XXV, June 2014.* Dili, Timor-Leste Central Bank.

Timor-Leste Direcção Nacional de Estatística (2007) The 2004 Population and Housing Census of Timor-Leste. *Direcção Nacional de Estatística.* Available from: http://dne.mof.gov.tl/census/2004_census/2004_population_housing/index.htm [accessed 16 November 2014].

Timor-Leste Direcção Nacional de Estatística (2008) *Final statistical abstract: Timor-Leste Survey of Living Standards 2007.* Dili, Direcção Nacional de Estatística, Ministério de Finanças.

Timor-Leste Government (2008) *Deklarasaun Kompromisu Dili, Investe ba Feto ho Labarik Feto: Investe ba Igualdade, Díli, 8 Marsu 2008.* Dili, Timor-Leste Government.

Timor-Leste Government (2010) *Millennium Development Goals 2010. Where are we now? Where do we want to be in 2015?* Dili, Timor-Leste Government.

Timor-Leste Government (2014) Strong growth in Timor-Leste's non-oil GDP confirmed by the 2012 National Accounts. Media release, 30 July. Available from: http://timor-leste.gov.tl/?p=10456&lang=en [accessed 30 July 2014].

Timor-Leste Government (2016) State Budget 2016 Budget Overview – Book 1. *La'o Hamutuk.* Available from: www.laohamutuk.org/econ/OGE16/15OGE16.htm [accessed 7 December 2016].

Timor-Leste Government & UNDP (2009) *2009 The Millennium Development Goals Timor-Leste.* Dili, Timor-Leste Government and UNDP.

Timor-Leste Ministry of Education (2011) *National education strategic plan 2011–2030.* Dili, Timor-Leste Government.

Timor-Leste Ministry of Education and Culture (2011) *Education statistical yearbook 2008/2009.* Dili, Timor-Leste Ministry of Education.

Timor-Leste Ministry of Finance (2008) *General Budget of the State 2008: Budget Paper no. 1.* Dili, Timor-Leste Government.

Timor-Leste Ministry of Finance (2009a) *2010 State Budget: Book 1.* Dili, Timor-Leste Government.

Timor-Leste Ministry of Finance (2011) *State budget 2011. Book 1: Goodbye conflict, welcome development.* Dili, MoF.

Timor-Leste Ministry of Finance (2013a) *State budget 2014. Book 1: 'Be a good citizen. Be a new hero to our nation'.* Dili, Timor-Leste Ministry of Finance.

Timor-Leste Ministry of Finance (2013b) *Summary report: fragility assessment in Timor-Leste.* Dili, Fragility Assessment Team, Ministry of Finance.

Timor-Leste Ministry of Finance (2014) *Timor-Leste Millennium Development Goals report 2014.* Dili, Ministry of Finance.

Timor-Leste Ministry of Finance (2015) *State budget approved 2015, Budget Overview, Book 1.* Dili, República Democrática de Timor-Leste.

Timor-Leste Ministry of Finance (2016) *Rectification budget 2016, Budget Overview, Book 1.* Dili, República Democrática de Timor-Leste.

Timor-Leste Ministry of Planning and Finance (2006) *General budget of the state 2006–07, budget document No. 1.* Dili, Timor-Leste Government.

Timor-Leste National Commission for Research and Development (2008) *State of the nation report. Volume I and II: Macroeconomic management and fiscal policy and thematic reports.* Dili, Timor-Leste Government.

Timor-Leste National Commission for UNESCO & Ministry of Education (2012) *Mother tongue-based multilingual education pilot program for Timor-Leste: a brief progress report on activities conducted January–May 2012.* UNESCO.

Timor-Leste National Statistics Directorate (2013) *Timor-Leste Household Income and Expenditure Survey 2011.* Dili, Timor-Leste Government.

Timor-Leste National Statistics Directorate & ICF Macro (2010) *Timor-Leste Demographic and Health Survey 2009–10.* Dili, USAID, AusAID, UNICEF, Timor-Leste Government, UNDP, Irish Aid, WHO, UNFPA.

Timor-Leste Planning Commission (2001) *East Timor 2020: our nation, our future.* Dili, Timor-Leste Government.

Timor-Leste Planning Commission (2002) *East Timor: national development plan.* Dili, Timor-Leste Government.

Timor-Leste Secretary of State for the Promotion of Equality (2007) *Initial report: the Convention on the Elimination of All Forms of Discrimination against Women (CEDAW) Timor-Leste.* Dili, Timor-Leste Government.

Timor-Leste Secretary of State for the Council of Ministers (2012) *Prime Minister explains government's policy on mother tongue in parliament.* Dili, Government of TimorLeste. Available from: http://timor-leste.gov.tl/?p=6454&lang=en [accessed 13 December 2016].

Timor-Leste Secretary of State for the Promotion of Equality (2014) *Timor-Leste Beijing Platform for Action national review and appraisal report.* Dili, Timor-Leste Government.

Trembath, A. & Grenfell, D. (2006) Oan Kiak: women and independence in Timor-Leste. *Arena Magazine*, 83, 10–12.

Trembath, A. & Grenfell, D. (2007) *Mapping the pursuit of gender equality: non-government and international agency activity in Timor-Leste.* Melbourne, RMIT.

Tripp, A.M. (2001) A new political activism in Africa. *Journal of Democracy*, 12 (3), 141–155.

True, J. & Mintrom, M. (2001) Transnational networks and policy diffusion: the case of gender mainstreaming. *International Studies Quarterly*, 45 (1), 27–57.

Turpin, J. (1998) Many faces – women confronting war. In Lorentzen, L.A. & Turpin, J. (eds) *The women and war reader.* New York, New York University Press.

Umapathi, N., Dale, P. & Lepuschuetz, L. (2013) *Timor-Leste: social assistance public expenditure and program performance report.* Washington, DC, World Bank.

Umapathi, N. & Velamuri, M. (2013) *Labor market issues in Timor-Leste: current state, prospects and challenges.* Washington, DC, World Bank.

UN Women Southeast Asia (2008) Gender resource centre will enhance equality for parliamentarians in Timor. Available from: www.unifem-eseasia.org/News/GenderResourceCentreEnhanceEquality.html [accessed 4 April 2011].

UNESCO (2011a) *2011 education for all global monitoring report. The hidden crisis: armed conflict and education.* Paris, UNESCO.

UNESCO (2011b) UNESCO organized a Statistical Capacity Development Workshop in Timor-Leste. UNESCO, 26 January. Available from: http://portal.unesco.org/geography/en/ev.php-URL_ID=13685&URL_DO=DO_TOPIC&URL_SECTION=201.html [accessed 16 November 2014].

UNICEF (2000) East Timor: what UNICEF is doing. *UNICEF.* Available from: www. unicef.org/easttimor/ [accessed 31 October 2014].

UNIFEM (2000) *Progress of the world's women 2000: UNIFEM biennial report.* New York, UNIFEM.

UNIFEM (2008) *Progress of the world's women 2008/2009: who answers to women? Gender and accountability.* New York, UNIFEM.

United Nations (2006) *Report of the United Nations Independent Special Commission of Inquiry for Timor-Leste.* Geneva, United Nations.

United Nations (2014) *List of least developed countries.* Available from: www.un.org/en/ development/desa/policy/cdp/ldc/ldc_list.pdf [accessed 16 November 2014].

United Nations Development Programme (2006) *Timor-Leste human development report 2006. The path out of poverty: integrated rural development.* Dili, UNDP.

United Nations Development Programme (UNDP) (2010) *Price of peace, financing for gender equality in post-conflict reconstruction, United Nations Development Programme synthesis report.* New York, UNDP.

United Nations Development Programme (2011) *Human development report 2011. Managing natural resources for human development, developing the non-oil economy to achieve the MDGs.* Dili, UNDP.

United Nations Development Programme (2013) *Human development report 2013. The rise of the South: human progress in a diverse world.* New York, UNDP.

United Nations Development Programme (UNDP) (2016) Timor-Leste: Integração da igualdade do género na orcamentação. *Pro PALOP-TL ISC.* Available from: http:// propaloptl-sai.org/index.php/pt/2015-02-19-12-51-50/recortes-de-imprensa/400-timor-leste-debate-a-integracao-da-igualdade-do-genero-na-orcamentacao-do-estado [accessed 7 December 2016]

United Nations Integrated Mission in Timor-Leste (2008) *International Women's Day (update).* Dili, UNMIT.

Unterhalter, E. (2013) Education targets, indicators and a post-2015 development agenda: Education for All, the MDGs, and the human development. *Working Paper Series – The Power of Numbers: A Critical Review of MDG Targets for Human Development and Human Rights.* Available from: http://dosen.narotama.ac.id/wp-content/ uploads/2014/11/Education-Targets-Indicators-and-Post-2015-Development-Agenda-Education-for-All-the-AMGs-and-Human-Development.pdf [accessed 8 December 2016].

Valodia, I. (2010) Conclusion and policy recommendations. In Grown, C. and Valodia, I. (eds) *Taxation and gender equity: a comparative analysis of direct and indirect taxes in developing and developed countries.* Oxon and New York, Routledge, pp. 299–313.

Van Eden, H., Bessette, F., Pedastsaar, E. & Nayer, H. (2010) *Public Financial Management Performance Report.* Dili, IMF.

Van Staveren, I. (1997) Focus groups: contributing to a gender-aware methodology. *Feminist Economics,* 3 (2), 131–135.

Varela, O.B. & Costa, S.F. (2009) Comunidade dos países de lingua official Portuguesa (CPLP): Comunidade 'lusofona' ou ficticia? *Tempo Exterior,* 19 (xullo/decembro), 23–46.

Vetten, L. (2005) 'Show me the money': a review of budgets allocated towards the implementation of the Domestic Violence Act (no. 116 of 1998). *Politikon,* 32 (2), 277–295.

Vetten, L., Budlender, D. & Schneider, V. (2005) *The price of protection: costing the implementation of the Domestic Violence Act (no. 116 of 1998).* Johannesburg, Centre for the Study of Violence and Reconciliation.

Victorino-Soriano, C. (2004) *Obstacles to effective participation of women in adult education program – focus on social: cultural factors.* Dili, Oxfam.

Voigts, F.G.G. (1999) *Development of an Education Management Information System (EMIS) in Namibia.* Paris, ADEA.

Wako, T.N. (2003) *Education Management Information Systems (EMIS): a guide for young managers.* Harare, NESIS/UNESCO.

Walby, S. (2005) Gender mainstreaming: productive tensions in theory and practice. *Social Politics,* 12 (3), 321–343.

Waring, M. (2010) *Women's political participation.* London, UK Department for International Development, International Development Research Centre.

Waylen, G. (2000) Gender and democratic politics: a comparative analysis of consolidation in Argentina and Chile. *Journal of Latin American Studies,* 32 (3), 765–793.

Waylen, G. (2011) Gendered institutionalist analysis: understanding democratic transitions. In Krook, M.L. & Mackay, F. (eds) *Gender, politics and institutions: towards a feminist institutionalism.* Chippenham, Palgrave Macmillan, pp. 147–162.

Wehner, J. & Byanyima, W. (2004) *Handbook for parliamentarians no. 6: Parliament, the budget and gender.* Paris, IPU, UNDP, World Bank Institute and UNIFEM.

Welch, D. (2009) *Helen Clark: a political life.* Rosedale, North Shore, New Zealand, Penguin Books.

Weldon, S.L. (2002) Beyond bodies: institutional sources of representation for women in democratic policymaking. *Journal of Politics,* 64, 1153–1174.

Weldon, S.L. (2004) The dimensions and policy impact of feminist civil society democratic policymaking on violence against women in the fifty US states. *International Feminist Journal of Politics,* 6 (1), 1–28.

Weldon, S.L. & Htun, M. (2013) Feminist mobilisation and progressive policy change: why governments take action to combat violence against women. *Gender & Development,* 21 (2), 231–247.

Whittington, S. (2000) The UN Transitional Administration in East Timor: Gender Affairs Unit. *Development Bulletin,* 53, 74–76.

Whittington, S. (2003) Gender and peacekeeping: the United Nations Transitional Administration in East Timor. *Signs,* 28 (4), 1283–1288.

Wilkinson, S. (1998) Feminist research: focus groups in feminist research: power, interaction, and the co-construction of meaning. *Women's Studies International Forum,* 21 (1), 111–125.

Wigglesworth, A. (2009) Young women and gender dimensions of change in Timorese civil society. In Leach, M., Mendes, N.C., da Silva, A.B., Ximines, A.C. & Boughton, B. (eds) *Understanding Timor-Leste Conference, Universidade Nasional Timor-Lorosa'e, Dili, Timor-Leste, 2–3 July 2009.* Hawthorn, Vic, Swinburne Press, pp. 242–247.

World Bank (2010) *Determinants and consequences of high fertility: a synopsis of the evidence.* Washington, DC, World Bank.

World Bank (2011a) *2012 World development report: gender equality and development.* Washington, DC, World Bank.

World Bank (2011b) *Learning for all: investing in people's knowledge and skills to promote development – World Bank Group Education Strategy 2020.* Washington, DC, World Bank.

World Bank (2011c) *Reproductive health at a glance: Timor-Leste*. Dili, World Bank.

World Bank (2011d) *World Bank group education strategy 2020*. Washington, DC, World Bank.

World Bank (2013) *Building evidence, Shaping policy – Findings of the 2012 Timor-Leste Education Survey*. Dili, World Bank.

World Bank (2014) *Harmonized list of fragile situations FY14*. Available from: http:// siteresources.worldbank.org/EXTLICUS/Resources/511777-1269623894864/ HarmonizedlistoffragilestatesFY14.pdf [accessed 27 October 2014].

World Bank Group & Independent Evaluation Group (2011) *Timor-Leste Country Program evaluation, 2000–2010: evaluation of the World Bank Group program*. Washington, DC, World Bank Group, Independent Evaluation Group.

World Health Organization (2015) *Trends in maternal mortality: 1990 to 2015*. Geneva, WHO, UNICEF, UNFPA, World Bank Group and the United Nations Population Division.

Wyeth, V. (2012a) *Interview with Emilia Pires, Chair of the g7+ Group of Fragile States. IPI Global Observatory*, 23 April. Available from: http://theglobalobservatory.org/2012/04/ interview-with-emilia-pires-minister-of-finance-for-timor-leste-and-chair-of-the-g7- group-of-fragile-states/ [accessed 16 November 2014].

Wyeth, V. (2012b) Knights in fragile armor: the rise of the 'G7+'. *Global Governance*, 18 (1), 7–12.

Young, J. (2005) Research, policy and practice: why developing countries are different. *Journal of International Development*, 17, 727–734.

Index

For Product Safety Concerns and Information please contact our EU representative GPSR@taylorandfrancis.com Taylor & Francis Verlag GmbH, Kaufingerstraße 24, 80331 München, Germany

Printed and bound by CPI Group (UK) Ltd, Croydon, CR0 4YY

01/05/2025

01858410-0002